"In exploring the post-9/11 Western in relati⟨ history of the cultural relationship between dle East, Kollin makes a forceful case for t western literary studies for understanding both how American empire is propagated and how it might be overcome."

—Alex Trimble Young, *Montana Magazine*

"Expertly analyzed. . . . We who have grown up on many a western motion picture, and have read a few books dealing with the fictional as well as the historical west, will appreciate this thought provoking book."

—Chuck Parsons, *Wild West History Association Journal*

"Groundbreaking in its analysis. . . . This highly original perspective is timely as well as relevant in our post-9/11 world with its so-called war on terror and its volatile ethno-racial and gendered politics."

—Stephen Tatum, author of *In the Remington Moment*

"Kollin presents a nuanced and brilliant discussion of intersections. . . . Most significant, the book is so engagingly and clearly written that anyone interested in analyses of the U.S. relationship to the Middle East will find it fascinating. . . . Stunningly original."

—Melody Graulich, coeditor of *Dirty Words in Deadwood*

"An exuberant study of the transposings of the American West and the Middle East in diverse popular cultural expressions. Kollin re-circuits the 'Western' away from its moorings in both the U.S. West and Western power to remap how its conventions have been transnationally informed and transformed by circulations through Arab itineraries and Iranian iterations."

—Timothy Marr, author of *The Cultural Roots of American Islamicism*

CAPTIVATING
WESTERNS

Postwestern Horizons

GENERAL EDITOR

William R. Handley
University of Southern California

SERIES EDITORS

José Aranda
Rice University

Melody Graulich
Utah State University

Thomas King
University of Guelph

Rachel Lee
University of California, Los Angeles

Nathaniel Lewis
Saint Michael's College

Stephen Tatum
University of Utah

CAPTIVATING WESTERNS

The Middle East in the American West

SUSAN KOLLIN

UNIVERSITY OF NEBRASKA PRESS
LINCOLN AND LONDON

Sections of chapter 3, "On Savagery and Civilization: Buffalo Bill and the East," originally appeared as "'Remember, you're the good guy': *Hidalgo*, American Identity, and Histories of the Western," *American Studies* 51, no. 1–2 (2010): 5–25.

Library of Congress
Cataloging-in-Publication Data
Kollin, Susan.
Captivating Westerns: the Middle East in the
American West / Susan Kollin.
pages   cm.—(Postwestern Horizons)
Includes bibliographical references and index.
ISBN 978-0-8032-2699-9 (hardback: alk. paper)
ISBN 978-1-4962-1423-2 (paper: alk. paper)
ISBN 978-0-8032-8663-4 (epub)
ISBN 978-0-8032-8664-1 (mobi)
ISBN 978-0-8032-8665-8 (pdf)
1. American literature—West (U.S.)—History and criticism.
2. West (U.S.)—In literature. 3. Middle East—In literature.
4. West (U.S.)—In motion pictures. 5. Middle East—In
motion pictures. I. Title.
PS271.K65 2015
810.9'3278—dc23
2015017650

Set in Sabon by L. Auten.

For Dan, Michaela, and Alexandra

CONTENTS

ILLUSTRATIONS

ACKNOWLEDGMENTS

I have incurred many debts in the process of researching and writing this book. First, I wish to thank the faculty and students at the American University in Cairo (AUC), who graciously welcomed me as a Fulbright Scholar in 2007–8 and offered useful feedback and suggestions during the early stages of this study. Particular appreciation goes to Ferial Ghazoul, Nicholas Hopkins, Robert Switzer, Walid El Hamamsy, and Mai Abbas.

I have had opportunities to present this work at AUC's Fifteenth Annual Research Conference, the ECLIPS: Work-in-Progress Seminar Series in the English and Comparative Literature Department at AUC, the "World Wide Wayne Film Festival" hosted by the American West Center at the University of Utah, "Connections and Ruptures: America and the Middle East" conference sponsored by the Center for American Studies and Research at the American University of Beirut, the English Department Colloquium at Montana State University, "The American Literary West: A Territory without Borders?" Third International Conference at the University of Basque Country in Vitoria-Gasteiz, the Michael P. Malone Conference on "The Wild West in Transatlantic Contexts" hosted by the Montana State University History and Philosophy Department, the "Dances with Words Visiting Author Series" at the University of Montana Western, and the Western Literature Association meetings in Boulder, Colorado, and Victoria, British Columbia.

I owe thanks to the audiences for their useful comments on earlier versions of this work and to the organizers, especially Matthew Basso, the Re/West Research Group at the University of the Basque Country, Robert Rydell, and Alan Weltzien.

I appreciate Krista Comer's invitation to participate in the American West / Américas Workshop at Rice University, during which time I enjoyed great conversations and discussions with members of the Spanish and Portuguese Department, as well as scholars in western American literary and cultural studies.

At Montana State University, I have had the privilege to work with thoughtful, creative, and supportive colleagues who have discussed and argued with me over the years about the topics I address in this study. I owe thanks to Michael Beehler and Robert Bennett, who initially helped me think about the "two Wests" during our three summers co-teaching an American studies institute for undergraduate students from the Middle East and North Africa, from 2005 to 2007. I also appreciate the intellectual support and advice I received from Dan Flory, Robert Rydell, David Agruss, Timothy Marr, Andrew Nelson, Liza Nicholas, Dale Martin, and Mary Murphy. Over the years I have had generous financial support in the form of several Research Enhancement Awards from the MSU College of Letters and Science, as well as Scholarship and Creativity Awards from MSU's Office of the Vice President for Research. The Interlibrary Loan staff at MSU, particularly Mary Guthmiller, fulfilled my numerous requests and went beyond the call of duty in tracking down sources for me. At the University of Nebraska Press, Kristen Elias Rowley, Marguerite Boyles, and Ann Baker, as well as freelance copyeditor Maureen Bemko, deserve my sincere appreciation for their patience and help with this book. Thanks also to the editors of *American Studies* for permission to reprint in chapter 3 sections from my article, which received the Stone-Suderman Prize from the Mid-America American Studies Association.

Over the years, students have helped me clarify many of the ideas I present in this study. I owe thanks in particular to members of my undergraduate courses and graduate seminars: "Literature of the American West," "Introduction to American Studies," "America in the World," "Fictions of the American West," "Visual Cultural Studies and the American West," "Metawesterns," "Westerns and Post-Westerns," "Memory and Counter-Memory in Western American Literature," and "Theorizing the Western."

For nearly two decades, members of the Western Literature Association have prodded and challenged me to develop more sophisticated understandings of critical regionalism, transnational American studies, and the Western. My thanks especially go to Chadwick Allen, José Aranda, Susan Bernardin, Christine Bold, Neil Campbell, Krista Comer, Nancy Cook, Audrey Goodman, Melody Graulich, William Handley, Richard Hutson, Victoria Lamont, Lee Clark Mitchell, Capper Nichols, Dana Phillips, Ladette Randolph, David Rio, Forrest G. Robinson, Sara Spurgeon, Stephen Tatum, and Alan Weltzien.

My daughters lived in Cairo and traveled throughout Egypt with me in 2007–8, during which time they were ideal cosmopolitan citizens. Throughout their lives they have accompanied me to numerous libraries, bookstores, and conferences. I appreciate their patience in accommodating parents whose academic work does not always stay at the office and often filters into all hours and corners of home life. Finally, my husband, Dan Flory, has been busy with his own projects in philosophy, critical race theory, and film studies but has always been a careful reader of this work at all stages of its development. I could not have written this book without his enthusiasm, love, and support. Any mistakes here are my own.

CAPTIVATING
WESTERNS

Introduction

Transnational Cowboys and the Middle East

> To examine the West in the twenty-first century is to think of
> it as always already transnational, a . . . routed and complex
> rendition, a traveling concept whose meanings move between
> cultures, crossing, bridging, and intruding simultaneously.
> —NEIL CAMPBELL

> How can you just sit there listening to wailing cowboys
> when our lives are falling apart?
> —*HOMELAND* (2011)

In the twenty-first century, transnational developments in scholarship have recast the field of western American literature and culture, with borderlands criticism, Pacific Rim studies, comparative
Indigenous theory, and environmental criticism offering important new frameworks for reconceptualizing the region. As both a
response to anxieties emerging after 9/11 and as part of a larger criticism launched against the U.S. war on terror and its "Lone Ranger"
foreign policy, western American fiction and film have also developed along transnational routes by featuring the U.S. cowboy hero
in an international setting, where his adventures often involve bat-
tling foes and restoring order on the global frontiers of the Middle
East. Just as the popular Western is not a monolithic genre but a
divided and contested form that has the ability to articulate ideas
across the political spectrum, recent narratives featuring the post-

9/11 cowboy likewise function in a variety of capacities.[1] Sometimes the texts celebrate American efforts to restore order and democracy across a global terrain, while at other times they cast doubt on these acts, laying bare the problems of defining freedom and independence as universal ideals or assuming that those conditions are even desired or welcomed by other populations.

The title of my study, *Captivating Westerns: The Middle East in the American West*, gestures toward the multiplicity and diversity of meanings in the genre, building on and extending competing ideas encoded in the form. The theme of captivity, for instance, has been central to the genre of the Western, with Mary Rowlandson's narrative from the Puritan era serving as the archetypal story of this encounter.[2] Recently, scholars have shifted focus to other geographical locations by examining tales that emerged in the 1790s and featured Americans taken captive in North Africa or the Barbary Coast. These captivity tales served a number of functions. As Paul Baepler argues, they offered Europe and the United States many of their initial representations of Africa, provided abolitionists and slave owners with a means of protesting or rationalizing the institution of slavery, helped create a foundation that later justified the colonization of Africa, and established some of the means with which to construct the boundaries between "barbarity" and "civility" used to police categories of whiteness and blackness in the United States.[3] Barbary captivity narratives are also important to analyze, as Gordon Sayre points out, because they advanced propaganda that led to the attack on Tripoli in 1801, which became the First Barbary War as well as the first U.S. military invasion of a foreign land.[4]

Because captivity narratives have often played a crucial role in establishing notions of an exceptionalist America by contributing to myths of the frontier, it is important to recognize that these narratives were not just produced and consumed by Americans but were multinational in scope. British authors also wrote stories about their captivity experiences in America, North Africa, and India. Spanish and Portuguese writers likewise produced accounts that detailed life in captivity in the early modern Atlantic. Eventually Moorish and Turkish authors also penned narratives that borrowed content along with various rhetorical elements from earlier tales of captivity.[5] These diverse experiences of captivity inform my uses of the term in this book. By placing captivity narratives within a larger global history, scholars may avoid replicating exceptionalist arguments about quintessential American genres. In the case of the popular Western, which draws on the captivity narrative and has likewise been regarded as a uniquely American form, it is important to recognize the transnational influences that shaped the genre, its overdetermined origins in other nations' literary traditions. While the Western was clearly influenced by tales of Puritan captivity and popular frontier stories, the genre also developed out of the British and European colonial adventure tale, which centered on the travels and exploits of a protagonist from the metropole whose adventures took place on the far edges of empire, with the heroes in these narratives often dividing the geographies and peoples they encountered into categories of savage and civilized.[6]

The Western in the twenty-first century carries traces of these earlier tales of contact and conflict and perhaps not surprisingly continues to shape U.S. multicultural encounters in the post-9/11 era. Derek Gregory's observations about American foreign policy in the twenty-first century offer insights into how the genre has frequently been deployed today. As he aptly notes in *The Colonial Present: Afghanistan, Palestine, Iraq*, the dominant tales the United States and Europe use to justify military invasion continue to be narratives about civilization's struggle against savagery.[7] These stories involve "myths of self-sufficiency in which 'the West' reaches out only to bring to others the fruits of progress that would otherwise be beyond their grasp."[8] The Western has frequently helped extend this tale of progress, borrowing the logics of orientalism in justifying contemporary U.S. foreign policy, especially in the Middle East, where it contributes to what Walid El Hamamsy and Mounira Soliman call the "old colonial 'savage'/'savior' binary."[9] The Western gains power in the twenty-first century as a narrative form that *captivates* popular audiences. In some instances, the genre may speak to larger anxieties about America in the world and a perceived sense that U.S. innocence has been *held captive by terrorists* from the Middle East. In other cases, especially as it is reimagined by authors and filmmakers in the Middle East, the Western becomes a useful means of critically examining how the nation has been *held captive to its own fears and anxieties*, with the war on terror resulting not in more freedom but in greater restrictions and fewer liberties.

Captivating Cowboys

Recent political thrillers, such as the Fox television series *24* (2001–10) and the films *Taken* (2008), and *Argo* (2012), draw on the codes and conventions of the Western, particularly its captivity and rescue story, by featuring Arab or Iranian captors and innocent Americans abroad. In these narratives, U.S. hostages are in need of a liberating cowboy hero who will bring them back home safely, renew the national mission, and restore American collective innocence. More recently, the political thriller *Homeland*, which first aired on Showtime in 2011, plays on the multiple possibilities entailed in the Western, especially in an episode from season one entitled "The Good Soldier." The story features a scene with American heiress Aileen Morgan (Marin Ireland) and her professor husband Raqim Faisel (Omid Abtahi), both of whom are low-level al-Qaeda operatives living in the United States and on the run from the CIA as well as their own al-Qaeda bosses. While hiding out in a cheap motel room, Aileen settles her nerves by watching television. Raqim accuses her of wasting time, asking how she can just sit there mindlessly captivated by stories of "wailing cowboys" at a time when their "lives are falling apart." Based on a popular Israeli television series, *Hatufim* (Prisoners of war), which aired from 2009 to 2012, *Homeland* positions itself ambiguously in the war on terror by blurring divisions separating enemies from allies and distinctions drawn between savagery and civilization.[10] The series plays on classic frontier anxieties in the Western concerning racial and cultural contamination by featuring U.S. marine sergeant Nicholas Brody (Damian Lewis) as the American captive finally making his way home. Brody is a complicated political figure whose

4   *Introduction*

experiences living with the enemy as a prisoner of war may have turned him against his own nation. At the start of the series, it remains open to debate whether the protagonist Carrie Mathison (Claire Danes) and her supervisors at the CIA are acting ethically in hunting down international terrorists or whether they in fact are barbarous in their security efforts. Like many Westerns, *Homeland* plays it both ways, questioning the Western's codes and conventions concerning savagery and the national mission yet at times seeming to provide an endorsement of America's global role in the post-9/11 world.[11]

The figure of the transnational cowboy fighting the war on terror across a new global frontier has also captivated a number of veteran authors and journalists. Their writings about the U.S. invasion of Iraq often employ remarks about the Western in general and John Wayne in particular. For instance, Evan Wright's *Generation Kill*, the basis for a seven-part miniseries that first aired on HBO in 2008, features a marine describing combat experiences as "John Wayne shit," while Colby Buzzell's *My War: Killing Time in Iraq* depicts a soldier "John Wayne-ing it" by shooting from the hip while firing at a civilian enemy.[12] In many of these memoirs, Iraq is portrayed as Indian country, a comparison that uses familiar frontier rhetoric to make sense of the new enemy in the war on terror. Tim Pritchard's *Ambush Alley: The Most Extraordinary Battle of the Iraq War*, which tells of the March 2003 capture of and subsequent mission to rescue Pvt. Jessica Lynch, references John Wayne in his role as the cowboy hero who defeats the Indian captors. In the mainstream U.S. press, the battle was infamously framed as a modern replay of Ethan Edwards's efforts to get Debbie back from the Indians in *The Searchers* (1956), an account that was later discredited by a number of journalists and scholars.[13] As Jodi A. Byrd aptly points out, "ideas of the Indian" have frequently operated as "the contagion" through which an American empire "orders the place of peoples within its purview."[14] She notes that "Indianness functions as a transit within empire" or a recurring entity through which the colonizing power "replicates itself by transforming those to be colonized into 'Indians' through continual reiterations of pioneer logics."[15] In John Crawford's *The Last True Story I'll Ever Tell: An Accidental Soldier's Account of the War in Iraq*, this new Indian country becomes a particularly dangerous battle zone; at one point, his memoir describes an eerie site of combat in Iraq as "the Wild West," a geographical space given a new name by U.S. soldiers who associate the area with particularly unsettling scenes of death, chaos, and violence.[16]

In *The Forever War*, Pulitzer Prize–winning journalist Dexter Filkins describes an odd moment he experienced while covering the Iraq War in 2006. One day he encounters two soldiers carrying "a life-size cutout of John Wayne, the American movie icon. It was one of the giant cutouts you stand next to at theme parks and get your picture taken." The journalist remarks that "no matter where you went in the Middle East, no matter what people thought of America, everyone loved American movies." In the large cutout figure that the soldiers carry, the Duke "was wearing a ten-gallon hat and a white kerchief round his neck and a gunbelt low round his waist. He was grinning like he'd just shot a bunch of cattle rustlers." Described as "a fan of John Wayne," one Iraqi official at the scene is told that the Duke was a "tough guy like you are, a sheriff in a bad neighborhood, and he gave the bad guys nightmares."[17] For Filkins, the moment is a strange confusion that places a fictional film icon into the reality of twenty-first-century war, turning the idealized cowboy that John Wayne famously played on-screen in Cold War Westerns into a captivating, real-life role model in the U.S. war on terror.

David Abrams's war novel, *Fobbit*, also references the popular Western, often comparing combat sites in the Middle East to the nineteenth-century U.S. frontier. *Fobbit* is written in the tradition of the American antiwar novel and offers a parody of the experiences U.S. Army employees have while stationed at a forward operating base during Operation Iraqi Freedom. The employees have relatively menial jobs compared to what U.S. soldiers face in combat, yet because they are also located in a war zone, they experience dangerous situations that contrast with the trivialities of their daily tasks. As the protagonist Chance Gooding Jr. explains in his diary, the battle zones in Iraq are largely beyond what he has previously encountered; he later resorts to anachronistic descriptions of these spaces, at one point describing the land as "biblical" terrain. In doing so, Gooding also positions the arid desert outside his own time, explaining that Triumph, the name of the forward operating base, is an *"American city unto itself. . . . Not unlike what you would have seen 150 years ago in Colorado, Nevada, Oregon, or Montana—slapdash communities nailed together by railroads, miners, lumberjacks, swollen with a flood of prostitutes, grocers, haberdashers, and schoolmarms, then just as quickly deflated as the mines dried up, the railroads moved on, and the forests were depleted. Just like frontier America."*[18]

Such descriptions help the characters make sense of the American military presence in the region. The particular Western that Gooding evokes here is not just any Western but the entrepreneurial Western, the story of capitalist industry arriving in an undeveloped region and laying waste to the natural environment, its boom-and-bust economy forever changing the landscape, as well as the lives of its inhabitants.[19] Later, another diary entry by Gooding notes that the px is the *"equivalent of the Old West general store. Its aisles are stocked with potato chips, beef jerky, cases of soda, sunglasses, baby oil, panty hose, tennis shoes, magazines (sans the porn, in deference to host nation Islamic sensitivities) . . . T-shirts ("My Daddy Deployed to Iraq and All I Got Was This Lousy T-Shirt") . . . paperbacks that lean heavily toward Louis L'Amour and Nelson DeMille."* Cataloging the numerous consumer items available to U.S. soldiers at the commissary, the narrator equates popular Westerns with other kitschy products, deeming them useless and trite material goods that offer temporary distraction but that, like pantyhose, ultimately have little purpose in the desert. Gooding later complains about the ubiquitous presence of such books and notes, saying that his trailer contains "enough Louis L'Amour paperbacks to choke a horse."[20]

Memoirs about U.S. combat in Afghanistan likewise gesture toward the genre, with Sean Naylor's *Not a Good Day to Die: The Untold Story of Operation Anaconda* using popular rhetoric from the

Vietnam War to describe a battle zone in central Asia as "Indian country."[21] Finally, in *One Bullet Away: The Making of a Marine Officer*, author Nathaniel Fick explains that Afghanistan reminds him of "Nevada and Arizona" and goes on to describe a scene in which a "sharp wind rustled the carcasses of plants still upright in the ground. Others rolled along like tumbleweeds in an old Western."[22] Encountering a threatening and dangerous terrain, the writer resorts to a domestic desert aesthetic, his sense of dislocation and displacement alleviated by a comparative landscape description that likens the incomprehensible and overwhelming war zones of Afghanistan to the familiar terrain of the U.S. Southwest while offering a triumphalist narrative framework that seeks to ensure a successful ending for U.S. soldiers in the region.

Such comparative landscape descriptions are not unique to recent military memoirs but have commonly appeared in the work of explorers, tourists, writers, and artists throughout U.S. history. As Audrey Goodman has pointed out, European Americans often struggled to translate their experiences as visitors to the desert American Southwest and frequently described these spaces using biblical language, turning what appeared to be useless, dry wastelands into antiquated but elevated sites much like the Holy Lands of the Middle East.[23] Richard V. Francaviglia extends these observations, tracing the ways the American West in general was often depicted as a New World Orient. In his study *Go East, Young Man: Imagining the American West as the Orient*, Francaviglia notes that it has been common in U.S. cultural history to describe the American West through an orientalist vision and that such descriptions have been largely positive and celebratory. As he explains, alongside stereotypes involving cowboys and Indians there may be found "another set of images of a West that is not West at all but has its origins in Asia and the Middle East." His study helps lay the groundwork for my examination of how the U.S. West has been frequently described as and likened to the spaces of the Middle East. As Francaviglia observes, the "paradoxical idea that the West can be East" may be widely traced in historical writings, many genres of literature, and contemporary popular culture.

Thus, in addition to the common frontier icons associated with the region, "Eastern or Oriental motifs also brand this otherwise characteristically western American locale."[24] Branding the West as an intriguing or captivating Orient—even at times as a New World Holy Land—enabled European Americans to transform what was largely an incomprehensible and unsettling terrain into something that could be reassuringly familiar and that provided a divine basis for exploration and conquest.[25]

In recent years, this "brand" has been subjected to criticism, with various novels, short stories, films, television shows, and music videos showcasing the problems of conflating the U.S. West with the Middle East, especially as the exchange unfolds during the war on terror. Ben Fountain's novel, *Billy Lynn's Long Halftime Walk* (2012), offers such pushback, reading the cultures of post-9/11 against the backdrop of the Western formula. His novel intertwines a portrait of U.S. soldiers in Iraq with the American cowboy hero, this time in the context of Texas football. Peppered with various references to the Alamo and Custer, the narrative takes place during a Dallas Cowboys game as the men of Bravo Company's second platoon tour the United States during a leave from service in Iraq. Here the brand linking the American West to war in the Middle East extends to the world of professional football and the various commercial enterprises that profit from the bodies of the players. Fountain folds a hyperbolic patriotism and over-the-top masculinity into the narrative as a way of drawing connections between the spectacle of sports, the U.S. military, American hypercapitalism, masculinity, and the Western. At one point the narrator notes that it "has been a frustrating game thus far" for sports fans, so "they blow off steam by spending money. Happily there is retail at every turn so the crowd doesn't lack for buying opportunities." Other references to American consumerism appear throughout the novel as readers learn "it's the same everywhere Bravo has been, the airports, the hotels, the arenas and convention centers, in the downtowns and the suburbs alike, retail dominates the land. Somewhere along the way America became a giant mall with a country attached."[26] Billy Lynn, the nineteen-year-old protagonist of the novel, soon comes to understand these moments as embodying what freedom and democracy finally mean for his fellow Americans, the war itself framed as not just bringing the fruits of civilization to populations who are allegedly stuck in a place of savagery but also as enabling an orgy of shopping and consumption in the process.

During the football game, Billy and other members of Bravo Company meet various Cowboys fans who enthusiastically express their support for the troops. These civilians often speak "'Merican," deforming keys words in their conversations, so that what Billy hears are almost incomprehensible and senseless utterings about the tragedy of "nina leven," the "terrRist" threat, the soldiers' "currj" in battle, their *"acks* of *sack*-rih-*fice*," their *"soooh-preeeeeme* sacrifice," the fight for "dih-mock-cruh-see," and the act of uncovering "dubya em dees."[27] So often do civilians repeat the same lingo that their comments become meaningless sound bites to Billy, his discomfort stemming in part from his belief that he and his fellow soldiers are attending the Dallas Cowboys game under somewhat false pretenses. As the story goes, the eight surviving members of the Bravo squad had courageously exchanged fire with Iraqis in the battle of Al-Ansakar Canal. The moment was filmed by an embedded news crew, but in the course of editing the filmmakers embellished the event. Later the men are named heroes by the mainstream press and are widely praised by the civilians they encounter during their tour. Soon there is talk about a blockbuster Hollywood film in production with actress Hilary Swank in the lead role.

Just as the battle becomes amplified in its retelling, so Billy notes the ways American culture itself seems overwrought, artificial, and supersized. He feels like an impostor during the football game and unfavorably compares his short-lived action in battle with the violence unleashed at the game in Cowboys Stadium. While his combat experiences were largely underwhelming and ended almost as soon as they began, the football game is a larger-than-war encounter. Fountain describes Billy's response to the spectacle of the Dallas football players:

He's not comfortable here. He feels exposed, diminished. If the painful truth be known, he feels less of a man right now than he did five minutes ago. The players seem so much more martial than any Bravo. They are bigger, stronger, thicker, badder, their truck-sized chins could bulldoze small buildings and their thighs bulge like load-bearing beams. Testosterone, these guys are cranking it, and their warrior aura ramps up exponentially as they assemble themselves for the game. As if these human mountains need more bulk? Elaborate systems of shock and awe are constructed about their bodies, arrays of hip pads, thigh pads, then the transformative lift of the shoulder pads, these high-tech concoctions of foams, fabrics, Velcros, and interlocking shells, with girdling skirt extensions to cradle mere mortal ribs.[28]

The sport of football is not just comparable to war but at times may even exceed some aspects of war in the violence and savagery it unleashes on the field. As Billy comes to believe, football appears to be the unfortunate end product of national progress, success, freedom, and economic growth. It is a strange spectacle that captivates these American audiences and provides an occasion for unleashing a violent patriotism that is expressed by coaches, players, fans, and the team owners throughout the game.

For Billy, such excess as a sign of civilization is deeply discouraging. He muses whether any other nation could sustain or want to sustain this overload, this American surfeit of power and resources:

Where else but America could football flourish, America with its millions of fertile acres of corn, soy, and wheat, its lakes of dairy, its year-round gushers of fruits and vegetables, and such meats, that extraordinary pipeline of beef, poultry, seafood, and pork, feedlot gorged, vitamin enriched, and hypodermically immunized, humming factories of high-velocity protein production, all of which culminate after several generations of epic nutrition in this strain of industrial-sized humans? Only America could produce such giants. Billy watches as tight end Tony Blakely pours an entire box of cereal into a mixing bowl, follows that with a half gallon of milk, and serenely falls to with a serving spoon. One. Entire.

Box. Any other country would go broke trying to feed these mammoths, who blandly listen as Norm speaks from the center of the room. *Real American heroes . . . freedoms . . . that we might enjoy.*[29]

The novel unfolds through other scenes that draw connections between the Cowboys, consumerism, patriotism, freedom, democracy, savagery, and war. Billy notes that the team's owner, March Hawey, is all western in the way he uses any opportunity to promote the Cowboys brand. Praising the members of Bravo, Hawey tells Billy that seeing them "John Wayne that deal" was a catharsis that gave him something to finally cheer about in the war on terror.[30]

Sporting an especially interesting pair of cowboy boots, the team owner is reminiscent of a character in William Gibson's 2003 futuristic thriller, *Pattern Recognition*. In what has been regarded as the first instance of the post-9/11 novel, *Pattern Recognition* features the aptly named Hubertus Bigend, the head of a multinational firm of "cool hunters" in search of new frontiers for his ever-expanding global enterprises. Bigend dresses in over-the-top western garb, including a huge cowboy hat and high-end cowboy boots, representing not the arrival but the end of various freedoms after 9/11, embodying the demise of the nation-state during the post–Cold War era along with the beginning of a powerful reign of hypercapitalism, and inaugurating the culture of surveillance and counterterrorism.[31] In Fountain's novel, Billy is allergic to these displays of national power and corporate wealth; he avoids crowds of rich, influential people and struggles to survive his encounters with the team's wealthy patrons. Growing up in a working-class family from a dead-end Texas town, Billy previously had trouble with the law and joined the Marine Corps in order to avoid a jail sentence, his decision to sign up less about heroically serving his country and more about saving himself. These motivations offer another reason Billy shies away from all the praise showered on them during the Cowboys game, another reason he feels like an impostor as a soldier and a true American hero.

Similar motivations shape the lives of two young westerners who sign up for military service in a story from Annie Proulx's

Fine Just the Way It Is (2009). In "Tits-Up in a Ditch," Proulx draws connections between the hypermasculine world of the U.S. cowboy and the cultures of the American military. The narrative centers on the life of Dakotah, an orphaned cowgirl raised by her working-class grandparents after she is abandoned by her single mother. The story takes place against the boom-and-bust economy of Wyoming's oil and cattle industries in a small town whose inhabitants often fight change because, as one character explains to an outsider, "Wyoming was *fine just the way it was*." It's a place that strongly believes in core American and western rural values, a town where not being "constrained by a seat belt was the pioneer spirit of freedom," a belief that comes to have dire consequences for a young character later in the story. In high school, Dakotah falls for Sash Hicks, "a skinny boy dressed perpetually in camouflage clothing, with a face and body that seemed to have been broken and then realigned." One day, her history teacher devises a clever way of making the subject more interesting to the classroom of disengaged students by assigning them an essay on outlaws of the Old West. Thumbing through the school's *Encyclopedia of Western Badmen*, Dakotah finds an entry on Billy the Kid and becomes captivated by his story: "It seemed Sash Hicks was looking up from the page, the same smirky triumph in the face, the slouched posture and dirty pants. Sash immediately gained a lustrous aura of outlawry and gun expertise. Now in her daydreams they rode away together, Sash twisting back in the saddle to shoot at their pursuers."[32]

Dakotah's romance with Sash—her imagined western hero—does not end up quite as she hopes it would. After the two run off to get married, she quits school, but the relationship doesn't last long because Sash wants a subservient wife, not a partnership of equals. Dakotah learns she is pregnant just after he leaves her, but she can't locate him because he's joined the army. His mother explains that Sash "didn't tell us where they was sendin him. Probably Eye-rack by now. He said he was bein deployed to Eye-rack." Dakotah gives birth to a boy but can't pay her bills, so she too joins up, leaving her young son in the care of her grandparents. Things continue to go downhill for her. She loses an arm to an improvised explosive device. At the army hospital where she is recovering, Dakotah learns that Sash is also there. He has lost both legs in the war and has suffered brain damage, "but Dakotah recognized him, old Billy the Kid shot up by Pat Garrett. More than ever now he looked like the antique outlaw."[33] In the aftermath of his tragic injury, she continues to be captivated by legends and stories of the Old West, even as she begins to note how western men often pay a huge price for their privileged role in these narratives.

Later, as Dakotah drives by the places of her childhood after her return from Iraq, she recognizes sites where tragic events had occurred, where too many boys had lost their lives living out their cowboy dreams of the Old West:

> She knew what blood-soaked ground was, knew that severed arteries squirted like the backyard hose. . . . They passed the Persa ranch, where the youngest son had drowned in last spring's flood. She realized that every ranch she passed had lost a boy, lost them early and late, boys smiling, sure in their risks, healthy, tipped out of the current of life by liquor and acceleration, rodeo smashups, bad horses, deep irrigation ditches, high trestles, tractor rollovers, and unloaded guns. . . . This was the waiting darkness that surrounded ranch boys, the dangerous growing up that canceled their favored status.[34]

Dakota's toddler son, who is already being groomed to take his place as a rightful Wyoming cowboy one day, loses his life in a horrific turn of events. While driving around town, her grandfather places the young boy with a dog in the open bed of a truck. The eighteen-month-old leans over the side of the truck to get a better view and is thrown from the vehicle when it hits a pothole in the road. He dies from his injuries. The older man is devastated by the child's death; he loved his great-grandson and just "wanted him to be tough."[35] Here the powerful narratives and belief systems that are responsible for constructing cowboy and cowgirl identity in the modern West often end badly. In this case, fantasies about the heroic possibilities of the Wild West are partly responsible for

Introduction

bringing these characters to the war zones of the Middle East, where their lives are eventually torn apart and destroyed. In Dakotah's case, she marries the wrong Western outlaw, ends up injured in the Iraq War herself, and loses her son in a horrible accident.

Like Annie Proulx, contemporary author Kim Barnes also reexamines links between Wild West heroism, economic opportunities, and American involvement in the Middle East. Her novel, *In the Kingdom of Men* (2013), features transnational cowboys living and working in the offshore oil fields of Saudi Arabia in 1967. Barnes takes a critical stance toward codes and conventions of the Western, particularly the divisions it erects between savagery and civilization on an imagined global frontier. Stephanie LeMenager notes the ways frontier discourses have enabled European Americans to negotiate their place in the world by allowing them to take refuge in a common disavowal. "In the collective imaginings of the United States," she writes, the frontier has "functioned to separate the USA from global imperial history, marking it as an exceptional national experiment." LeMenager goes on to note the powerful cultural uses of these discourses throughout American literary history. "If there is a single metanarrative that can be derived from the diverse iterations of frontier experience in US literature," she writes, "it is that the frontier performs the settler culture's failure of thought, the paralysis of its imagination in the face of facts too threatening, experiences too rare."[36]

Barnes critically employs elements of the frontier and the popular Western in her novel, revisiting Wallace Stegner's earlier account of petro-cowboys and Arab-Indians in the Middle East. Stegner's book, *Discovery! The Search for Arabian Oil*, was written in installments that initially appeared in *Aramco World* beginning in 1968 and were published as a book in 1971. The narrative may be understood in the tradition of what Amitav Ghosh calls "petrofiction," a genre whose protagonists meet in an "oil encounter" that includes "America and Americans on the one hand and the peoples of the Arabian Peninsula and the Persian Gulf on the other."[37] In a telling way, the comedian Mel Brooks's satirical Western musical *Blazing Saddles* (1974) manages to offer a brief reference to this oil encoun-

Fig. 1. The anachronistic posse of western outlaws, including Ku Klux
Klan members and an Arab horseman, in *Blazing Saddles*
(directed by Mel Brooks, 1974), from the DVD.

ter, specifically to the 1973 oil crisis. When the corrupt attorney
general Hedley Lamarr (Harvey Korman) tries to get rich quick
off a land purchase near a newly built railroad, he recruits a mot-
ley army of western outlaws to fight the townspeople. The gang
includes an anachronistic array of enemy figures, including members of the Ku Klux Klan and Hell's Angels, as well as Nazis and
an Arab horseman, the latter perhaps meant to embody a member
of the oil-rich Middle Eastern nations demonized by many Americans during the oil crisis of the 1970s.

Chronicling a different aspect of the oil encounter, Stegner's
book appeared as a nonfiction account of the early years of the
Arabian American Oil Company. In his study of the book, the historian Robert Vitalis skillfully analyzes the narrative, noting how
the text draws on and extends the popular Western in the context
of the Saudi oil encounter.[38] Hired by Aramco in 1955 to write a
history of the company, Stegner moved to Dhahran, Saudi Arabia, with his wife Mary. Vitalis notes how the celebrated western
author begins his account with references to "the ritual howling
wilderness, where history is set in motion by the coming of a civilizing agency," ending with the classic tale of declension and the
passing of the frontier.[39] The story Stegner provides in *Discovery!*
again borrows from a particular kind of Western—the entrepreneurial Western relocated to a global context. In this case, Stegner's

account chronicles the capitalist transformation of an undeveloped "wasteland" into a booming frontier town that finally ends as so many Westerns do—in regret and nostalgia for what has been lost and destroyed by the forces of economic progress.

In a similar way, Barnes's *In the Kingdom of Men* unfolds along a series of parallels that bring diverse populations together by linking the world of the Saudi hosts with that of their American guest workers, the transnational cowboys. The novel's protagonist, Gin Mitchell, is an Oklahoma girl raised by her grandfather, a strict Baptist minister. Gin's father had been drafted and deployed to Vietnam, and he dies in the war when she is a child. When she turns seven, her single mother dies of cancer, leaving Gin to be raised by her authoritarian grandfather. Gin is something of a wild child; she joins the girls' basketball team against her grandfather's wishes and doesn't tell him about it. The older man endorses a code of female modesty, disapproving of what he believes is an inappropriate uniform that is both too revealing and too much like what men wear. Later, she sneaks out of the house to meet her new boyfriend, Mason, the town's golden boy. Gin's grandfather finds out about these deceptions and beats her; Gin later runs away to marry Mason. Like the writings by Fountain and Proulx, Barnes's novel features the promise of class mobility as a motivating force for the American characters' journey to the Middle East. With new financial burdens now facing him, Mason takes a job with the Arabian American Oil Company in Saudi Arabia and sets up a household with his wife in the company's gated community in Abqaiq. There, her life is consigned to boring days of playing golf and endless games of bridge, to extended lunches and mindless shopping sprees with other American or European wives.

Gin passes the time reading stories in *Aramco World* magazine that could have been penned by Stegner when he was a hired writer for the company. The articles feature color photographs of Arabs and Americans working side by side in the desert, "building, paving, extracting, standing back to admire the progress they had made . . . the harmony and utility perfectly captured, the desert no more impossible than any frontier had been, the ingenious

Americans and their Saudi allies headed for sure victory over what-
ever lay between them and the massive fields of oil."[40] Like Stegner, Barnes stages the Saudi oil encounter through the genre of the
Western but does so for decidedly different purposes. A number of
the workers in her novel appear as cowboys decked out in classic
cowboy garb. One character in particular dresses in clothes purchased by wives of Aramco workers. Yousef, the Bedouin driver,
dons a "ten-gallon hat settled onto his jug-handle ears. . . . Instead
of a *thobe* and *ghutra*, he wore a Western snap-button shirt and
blousy cotton trousers, tucked into a pair of boots whose gaucho
heels added two inches to his height."[41] At another point, Gin
walks through the *souq*, which she likens to an "Old West town, a
mix of what once was and what was about to be," with its "adobe-
like buildings of mud and mortar, some centuries old and faded
to the color of sand, others newly constructed and limed a brilliant white."[42]

The gendered politics of mobility shaping the popular Western also curtail Gin's life in Saudi Arabia. Often consigned to her
home, Gin begins to feel like a captive in this world of new wealth
and privilege. Servants take care of her housework, a driver trans-
ports her everywhere, and she mostly mingles only with other
Americans or Europeans. "I wish I could explore the desert like
Lawrence of Arabia," Gin confesses one day to Yash, her Indian
housekeeper. He responds by telling her about the earlier exploits
of female explorers in the region and the stories of Gertrude Bell
and Freya Stark but warns her against these romantic dreams of
worldly exploration and imperial adventure. Such fantasies of
discovery, he says, are symptoms of "an illness" that has already
afflicted "white men of some privilege" who "see themselves as
golden-haired gods."[43] In another scene, she speaks with Abdullah,
an Aramco employee who previously trained as a petroleum engi-
neer in the United States but is demoted to working as a driver for
the company in Saudi Arabia. "In Texas, they probably thought
you were an Indian or something," she tells Abdullah, "you know,
like an Apache"; he replies that "they thought I was a Mexican . . .
and treated me with contempt."[44] The exchange causes Gin to

Introduction

reflect on the intersecting race and gender restrictions set up by the company, how Abdullah is not allowed onto the campus while she's not allowed to leave it.[45] Meanwhile, Mason faces problems of his own when he sides with the workers against the bosses in order to fight what he calls "corporate colonization."[46] In this scene and others, Barnes rethinks the Western and its treatment of multicultural encounters by locating much of the barbarism on the American side of the equation. Gin is not free in her marriage, a power imbalance that existed between her and her husband long before they arrived in the Middle East. Mason himself becomes a somewhat reluctant bringer of law to the region. The men he polices in this instance, however, are high-placed U.S. Aramco employees who cheat the company by keeping funds meant for various repairs in the oil fields and are finally responsible for the disappearance and death of Mason near the end of the novel.

Critical Regionalisms and the Transnational West

The project of examining connections between the Middle East and the American West as developed in fiction, film, and other cultural production requires critics to bring together bodies of knowledge that have tended to remain far apart in scholarship. Addressing this critical disconnection, Ella Shohat and Evelyn Alsultany argue for what they call a more "capacious and diasporic reconceptualization" of knowledge, especially in the context of area studies and ethnic studies. Building on these observations, the field of western American regional studies could address new areas of inquiry if placed alongside studies of the Middle East, such that the terrain of the U.S. West could be "mapped transnationally, subjected to a diasporic cross-border critique as a method of reading. What could be called a 'diasporic turn' would help us conceptualize all regions in a more flexible and non-finalized manner, wherein each geography constitutes not a point of origin or final destination, but a terminal in a transnational network."[47] While much of this work is being conducted by critics in Latinx, Asian American, Native American, and environmental studies, scholarship on the Western is still waiting to be placed in a productive relationship with area studies of the Middle East.

The postcolonial critic Ali Behdad recounts some of the difficulties faced by scholars engaging in such interdisciplinary border crossing. A member of UCLA's Department of Literature, Behdad teaches in a U.S. city that is home to the nation's largest population of Iranian Americans. When he first embarked on a study of immigration and nationalism in the United States, some of his colleagues expressed skepticism about his unexpected disciplinary leap, a move that marked for them a puzzling shift from the focus he developed in his prior scholarly interests—nineteenth-century European representation of the Middle East. Behdad describes how some of his well-meaning colleagues went so far as to warn him about "committing academic suicide" by delving into such "unknown territory." His new work on immigration and formations of U.S. national identity, however, helped him resolve a number of personal conflicts he faced, particularly the "disillusioning experiences and traumatic memories of being an Iranian immigrant in America." In better understanding this history, he was able to examine the larger social forces that simultaneously marked him in the United States as "an exotic 'oriental'" and "a decadent 'other.'"[48] Behdad chronicles how he had to retrain as an Americanist in order to gain a deeper understanding of the Iranian diaspora and postcolonial criticism about the Middle East, a transformation that may be instructive to western American literary and cultural scholars who perhaps now find themselves in a position where it may be increasingly necessary to retrain as comparatists in order to better understand the global dimensions of the region they are studying.

In doing so, an expanded body of texts and archives becomes available to scholars of western American culture, with new approaches enabling critics to read against the "imperial grain."[49] Such readings are already well under way in other locations, as the ironies of the Western and its civilizational narrative have not been lost on critics of U.S. foreign policy, particularly by those populations directly affected by these projects. An Iraqi female blogger who goes by the name Riverbend on the Internet, for instance, has written eloquently about her experiences with U.S. soldiers during the early years of the invasion of Iraq: "There was a time when people here felt sorry for the troops. No matter what one's attitude was to the occupation, there were moments of pity towards the troops, regardless of their nationality. We would see them suffering under the Iraqi sun, obviously wishing they were somewhere else and somehow that vulnerability made them seem less monstrous and more human. That time has passed."[50] The beginning of the blog entry appears as a reversal of the rescue mission, with the female writer taking pity on these lost young American savior/ soldiers who are held captive to their mission and the desert heat while suffering mightily in their military uniforms. As the invasion unfolds, however, the Iraqi author's empathy begins to wane as she notes the barbarity of the American military and the violence unleashed in the fight against terrorism. "Terror isn't just worrying about a plane hitting a skyscraper," Riverbend later writes; it is also about "watching your house being raided and knowing that the silliest thing might get you dragged away to Abu Ghraib where soldiers can torture, beat and kill. . . . Terror is trying to pick up the shards of glass resulting from a nearby explosion out of the living-room couch and trying not to imagine what would have happened if a person had been sitting there."[51]

In another context, the Western's central characters underwent a critical recasting during a visit by U.S. secretary of state Condoleezza Rice to Ramallah in 2007 when she was greeted by Palestinian protesters dressed as Native Americans and carrying signs that read, "Mrs. Rice, The Indian wars are not over. We are still here too."[52] The continuing critiques of U.S. frontier discourses in new contexts speak to the powerful ongoing nature of settler colonial projects. As Tom Lynch argues, it is important to note that settler colonialism is "complex, multifaceted, and enduring and typically persists into the indefinite future." He contends that we need to "recognize that settler colonialism is not contained within a singular, colorful, and celebrated frontier era that passes but is given meaning, justification, and continuing manifestation in the social, political, and cultural structures—including linguistic formations, rhetorical patterns, and cultural structures that persist."[53] In this context, a counterrhetoric has emerged, with references to American Indians becoming a means of critiquing colonization and dispossession. Such cross-cultural comparisons appear in the work of the Palestinian writer Mahmoud Darwish, whose well-known poem "Speech of the Red Indian" connects Palestinians and Native Americans as a way of laying bare comparative colonial practices.[54] The poem centers on the violence of occupations past and present and how Western imperialism and its civilizing missions continue to have dire consequences for both Native Americans and Palestinians.

In his study about the practice of "playing Indian," Philip Deloria notes how cross-cultural performances have historically enabled the negotiation of new political identities. The act of "playing Indian" allowed non-Indian Americans a means of working through unresolved tensions of national identity that involved an acknowledgment and disavowal of Indian presences in the land. Deloria explains that "there was, quite simply, no way to conceive an American identity without Indians. At the same time, there was no way to make a complete identity while they remained."[55] In the instance of Palestinian protesters, "Indian" performance allows them to stand not in the place of but alongside Native Americans, an act that makes visible different histories of occupation, as well as comparative projects of resistance. Rather than accepting the role of the savage enemy and perpetrator of violence, these Palestinians reference American Indian histories in order to engage in similar forms of resistance and survivance in the present era.[56] As Alex Lubin argues, such comparative critiques and cross-cultural allegiances may help dismantle "the logic of colonialism by exposing its technologies of governmentality" and by highlighting multiple "forms of violence perpetrated by settler colonial states" while disrupting "its projection of uniqueness."[57]

In reading the Western's travels across global spaces, certain questions emerge. What does it mean when the Western is no longer situated in the context of the American West? Do such texts somehow forfeit their right to the term if they do not adhere to standard geographical definitions of the U.S. West? Does it become necessary to coin a new term for such narratives, one that is no longer tied to a designated regional American space? To answer these concerns, it is important to note that the name "Western" came into circulation belatedly, as a way of narrating a certain type of American settler colonial activity, particularly as a way of depicting stories involving U.S. adventures in frontier spaces that entailed what were frequently violent multicultural contacts.[58] In chapter 1, I address the emergence of the Western in global contexts more fully, noting how a particular body of stories that took place in multiple international contact zones eventually became associated with a narrowly defined U.S. terrain. Over the years, numerous scholars have traced how the codes and conventions of the Western have adapted to new conditions, as "Indian country" becomes relocated overseas to places such as the Philippines, Cuba, Vietnam, Iraq, and Afghanistan.[59] Richard Dyer explains how the Western has been able to travel widely in this manner. As he notes, the genre is not static, nor tied to one fixed location, but is able to continually move into new geographical terrain by relying on conceptual possibilities entailed in ideas of the "frontier." At the center of the genre and its discourses of the frontier is an implied "teleological" movement or "destiny" that is "energetically and optimistically embraced, in the name of race." As he explains, "all this is dynamically crystallised in the image of the frontier," which is "both a temporal and a spatial concept . . . suggesting a dynamic that enables progress . . . it signals a border between established and unestablished order, a border that is not crossed but pushed endlessly back."[60]

In *Captivating Westerns*, two "Wests" continually emerge in a process that often poses difficulties for scholars who center their work on both geographical entities. Here I refer not only to a "West" that is an American region but also to a "West" that is a key term in postcolonial studies, itself an imagined concept necessarily set in relation to a constructed and often vilified "East." The critic Waïl Hassan has observed problems in defining this larger West as a geographical entity, noting that while Edward Said's critique of orientalism "succeeded in dismantling the concept of the Orient or the East once and for all, its discursive twin and polar opposite, 'the West,' has proved to be astonishingly resilient." Hassan points out that as a "product of early nineteenth-century colonial ideology," the term "West" is often made to "appear unproblematic, self-evident, unitary, and trans-historical not only by writers who see themselves as Western or as champions of the West, but also by many who would not countenance its discursive and ideological counterpart."[61] Ella Shohat and Robert Stam likewise recognize common East/West partitions of the world as a key component of imperial and Eurocentric thinking that is in need of revision. As they explain, such thinking "attributes to the 'West' an almost providential sense of historical destiny." It "envisions the world from a single privileged point. It maps the world in a cartography that centralizes and augments Europe while literally 'belittling" Africa. The 'East' is divided into 'Near,' 'Middle,' and 'Far,' making Europe the arbiter of spatial evaluation."[62]

For scholars of the American West, it is often difficult to employ "the West" as a geographical term referring to a U.S. setting without also calling forth the other, more expansive concept. As postcolonial critics would argue, however, this may be the point. The West as a region of the United States functions in the context of European expansion, as part of an ongoing transnational history of settler colonialism, and, like the other West, it encodes a powerful geopolitical vision and vantage point while ushering in what Shohat and Stam call a "providential" assertion of American "destiny." In a similar way, Krista Comer has noted that "Western-ness" is a "highly mobile" concept and that much of "its social force and moral credibility owes to a suppressed but sustained dialogue with that 'other' West: 'Western civilization.'" She argues that the "slippage" arises out of "parallel projects" of settler colonial cultures that are "undertaken in the name of civilizing, Christianizing, and modernizing 'non-Western' peoples."[63]

This study employs other concepts that also require some clarification. Although using the term "Middle East" is not unproblematic, it is nevertheless useful as a way of addressing a region that is continually stereotyped in the United States as the home of global terrorists and a land whose people allegedly suffer from a lack of American-style freedom and democracy. Karima Laachir and Saeed Talajooy also note that the term "Middle East" is useful as an inclusive term that frequently references North Africa. Yet, at the same time, they recognize the dangers in how "colonial legacies and imperial discourses have constructed the region and 'produced' it both geographically and discursively." The authors thus follow scholarly convention in opting to employ the term "Middle East" strategically as a means of examining the "negative and reductive production and reception of the region through the focus on its rich cultural production and artistic creativity."[64]

In tracing moments of cultural contact across transnational spaces, *Captivating Westerns: The Middle East in the American West* provides an examination of key moments that highlight how the U.S. region has been shaped and transformed by contact and conflict with the Middle East and North Africa. The first chapter, "'I Longed to Be an Arab': The Eastern Origins of the Western," examines the rise of the genre in different eastern geographies. While most accounts begin with the Western's origins in the U.S. East at a time when a powerful but anxious group of Anglo Saxon men positioned the region as a rejuvenating antimodern space of wild nature, an additional argument could be made for also understanding the Western's development in another East—in the Middle East and North Africa. Many of the central writers and artists who were influential in defining the genre had experiences outside the United States that shaped their imaginative production of the region and the western cowboy hero. Figures such as Mark Twain, Theodore Roosevelt, and Frederic Remington were influenced by their travels to the Middle East and North Africa, and those experiences later shaped their ideas about the American West, the Western, and the cowboy himself. Other popular writers of the Western, including Karl May and Owen Wister, were also fascinated by the horse cultures of the world and used elements from the region in defining the Western. These writers and artists brought another East into play in their constructions of the American West and the Western; their work provides important insights into the global foundations of what has been commonly misrecognized as a quintessential U.S. form.

Chapter 2, "From the Moors: The Easts and Wests of Willa Cather," remaps the literary history of the American West by excavating various Moorish influences in the region's cultural development as these elements arrived in North America through the New World travels of Spanish explorers. The writings of the celebrated author Willa Cather reveal traces of the global influences shaping the American Southwest, particularly in her novel *Death Comes for the Archbishop* (1927). The task of uncovering this history of cultural production, adaptation, and influence requires scholars to place regional studies into productive dialogue with other critical frameworks and to suspend rigid ideas of what counts as inside or outside and what qualifies as East or West. It also requires scholars to question understandings of what constitutes the "Arab world," a space in post-9/11 discourse that is seemingly far away and somehow utterly un-American. A transnational reading of Cather's writings about the Southwest, however, reveals the instability of these frontiers and borders and enables scholars to examine the many Easts that have shaped the cultures of the region. This remapping in turn allows readers to acknowledge the ways the United States itself and the American West in particular are indeed geographies that may be included in the so-called Arab world.

Chapter 3, "On Savagery and Civilization: Buffalo Bill in the East," examines how the World's Fairs and numerous Wild West shows staged throughout the country helped bring the first large wave of Arabs to the United States in the late nineteenth century, thus giving U.S. audiences some of their initial encounters with people from the Arab Middle East, specifically "Greater Syria," as it was called then. My argument focuses on how a competitive national ethos shaped the racial representations of these multicultural performances, especially as world horse cultures were pitted against each other in later Hollywood restagings of the Wild West shows. My discussion centers on how U.S. filmmakers became captivated by these performances and how they placed American cowboys and cowgirls in competition against Arab and other mounted riders of the world as a means of asserting an exceptional U.S. identity on a global stage.

In chapter 4, "The Persian Peddler and the Egyptian Elixir: Racial Intimacies in *Oklahoma!*," I examine how critics have often centered their readings of this celebrated Western musical on its racial silences and erasures. Native Americans are largely removed from the story and written out of the region's past—a perplexing absence, especially considering that the musical takes place in Indian Territory at the beginning of the twentieth century and that its source material was written by a Cherokee, Lynn Riggs. Alongside these removals, however, I argue that critics must also attend to how the story complicates other racial identities, including those of Arab and Persian characters, in order to better explain the complexities of national belonging in the twentieth century. Struggles over the category of whiteness become a central conflict, with determinations over which characters are worthy of membership in the community—and, by extension, American citizenship after statehood—operating as a primary theme in the story. The many adaptations of Riggs's story are important to examine because they provide an intriguing archive of the ways an orientalist presence has played a crucial role in defining the boundaries of whiteness, while activating and sustaining certain fantasies of the Americanness of the American West. Attention to the transformations across Riggs's writings allows scholars to restore to memory histories of racial intimacy across East and West, conflicted regional identities within the United States, and notions of citizenship that emerged throughout the twentieth century.

The next chapter, "Specters of Loss: Violence and the National Mission in Post-9/11 Westerns," examines how the Western has often emerged during times of collective crisis as a useful narrative for mediating larger national uncertainties. The post-9/11 era provides abundant instances in which the genre has functioned as a discursive weapon for the United States in its war on terror. At the same time, the period has also seen sharp criticisms of the triumphalist and exceptionalist uses of Wild West discourses and the dangers of American "cowboy diplomacy" following September 11, 2001. Focusing on *In the Valley of Elah* (2007), *The Hurt Locker* (2008), and *True Grit* (2010), chapter 5 traces how the Western has also been used to express deep ambivalence about the larger civilizing mission of American foreign policy. Even as the genre may foreground desires for new frontiers and new terrain, the Western is also haunted by the specter of loss, by the eventual and seemingly inevitable demise of those very forms of freedom frequently promised by the form. These films highlight the problems of censorship and restricted speech, as well as the pitfalls of narrowminded understandings of morality, justice, and revenge as issues that arose when the American cowboy moved to the new frontiers of the Middle East.

Chapter 6, "East of the Spaghetti Western: Global Travels of the Genre," notes how the genre of the Western has undergone important permutations throughout its recent travels in the Middle East, where it has experienced a process of adaptation and revision that recasts divisions between savagery and civilization. While the Western has made something of a comeback in the United States in the post-9/11 period, the genre has also circulated transnationally, capturing the attention of populations in Iran, Libya, and Egypt, where popular fiction and film have all recently reconfigured the possibilities of the form. My argument focuses in particular on how the codes and conventions of the Western have been revised by the very audiences who are targeted as threatening or dangerous in an age of terror. Here I attend to the routes through which the genre travels before it arrives in the Middle East, noting that in many cases, the Western loops back to a European context, specifically, to the critical cinema tradition of the spaghetti Westerns, where it undergoes important transformations and revisions before it arrives in the Middle East. The Western often referenced in these global texts is thus not the American Western per se but the Italian one, a reminder of the transnational influences that have shaped the genre and have been part of the form from its earliest days.

The concluding chapter, subtitled "Once Upon a Time in the Middle East," examines two revisionist uses of the genre in global popular culture. Both Beto Gómez's *Saving Private Perez* (2011) and "Ahlan Ezayak" (2007), a music video by the Saudi-Kuwaiti pop singer Shams, offer critical takes on the Western by decentering the United States and the American cowboy as benevolent providers of freedom and democracy. The storylines of both texts counter post-9/11 cowboy diplomacy by releasing the genre's traditional hostages—depicted here as a dangerous and threatening Mexican presence that must be contained, as well as a weak and feminized Middle East in need of saving. The logic of the popular Western is thus reworked in these two texts for decidedly anticolonial purposes that recast the traditional captive victim and the typical rescuing hero.

Ultimately, this study of the Middle East in the American West examines constructions and circulations of the Western in order to attend to a larger history of multicultural encounters between two regions that are often understood as existing far apart from each other. While the cowboy hero and his civilizing mission frequently appear as captivating elements in defining regional and national culture, this study places these entities within a broader transnational context. In particular, this book emerges out of a desire to revisit uses of the Western plot and cowboy hero in post-9/11 "Lone Ranger diplomacy." While various attempts to build a case for the U.S. war on terror referenced this quintessential American region, genre, and hero, such efforts largely overlook the ways in which these celebrated icons were not so uniquely American after all but were constructed through and against encounters with the Arab and Muslim Middle East. By tracing this history of contact, interaction, and influence, scholars are able to extend the scope of transnational studies and locate a powerful and productive presence of the Middle East in the American West.

ONE

"I Longed to Be an Arab"

The Eastern Origins of the Western

I read some of the many sets of American literary classics
(Cooper's *The Leatherstocking Tales*, Twain's travels and novels,
Hawthorne and Poe stories) with considerable excitement, since
they revealed a complete, parallel world to the Anglo-Egyptian
one in which I had been immersed in Cairo.

—EDWARD SAID

The transferability of empire's organizing metaphors is one of
the key distinguishing characteristics of colonialist discourse—
one that made possible the intertextuality of writing under
empire. Itinerant and adaptive, focusing on colonial myths,
activating imperialist agencies, what we shall call the traveling
metaphor formed an essential constitutive element of
an intensely imagined colonial system.

—ELLEKE BOEHMER

The tale commonly told about the development of the Western
usually begins with its origins in the U.S. East. According to this
story, a powerful but beleaguered eastern group of Anglo Saxon
men positioned the American West as a promising, wild terrain
of authenticity that helped alleviate their sense of disenchantment
with the course of modernization. In his classic study on the "eastern establishment" and the American West, G. Edward White

explains that, as a response to larger pressures emerging during the late nineteenth century, a group of urban elites relied on an interconnected set of social institutions such as boarding schools, Ivy League universities, college clubs, metropolitan men's clubs, and the *Social Register* to consolidate their social power.[1] These institutions created the means for developing self-identity, group allegiance, and a common value system, all of which helped concentrate power in the hands of a small set of influential families.[2] Frederic Remington, Theodore Roosevelt, and Owen Wister were prominent figures whose lives were enhanced by their ties to these eastern institutions and whose writings and artistic work served their class interests by creating a particular vision of the American West. Born within a few years of each other, these men grew up in an East whose economic development shaped their own coming of age; each of them also left the East in order to experience a new start in the American West and then publicized those experiences for audiences back home.[3]

Christine Bold's study of the popular Western builds on this argument to address what she calls the "frontier club." Extending White's discussion to include a larger group of elite easterners and emphasizing the problematic underside of their privilege and influence, Bold reexamines the networks of social power that emerged in the late nineteenth and early twentieth centuries and contributed to the rise of the Western, clinching "the formula which has long served as the most popular face of America."[4] Responding to threats from the new immigration and competition from new wealth, members of the frontier club worked hard to shore up their influence, not only by managing public opinion but also by directing federal policies in the areas of land use, race relations, and the popular press.[5] As Bold explains, their imaginative production of the American West as a space of rejuvenating nature and rugged outdoor experiences came into being through a system of violent exclusions. While they were advocates of numerous conservationist projects, the frontier club also established strict divisions between insiders and outsiders, between populations who could enjoy these spaces of nature and populations who were

"I Longed to Be an Arab"

kept out of them. The frontier club members favored Jim Crow laws, restrictions on immigration, and policies that dispossessed American Indians, ultimately advancing causes that "continue to benefit some of us" while leaving others to "count the cost." For Bold, what has been overlooked in histories of the popular Western are the ways in which the class, race, and gender interests of eastern elites helped constitute the genre and put in place a narrow understanding of the region that "furthered their own cultural, political, and financial interests while violently excluding less powerful groups."[6]

Focusing on similar exclusions at play in this period, Barbara Will examines the development of the genre by pointing to what she calls the "nervous origins of the Western" in the U.S. East. Will traces how cultural pressures in the late nineteenth century gave rise to what was diagnosed among elite easterners as "neurasthenia," a term made popular by the U.S. physician Silas Weir Mitchell to describe a variety of nervous disorders mostly afflicting class-privileged white Americans.[7] Treatments for neurasthenia varied greatly depending on the sex of the patient. As part of their "rest cure," upper-middle-class white women such as Charlotte Perkins Gilman were consigned to "bed rest, force-feeding, and massage" and were required to undertake "as domestic a life as possible" while never touching "pen, brush or pencil" as long as they lived.[8] Meanwhile, upper-middle-class white men—including Owen Wister, author of the highly popular Western *The Virginian* and one of the most famous frontier club members—were prescribed the "West cure," a treatment that involved seeking a "sturdy contest with Nature" through rugged outdoor experiences in the western regions of the United States. Will notes how "a whole generation of nervous men accordingly journeyed westward to recuperate not only by working on ranches and hunting game in the Rockies, but also by writing about their experiences."[9] Many of the codes and conventions of the Western came into being as a result of these "nervous" treatments for this group, with the genre centering on a white western hero who travels "within a sphere of self-contained masculinity, bringing order to an unbalanced environment" through the logic of "strenuous" efforts and "healthful" labors.[10]

These accounts of the eastern establishment's role in the formation of the Western make a compelling case for recognizing how an elite metropolitan group from the U.S. East helped develop the cultural form as a way of recuperating from the various social ills brought about by hypermodernization. My argument extends these histories by calling attention to the ways many members of the eastern establishment who popularized the Western as a key American genre and the Western hero as a quintessential American hero not only had adventures in the West but also journeyed outside the United States, gaining experiences that would shape their narrative visions of the region and the genre. My argument does not displace previous arguments about the emergence of the genre in the U.S. East but expands the sphere of influence beyond American borders and to a broader range of players in order to highlight how contact with another East—in this case, orientalist spaces of the Middle East and North Africa—also informed this history.

Edward Said's autobiography offers a useful opening for tracing some of these developments. In his memoir, *Out of Place*, Said recounts memories of being lost in books while studying at an American boarding school where as a young boy he recognized various continuities between the fiction of both U.S. and European imperial adventure. Here the author describes his sense of dislocation upon leaving Cairo for the United States in the 1950s. During his boyhood years, the boarding school's library rescued him from his feelings of displacement and from what he called the "insufferable daily routine" of scholarly life, an escape that came in the form of classic American fiction, including the writings of James Fenimore Cooper and Mark Twain. Said likewise recalls the books he read during his youth in Egypt, the stories of colonial adventures that chronicled similar intrigues of European heroes, played out across a variety of imperial landscapes. The author remembers devouring these narratives "with considerable excitement, since they revealed a complete, parallel world to the Anglo-Egyptian one in which I had been immersed in Cairo."[11] The intersections and affinities noted by a young student looking for escapist pleasures in the basement library of his boarding school provide glimpses into the common elements linking the imperial adventure tale and the frontier story, those worldly travels of adventuring heroes who encounter danger and intrigue across the globe.

Over the years, it has been common to classify the American version of these adventure stories as "Westerns," with Cooper's Leatherstocking tales typically considered proto-Westerns or what Scott Simmon calls "Eastern Westerns." As he reminds us, the Western was never merely regional or necessarily located in spaces associated with the present-day West but was always based in a geography that continually shifted, partly because, at one moment or another, all regions of the United States have had the opportunity to "claim their time as frontier."[12] In this way, the term "Western" can be somewhat misleading, as it narrows the geographical and thematic scope of the stories, restricting the area in which the genre took place and obscuring the connections the tales have with other nations' adventure narratives. The genre was never a quintessential or uniquely American form, as some critics have claimed, but rather an imitative one that revised, adapted, and extended elements found in other national literatures. Likewise, if the Western was never merely regional, it was also never merely national but always transnational and global, situated as it was on the dividing line between U.S. land claims and those of other nations.

In film studies, the Western is often regarded as a specifically American tradition, the nation's "distinctive contribution to the cinema" and "one of the few art forms native to the United States."[13] In the typical account of the genre, the filmic Western is an American-born tradition that emerges out of the literary Western, which itself may be traced to the frontier narratives of Cooper, who contributed to the production of a national myth and character in the early nineteenth century. According to this story, the later dime novels, with their tales of captivity and rescue, along with the melodramas of silent film helped further develop the literary and cinematic Western into the forms and conventions with which we are familiar today.[14] This well-known version of history tends to emphasize the Western's difference and distinction from European narratives and, as such, presents the genre as American in origin.

Rick Altman traces a development in film history that offers a different understanding of the Western by showing its origins in another cultural context. For Altman, the story begins with the early nickelodeon period, which saw the growing production of what today might be considered "pre-Westerns," or what were then called Wild West films, which were basically chase films, comedies, melodramas, romances, and epics that over time became solidified into a genre simply called "the Western." In the early days of film, the adjective "Western" pointed merely to the usefulness of a specific geography for the setting of a number of different plotlines. Only later did the term "Western" emerge as the name for a series of loosely connected films that played on audience interest in stories set in the region.[15] It was the film industry's move to southern California around 1908—in an effort to escape the patent restrictions put in place by Thomas Edison in New Jersey, where most films previously had been made—that helped solidify the Western as a recognizable genre. Only later did the "Americanness" of the genre develop more directly. With ready-made sets in which to feature their stories, a landscape that lent itself to a particular storyline, and a large body of trained actors and extras who could play the "cowboy," the "Indian," or the "outlaw," the Western became associated with a U.S. setting and site of production. It thus became more difficult to produce these films in Europe because of audience expectations regarding scenery, the absence of proper props, and a lack of appropriate actors who could play these established character types.[16]

Richard Slotkin likewise draws attention to the transformations in literary production occurring in the mid- to late nineteenth century that also reveal a more complicated transnational history of the Western in fiction. With the advent of printing technologies making production cheaper, a new type of publication emerged that was later called the dime novel. This literature was a key element in the development of the Western because, at its inception, it dealt with popular tales of action and adventure. Just as early films

"I Longed to Be an Arab"

set in the American West were not initially regarded as a genre in their own right, the writers of these texts did not understand themselves as creating "Westerns" per se. Instead they churned out hundreds of books that told the story of American adventure, and their contact zones were both domestic and foreign. Thus, before the Western was a noun, it was an adjective, part of a larger constellation of the adventure narrative that took place in various colonial geographies across the globe.[17] These tales of faraway adventure eventually split. While they retained their popularity overall, a significant body of this writing ultimately became identified as the "Western" and was distinguished from other forms of borderland adventures, such as the "oriental" or "African adventure narratives" taking place across the vast geographies of imperialism.[18] Much like the colonial adventure tales that place noble, upright, virile Europeans against degenerate, despotic savage "Others," the stories that became the Western typically feature an upstanding hero, often in the form of a cowboy or gunman who embodies civilization and who must defeat savagery in order to secure freedom, democracy, and justice.[19] Whether set in western U.S. contact zones or in the global outposts of empire, the primary conflict of these adventure tales centers on what John Cawelti has called the "epic" encounter between savagery and civilization.[20]

There are also some distinctions that may be made between U.S. adventure narratives and stories from the British and European tradition. Cawelti distinguishes, for instance, between conflicts facing the adventuring hero in various geographical contexts and the treatment of setting in these tales. In many colonial adventure narratives about the tropical jungle rather than the arid desert, the landscape typically embodies "both hostile and attractive qualities . . . savagery and raw nature that threaten the representatives of civilization." Cawelti goes on to note that, in contrast to the "fresh and open grandeur of the Western landscape," the qualities of the colonial jungle "are superficially attractive, but essentially subversive and dangerous." As he argues, landscape in the Western usually offers the means and setting for "a regenerated social order once the threat of lawlessness has been overcome," but, in the imperial adventure narrative, "the colonial landscape remains alien" to the hero.[21] While certain distinctions may be noted among imperial adventure narratives and orientalist discourses across different national literatures, my account points to more expansive transcultural and global contexts in explaining central developments in the Western. A diverse range of individuals wrote travel narratives and adventure tales set in contact zones across the globe, produced paintings and sketches based on their travels, and discursively employed an orientalist East in the production of the American West. Many of these writers and artists were fascinated by desert landscapes and the diverse horse cultures they encountered throughout the world, all of which in turn influenced their contributions to the genre.

Karl May is an important author to consider in this regard. The extremely prolific and popular German writer employed a diverse range of settings for his adventures stories, only some of which were set in the U.S. West. While he is mostly known for his series of frontier narratives modeled after Cooper's Leatherstocking tales, which feature the Apache chief Winnetou and the authorial stand-in Old Shatterhand—the *Westmann* or frontiersman—May also wrote a number of tales set in the Ottoman Empire.[22] In his Ottoman adventure narratives, Old Shatterhand becomes Kara ben Nemsi—Karl, son of the German—while his sidekick Winnetou is replaced by the Bedouin guide, Hadschi Halef Omar. In the U.S. English-language edition (1899) of May's oriental narrative *Im Lande des Mahdi*, however, the German adventurer becomes an American hero. The protagonist is renamed Jack Hildreth, perhaps in an effort to better sell these narratives to American audiences, who at the time might have been more interested in reading tales about U.S. imperial adventurers across the globe than about the heroic "son of the German" and his colonial endeavors. In *Jack Hildreth on the Nile*, the newly minted American protagonist describes his motivations for leaving the U.S. West, where May's earlier stories were set: "I began to get restless. I had no desire to return to the West, for with Winnetou, my adopted Apache brother, dead, there was little attraction to me in the scenes we had roamed together."

"I Longed to Be an Arab"

Bereft of his blood brother/Native American sidekick, Hildreth seeks new adventures in new lands: "Having once followed the star of empire in a westerly direction, I began to think of the East; I wanted, as Rudyard Kipling says, to hear 'the desert talk.'"[23] In the novel, the adventurer's travels take him to Egypt and Sudan, where he, like the heroes in May's American Westerns, must bravely fight against the forces of savagery.[24]

Other famous writers, including Theodore Roosevelt, Mark Twain, and Frederic Remington, also traveled to the Middle East and North Africa. Roosevelt's adventures, particularly his account of a trip he took with his family to the Holy Lands in 1873, may be read alongside Mark Twain's famous 1869 parody of American visitors to the Middle East and the ways they often employed a transnational nature aesthetic in describing their experiences in the region. Roosevelt's writings a decade later on the American cowboy and ranching life provide other instances of how a comparative landscape rhetoric and a cross-racial discourse came together in shaping these larger East-West relations. In the case of Remington, who traveled to Algeria in 1894 as an illustrator for a series of articles written by his friend Poultney Bigelow for *Harper's* magazine, encounters with the horse cultures and military life in North Africa provided knowledge of an equestrian tradition that differed from what he was familiar with back home, but that became a touchstone in establishing the western American cowboy as a national icon and an important figure in the popular Western. Finally, a particularly famous frontier club member, Owen Wister, also unknowingly referenced the East in positioning the cowboy as a crucial player in U.S. national discourse. While he initially acknowledged how the cowboy's identity was shaped by a larger global history, Wister later expressed ambivalence about this transnational influence and ultimately downplayed its importance in his writings on the West. These eastern establishment writers and artists all brought another East into play in their constructions of the American West and the Western and, in doing so, help draw attention to the global foundations of what has been commonly misrecognized as a quintessential U.S. form.

Fig. 2. Karl May dressed as the character Kara ben Nemsi from his
Ottoman adventure stories (1896). Reprinted with permission,
Karl May Gesellschaft. http://www.karl-may-gesellschaft.de.

Global Travels and the Eastern Establishment

The role Theodore Roosevelt played in the development of the American West has been well documented, particularly his efforts to popularize the region as a rejuvenating place of opportunity and adventure while elevating the role of the American cowboy in U.S. culture. A lesser-known story involves his experiences in the Middle East and his fascination with the desert landscapes of the region. As a ten-year-old boy traveling on a Holy Land tour with his family, Roosevelt began a diary chronicling his experiences. He continued writing in this journal from 1868 to 1877, until he was nineteen. His youthful writings about the Holy Land are important to examine for the ways they offer early instances of the continuities he saw between the landscapes of the Middle East and the American West, connections that were important to his elevation of the cowboy in the late nineteenth century and his celebration of the figure's achievements across the western United States.

During the nineteenth century, the Holy Land tour became a popular excursion for Protestant Anglo Americans, who developed a subgenre of travel writing about Palestine and the Holy Lands, which at that time were administered by the Ottoman Empire. When the Roosevelt family arrived in Alexandria in 1872 during their Holy Land journey, the young traveler could hardly contain his excitement at finally encountering a sacred geography that had long held his fascination. "How I gazed on it!" he wrote. "It was Egypt, the land of my dreams; Egypt the most ancient of all countries! . . . It was a sight to awaken a thousand thoughts, and it did."[25] For Roosevelt, Egypt was a much-anticipated destination, a romanticized space that captivated his youthful imagination. Indeed, the land that Protestant Anglo Americans like Roosevelt encountered on their tours was in many ways already "familiar" to them through their reading of the Bible and previous travel accounts about the region. These tourists also gained familiarity about the Holy Lands and the Middle East through stories from *The Arabian Nights*, a collection of tales that positioned the region as the fantastical and mythical Orient and that as Susan Nance points out remained highly popular and in steady demand throughout the United States during the nineteenth century.[26]

After their visit to Alexandria, Roosevelt's family traveled to Cairo, where they took an excursion to the Giza pyramids. While the women stayed behind, the men of the group ascended the structure, aided by locals who worked in the tourist trade. In his diaries, the young Roosevelt describes his surprise after one of the Egyptians tried to "boost" him "from behind" as he climbed up the steep rocks, an effort that eventually reaped its rewards after his arrival at the top. He wrote,

> The ascent of the Pyramid was like walking up an immense flight of stairs, with every stair four feet high and one or two feet broad, but as the arabs pulled you all the time the exertion was not nearly so great as I expected and as we were on the shady side we were not very warm when we got to the top where a most refreshing breeze was blowing. One poor gentleman almost fainted on the way however. Once on top the view was perfectly magnificent. On one side was Cairo and the valley of the Nile, all green and fertile and on the other stretched the vast, boundless, but by no means level desert of the Sahara. To look out on the desert gives one some what the same feeling as to look over the ocean or over one of the North American Prairies.[27]

Roosevelt's description of the Giza plateau from the heights uses a comparative language in making sense of the geography below. In his case, the view he encountered in Giza was meaningful in the context of a landscape aesthetic he employed transnationally, whereby the Nile valley that gave way to the vast boundless Sahara became a reminder of the familiar prairies of his home country. Hilton Obenzinger argues that U.S. travelers in the Holy Lands frequently saw the region "through American eyes," and what they viewed "often spoke to the formation of American cultural structures," elements that typically had very little relation to what was in fact "before their eyes."[28] The comparative descriptions they made were thus deeply entangled with "secular constructions of national destiny," as Anglo Americans repeatedly imagined continuities between the sacred histories and missions of the Old and the New World in bolstering their own understandings of nation and self.[29] This fixation with Holy Land travel may be understood as a symptom of larger anxieties shaping U.S. settler colonial culture, especially formations of religious and national identity. "With America conceived as the New Jerusalem," Obenzinger explains, "the old Holy Land was encountered as a terrain of crucial cultural dynamics both challenging and reaffirming America's narrative of settlement as divine errand."[30]

The discursive continuities between the Holy Lands and the U.S. West also appear in what is still the most popular account of the American Holy Land tour, as well as the most famous parody of such travel: Mark Twain's *The Innocents Abroad, or The New Pilgrim's Progress*. The book was published in 1869, a few years before Roosevelt traveled to the region, and offers a humorous send-up of tourist writings about the Holy Land and the comparative nature aesthetic U.S. writers often employed. Twain's narrative critiques common responses toward the sacred lands frequently expressed in American travel accounts, even as he himself engages in not a few of the literary sins he accuses his fellow travelers of committing. His writings of the tour, which were commissioned by newspapers in San Francisco and New York, parody the childish innocence displayed by U.S. tourists on board the *Quaker City* tour. At one point, Twain jokes about how a youthful familiarity with fantastical stories about the Holy Land frequently results in misguided contemporary views of the region among adult travelers:

> To see a camel train laden with the spices of Arabia and the rare fabrics of Persia come marching through the narrow alleys of the bazaar, among porters with their burdens, money-changers, lamp-merchants, Alnaschars in the glassware business, portly cross-legged Turks smoking the famous narghili, and the crowds drifting to and fro in the fanciful costumes of the East, is a genuine revelation of the Orient. The picture lacks nothing. It casts you back at once into your forgotten boyhood, and again you dream over the wonders of the Arabian Nights; again your companions are princes,

your lord is the Caliph Haround Al Raschid, and your servants are terrific giants and genii that come with smoke and lightning and thunder, and go as a storm goes when they depart![31]

The author wryly observes that upon their arrival in various locations, tourists often pulled out ancient maps to consult in an effort to ensure the authority of their own travels. They also read Bible passages and travel tales about Palestine that corresponded to the locations they were visiting as if to authenticate their own experiences in the region. Twain skewers such acts, noting that these efforts frequently had the unintended effect of creating fictional accounts rather than truthful reports. Indeed, in his own case, Twain confesses that the sacred images and information of the region he held did not match up well with the physical lands he saw firsthand, his previous textual encounters from his boyhood interfering with his actual experiences with the land. "Some of my ideas were wild enough," he muses. "I can see easily enough that if I wish to profit by this tour and come to a correct understanding of the matters of interest connected with it, I must studiously and faithfully unlearn a great many things I have somehow absorbed."[32]

The author tries to aid the process of unlearning by poking fun at earlier U.S. travel writers who often confuse and conflate the deserts of the Holy Land with the landscapes of the American West. He particularly satirizes William C. Prime, whose *Tent Life in the Holy Land* and *Boat Life in Egypt and Nubia* were published in 1857 and were widely read accounts in the period.[33] In his narrative, Twain refers to Prime as "Grimes," and he is especially annoyed by the language the author uses—a popular frontier rhetoric he transposes to the Middle East, thus enabling him to interchange Arabs and Bedouins with American Indians. In *Boat Life in Egypt and Nubia*, Prime describes a conversation he overhears among a group of Arab soldiers guarding a temple, their language replete with sounds of a "guttural *hugh*, like a North American Indian's expression of surprise."[34] At another point, the author writes about a Bedouin he encounters whose "resemblance to the North American Indian was startling. Every gesture was similar; and the eloquence was the same natural flow of fierce, biting, furious words, yet full of imagery and beauty."[35] Likewise, in *Tent Life in the Holy Land*, Prime describes his Arab travel guide and translator Abd-el-Atti as a "stout-built athletic Egyptian, with a light copper complexion, a very North American Indian countenance."[36]

In his own travel narrative, Twain offers a somewhat different portrait, describing the Holy Land inhabitants he encounters as an underwhelming and degraded presence. Leave it to James Fenimore Cooper, he complains, "to find beauty in the Indians, and to Grimes to find it in the Arabs."[37] For Twain, the latter do not inspire much admiration, partly because they fail to live up to their reputation as a formidable foe, as depicted by previous travel writers. Describing a side excursion on their tour, for instance, he expresses mock disappointment that he and his fellow travelers encounter no conflicts, nor any other people along the way, "much less lawless hordes of Bedouins."[38] Twain later tells of an alleged raid on their traveling party by a seemingly dangerous group of armed desert outlaws, who eventually turn out to be merely a few "cadaverous Arabs, in shirts and bare legs," a "guard of vermin" who are sent to protect the Holy Land travelers in the event of an actual attack.[39] Twain jokes that the sensationalized dangers of desert travel described by previous Holy Land writers do not stem from the violent cross-cultural conflicts but may instead come from closer quarters. "I do not mind Bedouins,—I am not afraid of them," he writes, "because neither Bedouins nor ordinary Arabs have shown any disposition to harm us, but I *do* feel afraid of my own comrades." The author goes on to describe his trepidation, recounting how his misguided fellow travelers arm themselves against a possible desert raid, shooting a "little potato-gun of a revolver" with its "startling little pop" and its "small pellet" flying through the air and more often than not missing its intended target.[40]

Although he dismisses the common racialized language found in typical Holy Land narratives, Twain himself employs the Bedouin-as-Indian or Arab-as-Indian comparison, imagining cross-cultural encounters through U.S. frontier discourses.[41] One of the more famous examples occurs when he describes the Bedouins as "ill-clad and ill-conditioned savages, much like our Indians," and goes on to dismiss both groups as "dangerous . . . sons of the desert."[42] The description continues throughout Twain's writings, with one Arab being "swarthy as an Indian" and a group of Bedouins characterized as "Digger Indians."[43] His denigrating racialized language culminates in an unsettling description about encountering "the usual assemblage of squalid humanity" made up of a group of mothers and their hungry children, who watch the Americans' "every motion with that vile, uncomplaining impoliteness which is so truly Indian."[44] For Twain, the response "makes a white man so nervous and uncomfortable and savage that he wants to exterminate the whole tribe."[45] Here the author's violent reaction to Arab and Bedouin poverty becomes a moral panic about race and nation. As Obenzinger notes, however, Twain seems largely unaware of the economic crisis facing the region. He appears to have no knowledge of the near collapse of the cotton market in Palestine and Egypt due to global fluctuations caused by the end of the American Civil War. Twain also seems ignorant of the devastating result of that year's crop failures, as well as the dire effects of locust plagues from the previous two years that further hurt the region's agricultural industry.[46]

Throughout *The Innocents Abroad*, Twain complains that the reality he encounters in the Holy Land rarely matches the images he carries in his mind, and he insists that readers evaluate and revise their own expectations about the region. The author applies this observation to his own knowledge of the region, at one point referring to the boyhood stories he heard about the talented horsemanship of the Middle East and denouncing their accuracy given his experiences in the present era: "To glance at the genuine son of the desert is to take the romance out of him forever—to behold his steed is to long in charity to strip his harness off and let him fall to pieces."[47] Twain goes on to explain the need to reassess these old childhood stories:

> I hope that in the future I may be spared any more sentimental praises of the Arab's idolatry of his horse. In boyhood, I longed to be

an Arab of the desert and have a beautiful mare, and call her Selim or Benjamin or Mohammed, and feed her with my own hands, and let her come into the tent, and teach her to caress me and look fondly upon me with her great tender eyes; and I wished that a stranger might come at such a time and offer me a hundred thousand dollars for her, so that I could do like other Arabs—hesitate, yearn for the money, but overcome by my love for my mare, at last say, "Part with thee, my beautiful one! . . . Away, tempter, I scorn thy gold!" and then bound into the saddle and speed over the desert like the wind![48]

Here the devoted relationship between the Arab of the past and his greatly esteemed horse almost resembles a courtship or love affair, so "fondly" and "tenderly" does the human owner treat the noble animal. Such fierce attachment and abiding dedication to their horses, however, cannot be found among the present-day Arab riders that Twain encounters on the tour:

If these Arabs be like the other Arabs, their love for their beautiful mares is a fraud. These of my acquaintance have no love for their horses . . . and no knowledge of how to treat them or care for them. The Syrian saddle-blanket is a quilted mattress two or three inches thick. It is never removed from the horse, day or night. It gets full of dirt and hair, and becomes soaked with sweat. It is bound to breed sores. These pirates never think of washing a horse's back. They do not shelter the horses in the tents, either; they must stay out and take the weather as it comes. Look at poor cropped and dilapidated "Baalbec," and weep for the sentiment that has been wasted upon the Selims of romance![49]

Twain's complaint that the Arab horsemen of his era do not measure up to the celebrated equestrians of the old legends functions as a way of diminishing the cultural authority of the Old World from a New World perspective. The author deflates American travelers' expectations about the Holy Land, Obenzinger suggests, in an effort to dislodge popular meanings assigned to the region and in the process alleviate U.S. settler colonial anxieties about their own nation-building projects and acts of conquest across the American West.[50]

The racialized language Twain offered in his travel account continued to appear in U.S. literature, taking on new significance as writers found the comparison useful for other purposes. Arab references, for instance, would shape encounters in the popular Western, in many cases as a way of addressing contested land claims in the region. Zane Grey, the author of more than sixty adventure narratives set in the West, frequently references Arabs in his stories, with one of his Anglo heroes in *Wildfire* (1910) describing a Navajo as "an Arab of the Painted Desert." In his best-selling novel, *Riders of the Purple Sage* (1912) and its sequel, *Rainbow Trail* (1915), Grey develops the racial connection further, offering a critique of Mormon polygamy as a foreign or anti-American practice by describing the custom as the western kin to the harems of the Middle East.[51] By the late nineteenth century, as the American cowboy had developed into a popular icon, and, as the Western emerged as a significant genre in its own right, the figure of the Arab also became a way of negotiating the meanings assigned to the genre's new national hero. In an interesting way, cowboys too would become Arabs, with popular discourse recognizing the American horseman's important links to a global history and his international inheritance. What is important to note in this context, however, are the ways the racial language operates at first as a way of elevating the American cowboy. It is only later that the discourse shifts and becomes more exclusive, downplaying this history in order to situate the cowboy as a unique and quintessential hero of U.S. origin.

Arabs and Cowboys

In his 1888 account of western labor and adventure based on his experiences in Dakota Territory, *Ranch Life and the Hunting-Trail*, Theodore Roosevelt employs a cross-racial comparison, building on romantic ideas of the orientalist East and the Arab horseman in order to lend legitimacy to the American cowboy. Illustrated by his friend Frederic Remington, *Ranch Life and the Hunting-Trail*

"I Longed to Be an Arab"

reads like a conduct book introducing metropolitan U.S. readers to the customs and behaviors found in the American West, especially regarding the pleasures of rigorous outdoor life on the range, where the primitive natural landscape promises rejuvenation and renewal. Twain himself employed a similar cultural comparison in *Roughing It* (1872) to elaborate on the charms of camp life in the West. "We are descended from desert-lounging Arabs, and countless ages of growth toward perfect civilization have failed to root out of us the nomadic instinct," the author explains to readers.[52]

Like Twain's introduction to western camp life, Roosevelt's narrative offers background about the world of the ranch and the horseman. In doing so, he locates the western figure within a larger global history, countering the negative associations many Americans held toward cowboys, who prior to the mid-1880s were often regarded as a marginalized class of violent men located on the social fringes, part of the seedy violent underworld of the western frontier. Throughout much of the nineteenth century, the term cowboy carried pejorative meanings. In the 1830s, it was often applied negatively to gangs of Anglo Texans who, as cattle thieves, notoriously threatened the livelihood of Mexican ranchers across the southwest.[53] Lonn Taylor and Ingrid Maar argue that cowboys were typically depicted in the popular press before the Civil War as bandits who were often "publicly drunk" and endlessly "engaging in reckless, lawless, and frequently murderous behavior."[54]

Roosevelt promotes the cowboy in his 1888 narrative, transforming him into a noble rancher on horseback, a rugged outdoorsman who lives a simple, primitive life in the West and who has ties with other important horse cultures of the world:

> Civilization seems as remote as if we were living in an age long past. . . . It is the life of men who live in the open, who tend their herds on horseback, who go armed and ready to guard their lives by their own prowess, whose wants are very simple, and who call no man master. Ranching is an occupation like those of vigorous, primitive pastoral peoples, having little in common with the humdrum, workaday business world of the nineteenth century; and the

free ranchman in his manner of life shows more kinship to an Arab sheik than to a sleek city merchant or tradesman.[55]

In Roosevelt's description, the western horseman appears as an independent man of the range whose honest and vigorous labors enable him to embody a dignified masculinity that connects him to a long line of free, master-less men. The comparison lends credibility to the horseman of the American West, linking him to a larger historical context and other elevated figures of the world. An important aspect of the horseman's redemption is that he now belongs to an international brotherhood of riders whose origins emerge in much older cultures and whose history provides a pedigree and status to the cowboy in the post–Civil War period. The cowboy on the western ranch gains authority because he shares a "kinship" with these other "vigorous" free men. In Roosevelt's account, the Anglo American horseman becomes an admirable and distinguished figure who has more in common with Arab sheiks than he does with degraded American workers back east.

The elevation of the cowboy to the status of an American icon emerged over time and as the result of several cultural developments. The nineteenth-century dime novelist Frederick Whittaker, for instance, is often credited with positioning the cowboy as the representative frontier hero in popular fiction, according to Christine Bold. Whittaker's novel *Parson Jim, King of the Cowboys; or, The Gentle Shepherd's Big "Clean Out,"* appeared in 1882 in Beadle's Dime Library. Its populist tale about the clash between large cattle barons and the small family ranches employing independent and hardworking cowboys would be retold and reworked by Owen Wister in his famous novel *The Virginian* (1902).[56] Locating the cowboy in a national symbolic role, a number of authors likewise created a lineage for him that borrowed from and relied on other national traditions. In Beadle's Half Dime Library, for instance, the figure of Buck Taylor, who was first fictionalized by Prentiss Ingraham in 1887 in *Buck Taylor, King of the Cowboys; or, The Raiders and the Rangers*, gains authority and prestige through his ties to other horse cultures of the world. As Bold argues, this cowboy's powerful frontier status may be traced in part to his chivalrous international ancestry, his identity and appearance becoming more flamboyant throughout the novel as he is increasingly displayed through "showy gun play" and described as "richly dressed in bejeweled, quasi-vaquero costume."[57]

Wister further positioned the western horseman as an iconic American in *The Virginian*, which was published in 1902, the same year that U.S. historian and naval expert Alfred Thayer Mahan invented the term the "Middle East."[58] Like other members of the frontier club, Wister reacted to the profound changes taking place across the nation by situating the U.S. West as the last surviving stronghold of real American values, what Liza Nicholas describes as a counterpoint to "the degenerate, emasculate, foreign influences" that the elites believed were increasingly controlling U.S. cities.[59] In 1891 Wister was already expressing concern about preserving the American West on the page. "Why wasn't some Kipling saving the sage-brush for American literature, before the sage-brush and all that it signified went the way of the California forty-niner, went the way of the Mississippi steam-boat, went the way of everything?" he lamented.[60] Like many elite Anglo Saxons who feared the rapid changes taking place in eastern U.S. cities, the author reacted strongly to this social upheaval, turning toward the values of the wild and the primitive. As Nicholas argues, "Wister, Remington, Teddy Roosevelt, and others of their social group, attributed the cataclysms that rocked the security of their upper-middle-class world—the Haymarket Riots of 1886, the Homestead Strike in 1892, the Pullman Strike of 1894—to the behaviors of uncontrollable, 'alien,' and unrepentant working classes and recently arrived immigrants. . . . The West . . . represented . . . an uncorrupted space in which they could imagine and create the sort of cultural icon needed to thwart the power of the problematic, 'un-American' working classes."[61] Intent on countering such disturbing upheaval and unsettling changes, elite easterners positioned the western horseman as embodying real American values—a solid work ethic, a sense of independence, and an uncorrupted masculinity. The cowboy was meant to be an authentic national symbol, a powerful response to the growing population of unruly, "un-American" workers who upset the larger social order. Yet, in deciding on the form of the horseman, elite easterners ended up choosing an icon whose origins were in fact un-American. Such a hero was actually not American by birth but rather a figure whose history ranged across world cultures, the cowboy version being merely the latest instance in a long line of previous global horsemen.

For some writers, the cowboy's mixed ancestry became a vexed issue. In Wister's well-known essay, "The Evolution of the Cow-Puncher" (1895), produced out of a dialogue with his friend Remington and intended as part of a longer but never completed project to be titled *The Course of Empire*, the author grapples with the prehistory of the American horseman, at first acknowledging his global antecedents and only later restricting them to an Anglo Saxon inheritance. Although he notes the figure's ancestry in the vaquero—"Let it be remembered that the Mexican was the original cowboy, and that the American improved on him"—Wister is reluctant to fully admit the cowboy's connections to a larger history of horse cultures outside of an Anglo Saxon context.[62] Wister takes care to set the American cowpuncher against the "debased and mongrel" population of the cities who represented the wrong kind of wild and primitive impulses, those "hordes of encroaching alien vermin" who reduced U.S. urban centers to a "hybrid farce."[63] In an effort to ward off contamination from such racial and national Others, Wister purges much of the threatening foreignness from the cowboy, leaving primarily the Anglo Saxon inheritance. The cowboy for him is not so much a modern figure of the frontier but the present-day embodiment of the age-old Anglo Saxon horseman whose "surviving fittest instinct . . . through the centuries" makes him into an exemplary "conqueror, invader, navigator, buccaneer, explorer, colonist, tiger-shooter," such that "the footprints of his sons" may now be found in all "corners of the earth."[64]

Wister's efforts to locate the cowpuncher in an Anglo Saxon heritage are marked by contradiction and ambivalence. He frequently notes how American cowboys borrowed from the tradition of Mexican horse cultures, which is particularly evident in

"I Longed to Be an Arab"

the terminology they adapted as part of U.S. ranch life, such as *ramuda*, *lobo*, *arroyo*, *riata*, *chapparajos*, and *cincha*.[65] Yet, the author's acknowledgments of these linguistic borrowings ultimately do not have much bearing on the meanings he assigns to the American cowboy, nor do they extend far enough by recognizing the prior borrowings from the horse cultures of the Moors. The historian Charles Colley points out that Spanish horsemanship was itself shaped by the Muslim occupation of Spain from the eighth to the fifteenth centuries. After several "disastrous encounters" with the Moorish cavalry, the Spaniards adapted various elements found in the riding style of the conquerors, including "the use of the light Moorish lance, Arabian and Berber horse breeds, and the varied techniques of maneuvering in battle."[66] Colley notes that ornamentations on saddles were also of Moorish origin and that Arabic words have historically informed cowboy life in the American Southwest. "*Alasán* is an Arabic word for sorrel," he explains, with other examples being "*moro* (gray), *cincho* (cinch), *jáquma* (anglicized into hackamore) and *barbuquejo* (the thong tied to the horse's lower jaw and used as a bridle by the Plains Indians.).*"[67] This international, hybrid mix found in horse cultures across North America needed to be managed, however, in order for the cowboy to become a quintessential U.S. figure. In his writings, Wister himself downplayed the non–Anglo Saxon elements in the cowboy's history and acknowledged the influences of the vaquero briefly, only to then set them aside.[68]

In writing "The Evolution of the Cow-Puncher," Wister collaborated with his friend Frederic Remington, who also contributed illustrations for the piece. During his twenty-one years as an artist, Remington became one of the most popular illustrators in the United States and was known primarily for his artwork featuring cowboys, Indians, bison, and military life in the American West. His training began in 1878, when he studied for two years in the art school at Yale. After completing his university education and experiencing some unfulfilling stints at various jobs while living at home with his widowed mother, Remington made his way out west to experience the invigorating and rejuvenating challenges of ranch life. He eventually settled in Kansas, where he invested in and subsequently lost much of his inheritance raising sheep rather than cattle. In 1885 the artist returned to New York, where he sold a drawing of a western scene to *Harper's Weekly Magazine*, thus beginning a long association that would eventually make him one of the most celebrated western artists of the period. Remington again enrolled in art school, studying under two former students of the famous French orientalist painter and sculptor, Jean-Léon Gérôme.[69] Years later when he illustrated Wister's essay, one of the images Remington produced, entitled *The Last Cavalier*, would be particularly striking for the ways it merged the riders of the world with the cowboy of the American West. The work points to the past glories of other previous military cultures, which now must give way to an American presence and its new forms of heroism as found in the mounted soldiers of the U.S. West.[70]

In the shadowy background of *The Last Cavalier*, Remington includes traces of the world's previous horse cultures, a global history his friend Wister references in his work and then ignores in his celebration of the cowboy. Remington's illustration for the essay showcases a ghostly procession of global horse cultures, a phantom line of Mongols, Moors, Crusaders, gauchos—a population of diverse riders set across a misty, dreamlike background with a U.S. cowboy and his horse featured prominently in the fore-ground, an embodiment of the ideas of Anglo Saxonism as the pinnacle of human "progress." Some critics have noted that Remington's western landscapes tend to remain rather underdeveloped, the natural terrain more often than not "effaced entirely by fore-grounded humans."[71] As Scott Simmon argues, "For all his fasci-nation with the cavalry and Indians," Remington never managed to figure out "how to depict western landscape, which even in his finished paintings tends to be featureless washes of color or veg-etationless sketches behind figures grouped in the foreground."[72]

I would argue that the effaced landscape in *The Last Cavalier*—its parade of blurred, spectral images of the world's previous horsemen—may capture in a telling way how Remington regarded the larger history out of which the meanings of the U.S. West and

"I Longed to Be an Arab"

Fig. 3. Frederic Remington, *The Last Cavalier*,
from *Harper's New Monthly Magazine*, September 1895.

the American cowboy emerged. This global context serves as a
fading backdrop that needed to eventually recede out of the picture in order for the cowboy hero to assume his elevated place in
American and world culture. Here the artist situates the American
cowboy at the center of the composition, as the only horseman in
full focus; two Spanish cavaliers look back at him from the right
corner of the frame. In Alexander Nemerov's description, it is as
though these side figures "announce some special affinity between
the two," with the movement across the frame suggesting that the
American cowboy represents "the last in an evolutionary line of
noble horsemen."[73] In this way, the human subject at the center
haunts himself. The title of the piece names the figure as the last,
the embodiment of an imperiled American West, and also signaled
the larger threat to the cowboy hero himself, a figure already on
the demise even as he was being situated as a national hero by figures such as Roosevelt, Wister, and Remington.[74]

Two years before he contributed illustrations for Wister's "Evolution of the Cow-Puncher," Remington produced artwork during a visit to Algeria with his friend from Yale, the writer Poultney

Bigelow, who had been editor of the school newspaper and was responsible for publishing Remington's first drawings during their university years. At the time, Remington wished to embark on an international trip, but he needed a sponsor to finance the venture. Lt. Powhatan Clarke was observing cavalry training in Germany, and Remington was particularly fascinated by the prospect of illustrating military life in different international settings. The artist had maintained an active correspondence with Clarke and at one point contacted him, writing "we must do a trip together.—Lets go down into the Balkan states or Hungary—or Algiers.—Let's do a 'Scout with the Buffalo soldiers in Algiers.'—would nt that be a world beater."[75] The lieutenant declined the offer but put Remington in contact again with his old friend Bigelow, who was then the editor of *Outing* magazine. Bigelow agreed to the excursion and invited Remington to accompany him on two international trips, first to Russia in 1892 and then to North Africa in 1893.

For their journey to Algeria, the two men arrived in Oran and then traveled by railroad to the Sahara, where they hoped to observe members of the French colonial military at their desert outposts. Remington mentioned how much he looked forward to encountering Arabian horses and North African riders firsthand; he likewise anticipated that Algeria would closely resemble the familiar Arizona desert he had previously illustrated for *Harper's* in 1886. During the train ride, the artist eventually moved from his first-class seat to the second-class compartment, where he smoked a cigar and enjoyed taking in what he called the "exotic odors" of the "Kabylles, Jews and Moors."[76] In his autobiography, Bigelow recounts that, at the time, he responded ambivalently to his companion's change of seats, noting that the second-class area was meant to be "where 'natives' ride, after the manner of our *Jim Crow* cars in the former slave states."[77] Remington didn't seem to notice these meanings and instead enthusiastically mingled with the "exotic" passengers on board the train. The two men eventually met a French couple on the ride, who offered to introduce them to Arab soldiers during their stay in Algeria.

In his essay for *Harper's*, Bigelow describes Remington's search for potential models and his good fortune in finally locating an Algerian cavalryman employed in the French service. This time it was Bigelow who would employ the racial trope, writing that "Arabs are very much like our North American Indians in their evasiveness. They carry away sheep with the greatest facility; they set fire to hay-stacks without ever being discovered. The white man who settles in the midst of the community cannot sleep secure unless he has paid blackmail to the Arabs about him." Bigelow then describes meeting Mustafa, an Algerian soldier whom Remington eventually decided he wanted as a model for his drawings: "At the door stood a Spahi orderly, straight as a Mohawk, and equally inscrutable. He saluted." Bigelow announces to the soldier that a "great painter has come to paint you—to paint your beautiful burnoose, your silver stirrups, your shining sash, your gorgeous saddle-bags."[78] Here the writer gives voice to barely concealed fears stemming from instabilities in the colonial order, an ambivalence surrounding the rule of occupied lands and the panicked sense of vulnerability that Anglo Americans seem to share with the French in Algeria. In his writings, however, Bigelow contains the threat by later presenting the Algerian horseman not as a menacing frontier foe but as a noble savage whose equestrian skills may be noteworthy but who is placed on a timeline that consigns him to a receding and distant past.

During his stay, Bigelow notes various similarities and differences among the world's military cultures, commenting on the Algerian saddle, which he calls a "frightfully heavy affair, weighing at least ten times as much as that used by an American trooper." He also observes that the "Arab stirrup alone weighs as much as one American saddle" and that instead of the blanket used by American troops, which is folded up under the saddle, the Arab riders use "half a dozen saddle-cloths of different colors, looking rather showy when the wind tossed them about, but not a very practical arrangement."[79] During their visit with the desert troops, a French officer shares his thoughts on the connections between the colonized inhabitants of occupied Algeria and the American West, telling Remington, "You would have equally good results with your

North American Indians if you treated them as justly as we do our Arabs."[80] The officer locates himself in the position of the experienced imperial advisor, offering the protocols of military rule and colonial management in French-occupied Algeria as a model for the United States to follow in managing and maintaining its own colonial power over Native Americans in the West.

Bigelow's attitudes toward Arab horsemen reveal social Darwinian notions of natural superiority, as in his belief that Algerians are closer to savagery on the alleged timeline of development rather than the embodiment of a present civilization, as is the U.S. cowboy. He observes distinctions between the horse cultures of Algeria and the American West, satirizing in particular how Arabs allegedly forge close physical relationships with their animals:

> It was like—but how unlike—the border life of our western territories. Here were horses of noble strain—loving companions to man—with noses that caressed like the cheek of a girl; great soft eyes, and nostrils that expanded or shrank as a barometer of exquisite sensibility. . . . Remington had known but the mongrel brutes we call mustang—the prairie horse. He survives as does the pariah dog and the product of our city slums through the very coarseness of his fibre. The mustang bucks and seeks to kill his rider; the Arab comes to his master and they whisper lovingly to one another.[81]

Bigelow's description of the partnership between Arab rider and horse exaggerates the attentiveness of the Algerian horseman toward his animal, which allows the author to locate North Africans closer to the nonhuman world and thus within the realm of nature itself, an embodiment of the savage and the primitive. In his writings, the close relationship that the human and animal share, having developed throughout the long history of Arab horsemanship, appears so intimate and familiar that it seems almost sexual in nature. Bigelow is left wondering if the wild horses or "mongrel brutes" of the American West finally prove superior to their North African counterparts, which, even though they appear domesticated and closer to human culture, are somehow lacking in comparison.

Such close relations between human and nonhuman animal

in the latter instance point to common understandings shared by European Americans who invented distinctions between so-called modern and premodern cultures and their relationship to the natural world. To be modern in this logic, John Berger observes, is to continually feel as if one is alienated from the natural world. He argues that, after banishing the natural from their everyday lives, modern cultures typically feel compelled to call back that very nature in what are often unusual new forms.[82] The cult of the primitive that figures such as Remington and other influential easterners located in the U.S. West and among Native Americans, as well as North Africans, serves as one way of calling wild nature into the modern world. At the same time, worship of the primitive allows them to maintain a contradiction whereby the human populations associated with the wild, the primitive, or the savage do not hold social power but instead yield ground to progress and to a new civilized order. T. J. Jackson Lears describes this belief within the context of what he calls "anti-modern modernism," an ambivalent structure of feeling among modern elites that cannot be categorized as "simply escapism" but must be understood as often coexisting "with enthusiasm for material progress." For Lears, the feeling went beyond mere nostalgia for passing cultures and served as a "complex blend of accommodation and protest" that "helped ease accommodation to new and secular cultural modes" for elite metropolitan Americans in the late nineteenth and early twentieth centuries.[83] Remington's antimodern modernism enabled him to maintain contradictory thoughts about national progress and racial superiority coexisting with the so-called primitive and the wild.

Such complex responses may be located in Remington's observations and art about the global horse cultures he observed on a visit to the Chicago World's Fair in 1893. In "A Gallop through the Midway," Remington reveals his fascination with the exotic international cultures on display, writing that, on a visitor's stroll through the fair, it is possible to "satiate one's appetite for strange sights and sounds, and regale one's self with several hundred distinct and separate odors."[84] In his study of the artist's continuing aesthetic and cultural significance, *In the Remington Moment*, Stephen Tatum aptly notes the ways Remington seems to position himself at the World's Fair with a certain modern detachment as a "blasé cosmopolitan wanderer," a persona particularly evident in the artist's summation of Cairo Street and the Midway.[85] "We did all the savages in turn, as every one else must do who goes there," Remington succinctly declares.[86] "Doing the savages" in this instance implies a kind of consumption or incorporation of the primitive's power on the part of the visitor.

Describing his stroll through the Midway, Remington is captivated by the diverse cultures he encounters. He writes about "the clank of a crooked sabre" carried by "a man in blue clothes, turban, and red leather shoes [striding] down the middle of the street . . . you feel with the sense of admiration creeping over you that if you were not an American you would be a savage of that type."[87] In his study of the meanings assigned to the international performers at the Chicago World's Fair by some audiences, Zeese Papanikolas argues that elites "have always been fascinated by a certain kind of primitive," their responses emerging in the belief that such societies are "prior to history, anteceding the social changes of industrial life and its democratic leveling—in short, all that threatens the superiority" of the elites "and their "supposedly 'timeless values.'"[88] As Papanikolas goes on to argue, however, the "code of the savage" ultimately shares much with the "code" of elites, both of which are regarded as favoring all that is "simple, inflexible, and impervious to the battering rams of economic and historical change."[89]

Remington's admiration for what he calls the "Wild East" continues in his descriptions of his encounters with cultural Others.[90] "I can understand why writers and artists have dwelt so long on the Bedouin," he writes, "for if he is not a dashing fellow, with his color and hightailed horse, nothing can be." The artist goes on to report an exchange he has with another fairgoer while viewing a performance of Bedouin women dancing in the Midway. The audience includes a group of "honest Illinois yeomen seated about on chairs, grinning cheerfully as the dancing women whirled. They ruined the environment and consequently the dance." Reming-

"I Longed to Be an Arab"

Fig. 4. Frederic Remington, *Columbia Exposition—a Note from the Wild East in the Midway Plaisance*, from *Harper's Weekly*, October 21, 1893.

ton writes that his companion "fired Arabic at the women, close range, and they replied" and that afterward, "one old lady asked me if I was a Turk—because I looked so intelligent as the conversation proceeded, I supposed—and I said: 'Si, señora, me heap Turk.'"[91] Here the artist offers an invented language of hybridity to reference the diverse cultures on display at the World's Fair. Such transnational encounters shaped the work Remington produced about the West. Yet, while he and other writers relied on the cultures of the orientalist East to lend authority and cultural power to the region and its iconic hero, these references would pose a threat to their constructions of the American West and the rising status of the frontier horseman as a unique national type. Even as encounters with the people, cultures, and landscapes of the Middle East and North Africa were a structuring factor in their representations, such influences were often invoked only to be dismissed and disregarded, a disavowal that still haunts the American West and the Western and that continues to frame how the region and the genre are constituted in popular U.S. culture and political discourse.

"I Longed to Be an Arab"

TWO

From the Moors

The Easts and Wests of Willa Cather

Islam stands as one of the primary exclusions upon which both
national and hemispheric exceptionalisms in the Americas have
been constructed. The diverse world of Islam (*dar-ul-Islam*) is
the most formidable frontier of alien difference embracing
the breadth of the continents that are not American.

—TIMOTHY MARR

The question of beginnings . . . can be narrated in very diverse
ways. . . . When and where does Orientalism, and the critique of
Orientalism, actually begin? . . . How to study transnationally a
Middle East that is not merely "over there" but also "back here"?

—ELLA SHOHAT

In the post-9/11 era, the American West faces ongoing pressures
to shore up its borders against potential terrorists and other vilified groups. The region is a space whose long history of geopolitical conflict and violence frequently shapes life in the present
era, as official policies and restrictions continually seek to contain
various threats haunting the elites on local, national, and transnational levels. Neil Campbell argues that the West is often constructed in a way that meets "the needs of a modern state to present
a solidity and unity at its heart" but whose alleged boundedness
as an American geography has been deeply contested by the pop-

ulations who reside there and by scholars working in the fields of ethnic studies, borderlands studies, critical regionalism, and area studies.[1] The traditional East-West trajectory of successive frontiers that informs the Turnerian paradigm of Anglo American nation-building moving continuously from the Atlantic to the Pacific, for instance, has been reconfigured by more complicated models focusing on different directional movements and flows of global populations.[2] As work in critical regional studies reroutes scholarship on the American West and displaces the long privileged trajectory of the Turnerian model, a new set of questions emerges involving a different East that has played a significant role in the historical and cultural development of the region.

The Bush administration tried to sell its war on terror by disseminating popular discourses of the "Wild West" in which the avenging cowboy rejuvenates and revitalizes a threatened America.[3] But what was lost on the administration was a realization that much of what were being hailed as core patriotic elements of Americanness actually had un-American origins and had emerged in part out of cultural developments arising elsewhere.[4] In accounting for such influences, this chapter troubles dominant conceptions of the U.S. West by excavating an Islamic and Moorish presence shaping the region's literature and history as it arrived in the Americas through Spain's New World exploration and conquest. Wai Chee Dimock suggests that the process of recovering what has been silenced and overlooked in cultural history may require critics to adopt approaches that are not "dictated by the obliterating myth of 'newness'" but that instead "throw into the mix" the geographies and histories that have been there all along but that have "so far been set aside."[5] Her work locates the long presence of Islam and the Middle East in American literary studies and in turn examines the "coordinates that emerge when we remap the world" through different "itineraries."[6] While there often appears to be a vast and strict divide between the American West and the locations of Islam or the region of the Middle East and North Africa, a study of transnational flows reveals problems in these divisions, as much of the culture associated with the American West has deep connections to this larger space of the East.[7]

The fiction of Pulitzer Prize–winning writer Willa Cather, one of the region's most well known and celebrated authors, reveals important traces of a Moorish presence shaping the cultures and histories of the American Southwest. Such elements are particularly apparent in *Death Comes for the Archbishop* (1927), a novel that former First Lady Laura Bush herself once named a "family favorite."[8] The task of restoring to memory this history of transnational influence requires scholars to place regional studies into productive dialogue with other critical frameworks. Indeed, the project demands that critics suspend ideas of what counts as inside and outside, rethink narrow notions of East and West, and abandon preconceived maps of American spaces. A transnational reading of Cather's writings about the American Southwest allows critics to recognize the fluidity of frontiers and borders, to understand how imaginative and real worlds connect, and to acknowledge the ways the United States itself and the American Southwest in particular are indeed geographies that may be included in the so-called Arab and Muslim worlds.[9]

The American West Unmoored

The process of globalizing western American studies has brought with it productive new conversations across fields and disciplines whose practitioners may not have previously thought they had much in common. The postcolonial critic Ella Shohat, for instance, argues a case for bringing together area studies with ethnic studies, with her analysis of the genealogy of orientalism foregrounding how histories of the Middle East have productively interacted with and influenced developments in Latinx studies and have thus impacted regional and national histories.[10] An examination of the European conquest of the Americas allows Shohat to write a different history of the global development and transmission of orientalist ideas than what the critic Edward Said initially envisioned in 1978. She sees a history that is "not merely longer but also more multifaceted and multidirectional than might at first appear" and that begins with Columbus's own "spatial disorientation" in 1492.[11] As Shohat argues, Columbus "could be regarded as the first Orientalist of the Americas, even in the sense of imagining himself, as his diaries indicate, to be actually in the Orient, in the land of the Great Khan."[12] The task of rewriting the "traffic" in orientalist ideas requires an expanded vision of Middle Eastern studies that includes the conquest and exploration of the Americas and that in turn calls for more nuanced studies of Latinx histories, area studies, regional formations, and U.S. national identities. The "intersectionality of regions and cartographies of knowledge allow us to redraw static maps of scholarly terrain, stretching and broadening the field," Shohat argues. "The study of cross-border movements through interarea studies approaches deterritorializes regions as stable objects of study, and offers new angles on the ongoing critique of the essentialist fixity of East-versus-West and North-versus-South."[13] Such critical allegiances become especially important to foster during the war on terror, Shohat points out, as xenophobia and Islamophobia come to operate hand in hand, with the American Southwest especially drawn into this sphere of anxiety as the violence of increased border patrols and racial profiling against Latinxs foreground heightened fears about the threat of the terrorist Other within.[14]

In this context, *Death Comes for the Archbishop* offers a particularly rich archive for analyzing these regional influences, which have not been fully excavated or examined. Ann Laura Stoler notes how scholarship is often "produced in uneven waves of reaction and anticipation, sometimes prescient about that which has not yet entered the public domain, at other times struggling to keep up with seismic shifts and unanticipated events that render our observations belabored and late."[15] Critics have tended to focus on the traces of Europe in Cather's West, especially the travels of Spanish explorers and French Catholic missionaries in the region. Cather's novel, however, reveals the important prior influences of the Moorish culture in American Southwest histories and, in particular, the interconnections and cultural borrowings that link Christians with Muslims in different global settings. *Death Comes for the*

Archbishop tells the story of two French Catholic missionaries—Bishop Jean Marie Latour and Father Joseph Vaillant—who seek to establish a diocese in New Mexico territory in 1848 after the end of the U.S.-Mexico War and who face the task of bringing a reformed Christianity to the Indigenous and Spanish Mexican populations in the region. Tracing the friendship between the two men over several decades, the story depicts their initial sense of displacement in facing what they regard to be an alienating desert landscape, as well as the struggles they encounter in confronting the resistant Ácoma population and the rebellious Spanish Mexican clergy they are meant to replace.

In a scene that takes place in Santa Fe early in the novel, Latour wakes to a ringing church bell, a noise that is unexpected and momentarily unfamiliar to him.[16] Cather writes that the bell's uncanny sounds initially convince him that he has been transported to another world. She explains that "he yet heard every stroke of the Ave Maria bell, marveling to hear it rung correctly. . . . Before the nine strokes were done Rome faded, and behind it he sensed something Eastern with palm trees,—Jerusalem, perhaps, though he had never been there. Keeping his eyes closed, he cherished for a moment this sudden, pervasive sense of the East." Vaillant then elaborates on the unusual sound of the bell, explaining that he found the angelus abandoned in the basement of an old church: "They tell me it has been here a hundred years or more. There is no church tower in the place strong enough to hold it—it is very thick and must weigh close upon eight hundred pounds. . . . I taught a Mexican boy how to ring it properly against your return." Vaillant goes on to explain how the bell initially arrived in New Mexico, noting that "the inscription is in Spanish, to St. Joseph, and the date is 1356. It must have been brought up from Mexico City in an ox-cart. A heroic undertaking, certainly. Nobody knows where it was cast. But they do tell a story about it: that it was pledged to St. Joseph in the wars with the Moors, and that the people of some besieged city brought all their plate and silver and gold ornaments and threw them in with the baser metals."[17]

The two men ponder the worldly movements of the bell and

the vast geographies through which it traveled before its arrival in the basement of the old San Miguel church. Latour comments with wonder, noting that "the silver of the Spaniards was really Moorish, was it not? If not actually of Moorish make, copies from their design. The Spaniards knew nothing about working silver except as they learned it from the Moors."[18] He further elaborates by claiming, "When I heard it this morning it struck me at once as something oriental. A learned Scotch Jesuit in Montreal told me that our first bells, and the introduction of the bell in the service all over Europe, originally came from the East. He said the Templars brought the Angelus back from the Crusades, and it is really an adaptation of a Moslem custom. . . . The Spaniards handed on their skill to the Mexicans, and the Mexicans have taught the Navajos to work silver; but it all came from the Moors."[19]

Cather's representation of the much-traveled bell may be read in the context of the movements and flows shaping and connecting Middle East studies with western U.S. regionalism, borderlands criticism, and American studies. Here the bell's travels from the Moors to the New World make an uncanny reappearance, emerging ghostlike from the basement of the old church, its presence calling back a history that has been overlooked or consigned to the basement of regionalist and Americanist scholarship. In particular, it calls back the history of Moors in Europe and the Americas, the latter a history that begins in 1536 with the arrival of Estevanico or Esteban the Moor, the first Muslim and the first African to travel to the present-day continental United States as part of the Spanish Narváez expedition with Álvar Núñez Cabeza de Vaca. The appearance of the bell, which Latour recognizes as something "oriental" and that Vaillant worries may make the object "out an infidel," carries traces of the histories of conflict between Islam and Christianity. Located in the old San Miguel church in Santa Fe, the bell represents a return of a repressed history of encounters, where the Middle East does not remain "back there" but erupts "over here" in a New World setting.[20]

Theorizing the complexities of what she calls "imperial debris," Stoler focuses on colonial ruins for the ways they "draw on residual pasts to make claims on futures."[21] Frequently portrayed as "enchanted, desolate spaces, large-scale monumental structures abandoned and grown over," imperial ruins "provide a favored image of a vanished past, what is beyond repair and in decay."[22] Her study draws particular attention to "'ruination' as an active, ongoing process that allocates imperial debris differentially and *ruin* a violent verb that unites apparently disparate moments, places, and objects."[23] Stoler's meditations on imperial debris and colonial ruins enable critics to examine the ongoing processes by which the American West as a transnational space becomes "unmoored." The relic found in the basement of the San Miguel church is understood as meaningful primarily as a symbol of conquest, an "enchanted" sign for the European crusades, which becomes significant in a new context as the Catholic missionaries wage another battle for souls in the American Southwest.[24] The relic operates as a reminder of the allegedly vanquished cultures of infidel Others, a symbol of Christian Europe's triumph over the Islamic East; it represents a force that has been seemingly put to rest and no longer deemed a religious or political threat in this context.

This East does not remain at rest in the novel but makes a spectral appearance throughout the story. Back in Rome at the beginning of the novel, Cather provides an opening for this presence when she describes the physical features of the Catholic clergy gathered at an Italian villa. Her depictions employ a language of racial demarcation and microranking, especially as it pertains to Mediterranean populations, an ideology of race that gained prominence in the United States particularly during the first half of the twentieth century, when Cather was writing.[25] "The French and Italian Cardinals were men in vigorous middle life—the Norman full-belted and ruddy, the Venetian spare and sallow and hook-nosed," she notes. "Their host, García María de Allande, was still a young man. He was dark in colouring, but the long Spanish face, that looked out from so many canvases in his ancestral portrait gallery, was in the young Cardinal much modified through his English mother. With his *caffè oscuro* eyes, he had a fresh, pleasant English mouth, and an open manner."[26] Here Cather's descriptions of a "sallow" man with a "hook" nose or a character with a "dark," long Spanish face and coffee-colored eyes build on familiar stereotypes about the physical features of Jews and Moors, using anti-Semitic and Islamophobic discourses that carried meaning in her culture and that could be traced back to Spain's *limpieza de sangre* (cleansing of blood)—the expulsion edicts of the Reconquista against Jews and Muslims.[27] The description draws attention to Cather's take on the multicultural and hybrid world of the Mediterranean, where religions and races have long joined up—Islam with Judaism and Christianity, East with West, and North with South, as well as Africa with Europe and the Middle East.[28] This complex hybridity is tempered in the young Cardinal María de Allande, Cather writes, through the modifications of an "English mother," who promises to expel the history of a previous darkness, a maternal inheritance that lends his features "a fresh," "pleasant," and "open manner," which neutralizes what is depicted as an unsettling element of racial and religious difference in the novel.

Later in the scene, Cather offers spectral references to the world of the East as she describes the interior of the villa where the cardinals and missionary clergy convene. The author depicts in detail how the sunlight hits the interior of the villa in a way that is "both intense and soft. . . . It warmed the bright green of the orange trees and the rose of the oleander blooms to gold; sent congested spiral patterns quivering over the damask and plate and crystal."[29] Here the sun highlights among other things the elaborate coverings of the furniture decorating the Italian villa, in this case the rich damask, a term deriving from the city of Damascus, where the cloth was first produced. Lingering over the details of the interior spaces of the villa, Cather offers a reminder of the vast and centuries-long cultural flows across the Mediterranean world and thus the Eastern presence in the Roman Catholic world. In addition, she offers—through descriptions of the riches of the villa as captured in the damask furniture coverings, intricate landscaping, and crystal tableware—visions of the material wealth and power of the Catholic Church, an authority that is being challenged in the Americas and thus in need of a vigorous and renewed presence.

Throughout Cather's novel, other cultural items take on particular significance, permitting glimpses into the ways the world joins up. Theorizing what he calls the "material unconscious" of literature, Bill Brown examines the capacity of literature to provide new archives for scholars and to "preserve (however marginally) residues of phenomena that remain in some sense unrecognizable (if not unrepresentable) in our existing historiographic genres. Within literature the detritus of history lingers, lying in wait."[30] In reading the material unconscious of literature, he argues, critics are able to grant "dimensionality to a passing reference or impression" and "confront an image of the past that otherwise inexplicably renders the text as a whole, and its moment to history, newly legible."[31] By recuperating such aspects of a text, scholars in turn gain a means of entering the otherwise lost "knowledge that literature can energize."[32]

In her well-known essay "The Novel Démeublé," Cather offers a theory of objects in modern fiction that is useful to consider in the context of Brown's argument. In her essay, Cather breaks with conventions of nineteenth-century literature, arguing that the "novel, for a long while, has been over-furnished."[33] Dismissing the tendency to clutter the pages of fiction with unsparing details about the physical items of fictional worlds, Cather contends that such obsessive efforts effectively close off avenues for more productive endeavors in literature.[34] In striving to achieve the exactness of journalism, the realist writer fails to treat the novel as a creative form in its own right. "It is the inexplicable presence of the thing not named, of the overtone divined by the ear but not heard by it, the verbal mood, the emotional aura of the fact or the thing or the deed, that gives high quality to the novel or the drama as well as to the poetry itself," she explains.[35] Cather suggests that twentieth-century novelists should instead follow the example of contemporary modernist painters in carefully selecting elements that will enable them to "present their scene by suggestion rather than enumeration" and thus better capture the emotional or inner lives of their characters.[36] "How wonderful it would be if we could throw all the furniture out the window; and along with it, all the meaningless reiterations concerning physical sensations, all the tiresome old patterns, and leave the room as bare as the stage of a Greek theatre," she proclaims.[37]

Literary critics have devoted much attention to the significance of "The Novel Démeublé," which they regard as crucial to understanding Cather's theory of fiction. Indeed, the author herself once emphasized the piece to her editor, explaining that she thought the essay to be the strongest writing included in her collection, *Not under Forty*.[38] Since the mid-1980s, when Sharon O'Brien's groundbreaking study of Cather's indirect and allusive means of representing lesbian identity and same-sex desire appeared in the feminist journal *Signs*, "The Novel Démeublé" has inspired important queer readings of her work.[39] In particular, Cather's comments about "the thing not named" have attracted the interest of critics such as Christopher Nealon, who excavates what he calls the "major languages" of queer feeling and affiliation that circulated in American culture prior to Stonewall.[40] Likewise, Cather's use of the familiar "house of fiction" trope has interested scholars who trace the author's contributions to the development of literary modernism. Having eschewed realism's excessive efforts at chronicling the details of everyday life, Cather developed an approach to modernist figuration that relied on minimalism and suggestion as a means of grappling with the interior and emotional lives of characters. Indeed, the two concerns about removing the excessive details from the novel and about capturing "the thing unnamed" in modernist literature frequently come together in critical readings of the author's work.

It may be tempting to take Cather at her word, noting the ways she helped wrestle the novel away from the obsessive "interior decorators" of the nineteenth century, liberating the form from compulsive hoarders who tended to clutter their fiction with unnecessary furnishing.[41] In doing so, however, critics risk overlooking aspects of Cather's writing that do not follow this minimalist approach.[42] While she may have sought to remove excess furniture from her house of fiction, Cather failed to get rid of a particular type of ornamentalism in her literary work. Although she famously criticized realist writers for "cataloguing . . . a great number of material objects," much of her fiction nevertheless contains excessive decoration and embellishment.[43] One might even describe these overwrought details as a form of kitsch and, in the case of this argument, as a kind of orientalist kitsch. Such elements indeed clutter Cather's work, including references from *The Arabian Nights* and biblical stories of the Holy Lands, as well as descriptions of Egyptian mummies and obelisks and comments about European traditions of orientalist painting and even Arabian spices.[44] What is striking about Cather's literature is the sheer number of orientalist objects that adorn the worlds of her fictional characters: items that decorate offices and living rooms, artwork on display at famous museums, and various ephemera that otherwise occupy the restless imaginations of her characters. Orientalist elements take on cultural significance in her writings precisely because they reappear as the very ornamentation allowed to stay on the pages of her fiction. The meanings these objects hold are often connected to the role Cather assigned to the artist in the modern world and to her ongoing efforts to articulate non-normative experiences of gender and sexuality in the first half of the twentieth century. The kitschy orientalist objects not removed from Cather's fictional worlds open up questions about the author's uses of the East in determining and directing the meanings of the American Southwest in the twentieth century.

Frequently centered on the lives of rural people in the Midwest who occupy what seem to be empty, dead-end spaces, Cather's fiction typically focuses on the struggles of desperate, lonely, and creative young Americans in search of broader cultural horizons. Their struggles often entail efforts to grow as artists, and, although at times coded and indirectly described, these dreams tend to involve desires for same-sex relationships and communities in locations found someplace else.[45] Indeed, the two dreams typically connect in her writings in productive ways. Christopher Nealon argues, for instance, that in Cather's work artists appear as "another type of person altogether."[46] The complex task of achieving a satisfying life beyond the restrictions of heteronormativity and as artists living and working outside mainstream standards of success requires Cather's characters to become a different type of person, which often means abandoning their rural communities for more exciting, exotic, or cosmopolitan lands elsewhere.

While place and space take on important meanings in Cather's writing, time and history likewise figure in her writings in complex ways. Nealon notes, for instance, that Cather understood queer identity as "gender inversion," that is, through the sexual models that were available to her at the time she was writing; he goes on to argue that, as a result, the author often reconfigured "gender inversion" as "historical backwardness."[47] The aspiring artist Thea in *The Song of the Lark* thus finds possibility and promise in the ruins left by the cliff dwellers who previously inhabited Panther Canyon, Arizona. The abandoned architecture and particularly the domestic items once occupying the homes of these "ancient people" provide the main character with a way out of the compulsory marriage plot and with a genealogical link to a previous era's artists and creators.[48] Cather writes that across the landscape "there still glittered in the sun the bits of their frail clay vessels, fragments of their desire."[49] Spatiality, temporality, and non-normative sexuality come together in meaningful ways here; for Nealon, the scene reveals how Cather figures the ancient people as "initiating Thea into a secret, cross-racial nationality of art, of desire expressed as a secret but confirming genealogy."[50] The moment likewise reveals her as a character "more ancient than modern," a figure whose "affinity" for the past helps the narrative thwart the conventional marriage plot of the novel.[51]

Nealon's attention to the submerged languages of queer desire and identity offers ways of understanding the interconnections of place, time, and identity in Cather's work. Building on these observations, critics may examine other "ancient" elements that the author likewise borrowed and incorporated into her fiction, elements that arose out of particular forms of American orientalism circulating in the United States during the time she was writing. In some cases, her work engages a tradition of American orientalism that emerged out of a popular wave of Egyptomania,

the national obsession with archaeological findings, desert exca-
vations, and the attendant debates about human origins, which
swept the nation in the late nineteenth and early twentieth centuries.[52] In other instances, Cather borrowed from and developed
a form of orientalism that circulated in the United States through
a more elusive route, namely through the buried histories and cultural ruins of the American Southwest, an intriguing and meaningful landscape she returned to time and again as a productive
setting for her fiction. As a culturally diverse and historically rich
terrain just beginning to enter the popular Anglo American imagination, the Southwest offered a space of enchantment and fascination for many modernist artists and writers in the early twentieth
century.[53] The desert spaces and cultural ruins of the region were
often viewed as New World analogs of ruins in the ancient Middle East, particularly of the Holy Land and Jerusalem itself. The
Southwest in turn became a landscape of exotic otherness and
intrigue, a region assigned a similar imaginative function that ori-
entalized and colonial spaces served in the European metropole.
The Southwest desert thus became a site of ancient cultures whose
ruins provide opportunities for adventure and discovery about the
past, a place whose current inhabitants, however, do not live up
to these previous glories and who now represent the savage, the
backward, or the anachronistic—a stark contrast to the seemingly
civilized Anglo American modernists who arrived in the region
from elsewhere.

Cather's decorated and adorned novel, *Death Comes for the Archbishop*, also serves as an important archive of another Eastern element not mentioned here yet, that is, a tradition of the Eastern
Christian church, which appears threatening in its distance from
the center of Europe and too close to the influences of Islam.
When Latour visits the Mexican families, for example, he notes the
wooden figures of the saints decorating the interior spaces of their
homes. Cather writes that "he had never yet seen two alike. . . .
The wooden Virgin was a sorrowing mother indeed—long and
stiff and severe, very long from the neck to the waist, even longer
from waist to feet, like some of the rigid mosaics of the Eastern

Church."[54] Latour's descriptions of the wooden Virgin reference the long-standing ecclesiastic schism in Christianity between its Eastern and Western churches, calling to mind how the Christian traditions of Eastern Europe and the Middle East have often been perceived as threatening outliers by officials in Rome, as they are located far away from the center of the Church, in close proximity to the influences of its religious rivals in the Islamic East, a conflict that is similar to what the clergy face as they encounter New World Christian traditions located within the Indigenous and Spanish Mexican populations in the American Southwest.

Eastern references are significant in Cather's work in other ways as well. Critics have noted, for instance, how she, like many Anglo American writers in the twentieth century, often depicted the U.S. Southwest through orientalist imagery, describing the land with Holy Land metaphors as an American Eden or New World Jerusalem.[55] Encountering what was for them a geography whose terrain could not be easily classified through previous landscape categories used to describe other U.S. spaces, Anglo American writers of the Southwest often made sense of the region through a comparative desert aesthetic that linked the Middle East with the American West. Hilton Obenzinger's observations about American Holy Land mania in the nineteenth century may be extended to Anglo responses about the U.S. Southwest, with their biblical appropriations operating in the context of "secular constructions of national destiny" as a means of "negotiating American settler identity" across a contested geography.[56] Thus, upon his arrival in New Mexico, Latour sees "people beat out their grain and [winnow] it in the wind, like the Children of Israel," his mission in the Southwest understood, interpreted, and justified through comparative references to the Holy Lands of the Middle East.[57]

Latour later remembers his first approach into the region. "One thing which struck him at once was that every mesa was duplicated by a cloud mesa, like a reflection, which lay motionless above it or moved slowly up from behind it," Cather writes. "These cloud formations seemed to be always there, however hot and blue the sky. Sometimes they were flat terraces, ledges of vapour; sometimes they were dome-shaped, or fantastic, like the tops of silvery pagodas, rising one above another, as if an oriental city lay directly behind the rock."[58] Here Latour's thoughts derive first from ancient biblical history and then borrow from a later medieval era. Riding into the town, the missionary imagines himself encountering an "oriental city," the space fantasized in his mind as akin to the Eastern geographies that Christian crusaders battled in their centuries-long wars against Islam. The colonial debris of the scene, in this case located in the missionary's geographical hallucination that links the imagined with the real world, indicates too how the past is not past in this American Southwest setting but instead operates in terms of what Ato Quayson calls an "active presence of imperial significance upon social relationships in the present."[59]

Just as her characters struggle to make sense of the Southwest landscape, so Cather elsewhere in her writings seeks to explain the strange effect the region evokes in her as a writer. In letters to Elizabeth Shepley Sergeant written from Winslow, Arizona, in spring 1912, for instance, Cather describes a sublime sense of fear, inspiration, and artistic freedom she felt in the desert: "The West always paralyzes me a little. When I am away from it I remember only the tang on the tongue. But when I come back [I] always feel a little of the fright I felt when I was a child. I always feel afraid of losing something, and I don't in the least know what it is. It's real enough to make a tightness in my chest even now."[60] Although Cather begins her letter by describing the Southwest desert as unsettling and disturbing—an unknown land that inspires a childlike anxiety and terror in her—later in the note she suggests that the region offers immense possibilities for new artistic and literary endeavors: "It is the most beautiful country I have ever seen anywhere. . . . There is a strong pull about the place, and something Spanish in the air that teases you. Such color! The Lord set the stage so splendidly there. . . . There really must be a new hope yet to come—a new tragedy or a new religion, some crusades or something. It is too utterly splendid, from Trinidad to Albuquerque, to go to pot."[61]

The Spanish past becomes a haunting presence for Cather, its history carrying a "strong pull" that leaves a spectral trace "in the air"—a ghostlike element and phantom presence that "teases" the author. Eventually the author devises a way of using the land as a literary resource, finding in it a "new hope" and inspiration for the production of creative work, such as what is found in "new tragedy" along the lines of "some crusades or something." What is needed, she argues, is a writer who will put this region to good literary use, thus preventing the land from falling into obscurity and going "to pot."

As evidenced in her fiction, Cather does not consign the region to the fate of abandonment but instead reframes multicultural encounters, making imaginative use of the region through references to the religious battles of another era and geography. For instance, when Latour meets up with Don Manuel Chavez, a powerful and wealthy Mexican ranchero who is a companion of Kit Carson,

> Chavez boasted his descent from two Castilian knights who freed the city of Chavez from the Moors in 1160. . . . He loved the natural beauties of his country with a passion, and he hated the Americans who were blind to them. He was jealous of Carson's fame as an Indian-fighter, declaring that he had seen more Indian warfare before he was twenty than Carson would ever see. He was easily Carson's rival as a pistol shot. With the bow and arrow he had no rival; he had never been beaten. . . . When he was a lad of sixteen Manuel Chavez had gone out with a party of Mexican youths to hunt Navajos. In those days, before the American occupation, "hunting Navajos" needed no pretext, it was a form of sport.[62]

Chavez traces his ancestry to the Castilian knights who fought the Moors in the twelfth century, his lineage creating a stream of connection between the Crusaders who battled Islam and what Cather describes as the Spanish Mexican "Indian-fighters" of the Americas. In doing so, the scene provides insights into how European racist and religious discourses were transposed onto the Americas, contributing in turn to what Alex Lubin calls the vast archive of the "Arab-as-Indian" trope in U.S. culture.[63] Beginning in the fifteenth century, Spanish explorers frequently compared the Indigenous populations they encountered in the Americas to a previous population they had already marginalized and expelled back home. In the sixteenth century, for instance, the Spanish explorer Francisco Vásquez de Coronado likened the Querechos and the Teyas as a group to the Bedouins, Arabs, Moors, and Turks.[64] As Ella Shohat and Robert Stam note, this discourse of otherness arose in Europe, then later "crossed the Atlantic with the Spaniards, arming the conquistadors with a ready-made racist ideology."[65] Thus, when Vaillant panics about the "infidel" Islamic history shaping the bell and its connections to the Moors, the threat that he and other missionaries face in the New Mexico territory is sifted through a prior encounter with Islam, with the Indigenous populations of the Southwest treated as a reminder of and substitute for an older clash with Spain's previous racial and religious Others.

A number of scholars have noted how this linkage of racial and religious otherness has been intimately tied into the global history of Islamophobia, which traveled from Europe to the Americas, creating in the process a specific strain of orientalist discourse in the New World, particularly in the Arab-as-Indian trope. Junaid Rana argues, for instance, that from the "conquest of the New World to the trans-Atlantic slave trade, Islam figured as an important aspect of the early formation of the U.S. racial formation across a Black and Brown Atlantic."[66] In fifteenth- and sixteenth-century Spain, the linkages between religion and race resulted from the larger conflict between Catholic Spain and Jews and Muslims; reconstructing this genealogy reveals "a complex and overlapping" set of categories, "such as Black and Brown with religious categories such as Islam and Muslim."[67] Rana goes on to explain that "as empires were shifting, power was also displaced in the ideological containment of both Jews and Muslim." For Spanish explorers in the Americas, "Muslims and Jews constituted an early category of religious racial other to transpose onto indigenous groups of the New World in the form of racial thought. . . . The triangle that emerged in these points of contact was between the heathen Indian, the Christian, and the infidel Muslim. As recent scholarship on the encounter between the Old World and the New has shown, Native Americans were made sense of through stereotypes of Muslims. Contact with the Spanish led to a configuration of Indian-as-Muslim."[68]

This history is made visible in the physical descriptions Cather provides of the Catholic church Latour visits at Ácoma. The missionary regards its architecture with a certain dismay and disappointment, describing it as an "old warlike church. . . . Gaunt, grim, grey, its nave rising from seventy feet to a sagging, half-ruined roof, it was more like a fortress than a place of worship."[69] The church's appearance is an unsettling and unwelcome reminder to him of Christian Europe's battles against its various Others on both sides of the Atlantic. The site also embodies violent memories of what Walter Mignolo describes as the "colonial wound," building on Frantz Fanon's work in *The Wretched of the Earth* and Gloria Anzaldúa's observations in *Borderlands/La Frontera: The New Mestiza.*[70] To recognize the colonial wound—a physical and psychological consequence of racism—is to "shift the geo-politics of knowledge" whose foundations derive from modernity, a colonial project "disguised as the natural course of universal history."[71] As Mignolo points out, the language of modernity is typically erected upon offers of a "promising salvation for everybody in order to divert attention from the increasingly oppressive consequences of the logic of coloniality."[72] As is evident in the warlike fortress of the old Catholic church, this "promising salvation" does not seem to have been well received by the Ácoma population, who not only resisted but sought to forcefully repel the colonial project and gifts of salvation from their homeland.

In *Death Comes for the Archbishop*, the European conflict with Islam does not stay in place "back there" but travels "over here," informing and shaping the religious missionary projects in the American Southwest. The narrative itself is preoccupied by the question of history, by the presence of ruins, and by the ways in which the region's past will be recorded in the nation's larger unfolding story. Toward the end of the novel, for instance, the aging Latour recalls to "a young disciple certain facts about the old missions in the diocese; facts which he had come upon by chance and feared would be forgotten. . . . Those truths and fancies relating to a bygone time would probably be lost," he fears.[73] The stories he dictates to the young disciple are tales of extreme hardship in the land, "Spanish Fathers" who arrived in "hostile country, carrying little provisionment but their breviary and crucifix. . . . A European could scarcely imagine such hardships. The old countries were worn to the shape of human life, made into an investiture, a sort of second body, for man."[74] The Southwest desert in Latour's account becomes a unique and challenging terrain for the earlier Catholic missionaries, a land of hardship and struggle, and a place whose history of conquest and settlement must be recorded for future generations of the expanding nation.

By the end of the novel, Cather brings the land into the U.S. American and Catholic fold; it is no longer a space of many religions but a terrain enabling the heroic birth of a new self: "Those early missionaries threw themselves naked upon the hard heart of a country that was calculated to try the endurance of giants. They thirsted in its deserts, starved among its rocks, climbed up and down its terrible canyons on stone-bruised feet, broke long fasts by unclean and repugnant food." The "scenes of martyrdom" in the old missions appear as remarkable events of bravery and heroism, with Latour's oral histories important as a record of the "triumphs of faith" that "happened there, where one white man met torture and death alone among so many infidels, or what visions and revelations God may have granted to soften that brutal end."[75] Cather's movement from a cosmopolitan and global vision of the land to a narrowly defined nationalist and regionalist perspective may be understood through developments in the literary history of U.S. modernism. As Bill Brown writes, such spatial constriction in American literary modernism was itself linked to a cycle of globalization that "provoked a romance of the local and an insatiable desire to know about innumerable locales. Most every region of the nation was reproduced as knowledge that could be incorporated, no matter how eccentric, into the nation's knowledge of itself—the eccentricity being an effect of the knowledge itself."[76] While modernism is often recognized for its "international, cosmopolitan aesthetic drive," alongside these developments there also exist elements Brown describes as "intensely nationalist and nativist."[77] The literature of difference and diversity in Cather's novel thus becomes unmoored from its cosmopolitan and multi-religious histories, where it is recast as a provincial tale confined to narrating the foundational story of a mythically bounded nation.

Cather and the Transnational Southwest

Death Comes for the Archbishop reveals traces of how U.S. Southwest histories and cultures were shaped by a Moorish presence and how orientalist discourses such as the Arab-as-Indian trope brought earlier European religious and racist ideologies into play in Spanish encounters with Indigenous populations across the Americas. In other writings by Cather, traces of a Moorish presence may also be excavated, particularly in the history and culture of American cowboys themselves. This work offers a variation on the familiar trope that Lubin describes, providing us not with the "Arab-as-Indian" comparison per se but with glimpses into the history of the "cowboy-as-Arab."

In *My Ántonia* (1918), Cather's novel about Nebraska immigrants and the making of the national landscape, the U.S. West again appears as an extension of Spanish North America, particularly as Jim Burden recounts a story about the recovery on a farm near Black Hawk of a Spanish sword, a relic engraved with the name of its maker in Cordova. Jim interprets this discovery as evidence that Francisco Vásquez de Coronado's expedition must have traveled much farther north than previously reported by historians, advancing beyond central Kansas to the southern parts of Nebraska. Mike Fischer suggests that Cather's "inclusion of this apparently inconsequential romantic detail" about a military weapon that somehow did not accompany its owner back to Mexico may be read as an allusion to an actual Spanish expedition that—unlike Coronado's—did arrive in this part of Nebraska. In the summer of 1720, Lieutenant-General Pedro de Villasur left Santa Fe on a mission to regain Spain's control of the Great Plains. Traveling with nearly fifty Spanish soldiers, a Catholic priest, and more than sixty Native Americans, as well as an interpreter, the expedition was later ambushed by Pawnee Indians, with most of the Native American soldiers escaping and only thirteen of the Spanish soldiers making their way back to Santa Fe.[78]

Just as she locates Spanish explorers in the Great Plains of her Nebraska settler narrative but credits the wrong figure in the process, so Cather also provides a transnational genealogy of the American cowboy, an account that is limited by its sole focus on the contributions of the Spanish vaqueros. For instance, in a letter to Sarah Orne Jewett written a decade before she completed *My Ántonia*, Cather speaks of Spain's role in shaping the American West, an element she hoped to capture in her own fiction. As a regionalist author writing to another regionalist, Cather explains the local culture she tried to depict in her work. For the author, the western setting provides an important departure from the landscapes with which most U.S. regionalists were familiar, and thus the natures and cultures Cather describes would likely be quite "different from the things" that Jewett knew as a child in New England. "In the West we had a kind of Latin influence, as you had an English one. We had so many Spanish words, just as you had words left over from Chaucer. Even the cow-boy saddle you know, is an old Spanish model," Cather explains.[79]

Later, the author finds herself having to defend the Spanish cultural influences she recorded in *Death Comes from the Archbishop* after the French writer Marguerite Yourcenar embarked on a new translation of the novel. In her letters, Cather expresses dismay that the Spanish terms she employed would be omitted in the French edition, and she complains about the translator's lack of knowledge about the region. Yourcenar had "never been in the Southwest at all, and seems to have no conception of how very different that country is from any other part of the United States. She has not informed herself about its people or customs—which, after all, are today very much as they were in Archbishop Lamy's time. In so far as that country and people are concerned, her mind is an utter blank," Cather writes.[80] Objecting to the translator's plan to paraphrase the Spanish terms in the novel, Cather complains that Yourcenar "speaks of these passages as descriptions of 'American landscape'; as you know, it is Mexican landscape, not 'American.'"[81] In a fascinating way, Cather anticipates many Latinx studies scholars who argue a similar case for recasting the region using a different geographical lens. Krista Comer puts it succinctly when she asks, "What if 'the West' were *not* about America[?] . . . One obvious alternative to dominant east-west spatial renderings underwriting the social space known as 'the West' can be found in the geographical imagination of Aztlán. . . . Suppose that critics reframed regionalism so that, for instance, the American Southwest signaled alternatively, as Paredes claimed it did, Greater Mexico?"[82]

In her letter, Cather asserts the rightful presence of Spanish words and names in her novel, noting the land as being "Mexican" and not "American." She writes with displeasure that Yourcenar had informed her it would be impossible to use the local names of objects, including "nouns such as burro, mesa, adobe (both a noun and an adjective), casa, arroyo, hacienda, etc., etc. These words were, of course, originally Spanish, but they are now common words everywhere in the southwest." To illustrate her point, Cather notes the unself-conscious manner in which all the "American farmers and railroad workmen use them without knowing they are Spanish. There are simply no other names for these things. You cannot call an arroyo a ditch or a ravine." She finally counters such practices by praising an Italian edition produced by Alessandra Scalero, noting that the Italian translator had employed Spanish words and phrases in that edition "exactly as I used them myself. The only difference being that she puts all these foreign words, even such simple ones as 'poker,' 'rancheros' and 'hacienda,' in italic. She has very clear and enlightening footnotes on such words as 'trapper,' 'gringo,' and very short footnotes telling clearly what a 'mesa' is, a 'hogan,' 'wampum,' etc."[83]

Cather's efforts to retain the Spanish terminology in her novel and keep the land Mexican offer a means by which to better understand the iconography of the West and particularly the non-U.S. origins of much of this culture. Yet, there are additional influences on the culture that Cather does not fully acknowledge; they remain unrecognized because they derive not from elsewhere in the Americas through Spain but arrive from elsewhere in the world, in this case from the horse cultures of the Moors, which influenced the equestrian traditions of Spain. As Gary Paul Nabhan explains—and as I addressed in the previous chapter—much of the cowboy lingo and culture that exists today in the Southwest has a Moorish ancestry. "Spaniards—including Arab and Berber refugees—took along their horses, and the Arabic-origin words they brought with them for managing them are now deeply lodged in 'cowboy lingo[,]' the vernacular English and Mexican Spanish of the desert borderlands" of the United States and Mexico, he explains.

> Sonoran *vaqueros* and the horsemen who've worked with them may still call their saddle an *albardón*, derived from the Iberian term *albarda*, which now means packsaddle and which came from the Arabic *al-barda'a*. Among the other tack such cowboys use is a leather belt they call an *acion*, from the Arabic *as-siyur*. A whip they call an *azote*—from the Arabic *as-sut*. Ringing straps are called *argollas*, from the Arabic *allgulla*. Perhaps my favorite Arabic-derived tack term is a widely used word for a headstall or rope halter: hackamore. It came straight from the Andalusian *jaquima*, which echoes the Arabic *sakima*, something worn on the head.[84]

Nabhan's genealogy of the origins of cowboy culture helps restore to memory the multiple prior transnational influences on this seemingly quintessential U.S. American figure, much of whose intrigue and authenticity derive from an absence, from the cowboy's unknown and shadowy past.[85] As I noted in chapter 1, the cowboy has frequently functioned as a national archetype, the embodiment of the mythical American Adam, an Anglo individual cut off from the past, bereft of history and ancestry.[86] Indeed, this cowboy is the product of a constructed fantasy of the hypermodernized American East devised in order to shore up a beleaguered white masculinity.[87] As Nabhan points out, however, another East played a role in the construction of the cowboy. This history has been largely relegated to a shadowy past but is increasingly being recovered in transnational scholarship, where it complicates the taken-for-granted U.S. Americanness of the popular cowboy.

Finally, the presence of the Middle East in the making of the cultures of the American West provides insights into not only the Arab-as-Indian figuration but also the ways minority groups in the Americas in general may be regarded as the ideological descendants of the first Moors. Anouar Majid explains this chain of signification, reminding scholars that the discourses used to vilify Indigenous Americans during the Spanish conquest came out of an earlier religious and racial othering of the Moors. He argues that "since the defeat of Islam in medieval Spain, minorities in the West have become, in many ways, reincarnations of the Moors, an enduring threat to Western civilization."[88] Hispanics in particular, as they increasingly face border restrictions and the continuous threat of expulsion, serve today as the "Anglos' Moors," a comparison Majid admits is not a precise mirror but does help us make some sense of how national belonging and racial identity are currently being reconfigured in the post-9/11 era.[89] To return to Cather, it appears that perhaps a great deal of the iconography and identity of the U.S. West may indeed be traced back to the Moors, as East and West continually join up in the present era, with elements of the Arab world deeply informing the cultures of the United States and the region and thus questioning the bounded and quintessential U.S. Americanness of the American West itself.

THREE

On Savagery and Civilization

Buffalo Bill and the East

> I wanted a name that would be easy for the Western world to
> pronounce, one that was easy to remember. . . . What name
> is going to be easy for the Americans, the English, or the
> Europeans? . . . There was Omar Khayyam, whom everyone
> knew, and Omar Bradley, the famous American general. And
> then I thought of the sheriffs, the ones in the Westerns,
> and I decided Omar Sharif was a good combination.
>
> —OMAR SHARIF

> All I want to be is a pink and white lady.
> —ANNIE GET YOUR GUN (1950)

While Frederic Remington and other American visitors to the
Chicago World's Fair may have regarded the Arab performers at
the Midway as exotic figures only temporarily visiting the United
States from their homes in faraway lands of the East, it was actually the World's Fairs of 1876, 1893, and 1904, in Philadelphia, Chicago, and Saint Louis, that brought the first significant wave of
Arab immigrants to the United States and eventually the American
West.[1] As the historian Sarah Gualtieri notes, a majority of these
first immigrants came from what was at that time called Greater
Syria, which was part of the Ottoman Empire.[2] These immigrants
did not understand themselves as "Arabs" or as a racial group per se,

even though they were widely treated as such at the time of their arrival and would continue to be inconsistently racialized throughout American history.[3] Most of the early Syrian immigrants in the United States instead identified themselves through other means, primarily through religious affiliation and family ties.[4] Some of the Arab performers at the World's Fairs would later go on to find work outside the confines of the fairgrounds, making a living for themselves by selling souvenir items that they advertised as originating from the Holy Lands and by working as pack peddlers offering various household goods for sale to a broader population of Americans throughout the country.[5]

Along with the World's Fairs, the Wild West shows—which also employed Syrian horsemen for the performances—gave American audiences some of their first encounters with Arab populations in the United States. Buffalo Bill's show, one of a number of Wild West extravaganzas that toured the United States and Europe in the late nineteenth and early twentieth centuries, featured diverse riders from around the world as representative figures of not only distinct international horse cultures but also various civilizations allegedly in different stages of development, stagnation, or decline. These shows reenacted battle scenes from western American history as well as various military excursions overseas. The performances often opened with a parade featuring different groups on horseback, with the riders displaying their own distinctive costumes and horse cultures and pitting their skills against one another alongside the American cowboy.[6] Paul Reddin contends that the show's audiences generally understood the group comparisons within the logic of social Darwinism. A "horse race between a cowboy, a Cossack, a vaquero, a gaucho, and an Indian was a 'race between races,'" with "national pride" and the "glory" of one's race motivating each contestant. Not surprisingly, in the context of the Wild West shows, the Anglo cowboy usually won the race.[7]

Eventually, American moviemakers became fascinated by the spectacle of U.S. competition with other nations and staged reenactments of Wild West shows in a number of films, placing American cowboys against Arab rivals, as well as other talented performers of the world. In doing so, these films featured a global contest in which the exceptional U.S. hero won out over other national contestants as the most talented and culturally advanced performer in the show. This chapter focuses on how ideas of nation, race, savagery, and civilization circulated in cinematic representations of Wild West shows, particularly in popular Hollywood Westerns. Discussing American interactions with the Middle East in contemporary U.S. cinema, Tim Semmerling notes how the Western has often been mobilized as a means of framing these encounters and has worked alongside an American orientalist discourse in resolving threats to U.S. national identity in times of global uncertainty.[8] The film scholar Philip French explains how the Western could be useful in this context, noting that while the historical background of the genre is often used for larger mythical stories of adventure and intrigue, the plots of individual Western films are "as much about the hopes and anxieties of the time in which they were made as the period [in which] they were set."[9]

In *Annie Get Your Gun* (1950), post–World War II American film audiences travel back to the era of the Wild West shows as a way of containing collective anxieties emerging from the United States' new global role and its civilizing mission across the world. Later, during the war on terror, as the cinematic Western entered a new and complicated cycle of popularity at the American box office, the film *Hidalgo* (2004) returns to the era of Buffalo Bill, centering on the exceptional U.S. hero, the western cowboy, this time as he engages in adventures in foreign lands. Throughout both of these films, ideas about whiteness operate centrally in larger debates about nation, civilization, and savagery—especially as the narratives tap into the theme of captivity and rescue, a key element shaping both the Wild West shows and popular Westerns throughout their historical development.

"Anything you can do, I can do better"

The film historian Stanley Corkin argues that after World War II, as the United States sought to secure its role as a global superpower, the project of developing and maintaining American foreign policy "caused untold strains domestically." Cinematic Westerns in this period were made in numbers that rivaled any other moment in American history, and Corkin argues that their popularity at the box office may have to do with how they helped mediate national problems "by grafting the historical onto the mythic" in an effort to enable viewers to "adjust to new concepts of national definition."[10] Nineteenth-century frontier mythology provided resolution to a nation undergoing great upheaval domestically and internationally in this period. Half a century before, when Anglo Saxon power faced threats in the form of increased immigration, a dehumanizing industrialization, and rapid urbanization, the myth of the frontier offered a promise of rebirth and renewal through encounters with the wild natures of the American West. The frontier narrative gave a beleaguered Anglo Saxon civilization another chance to triumph. The story suggested that the values and social structures of this once powerful group could be reclaimed and given a new lease on life in the American West. This narrative gained significance again by the mid-twentieth century, with Westerns becoming a useful means for making sense of America as a superpower on a new global frontier.[11]

The historian Melani McAlister also notes how the United States in the post–World War II period faced challenges internationally and developed various means of negotiating its new role. Particularly in U.S. dealings with the Middle East, postwar American interventions emerged through a discourse of "benevolent supremacy," a framework that sought to distinguish American overseas power from that of previous European nations and that justified U.S. policy in those regions. McAlister contends that the term "post-Orientalist" best describes the changes in representation that emerged during a time "when American power worked very hard to fracture the old European logic and to install new frameworks."[12] Such frameworks built on exceptionalist American ideologies, which the Western also popularized, its cowboy hero frequently becoming an exceptional figure in shaping American "benevolent supremacy" in the world. Often involved in various captivity and rescue missions, many of the cowboy heroes of post–World War II West-

On Savagery and Civilization

erns gave assurances that American-style democracy and freedom could prevail throughout the world.

The popular Western musical *Annie Get Your Gun* references the theme of captivity and rescue, as well as larger ideas about gender, race, savagery, and civilization, in reimagining historical events surrounding the travels of the Wild West show. *Annie Get Your Gun* centers on the life of the famous female sharpshooter (portrayed by Betty Hutton) and her romance with the celebrated marksman Frank Butler (portrayed by Howard Keel). Annie Oakley's story has been featured in a number of films over the years. The character first appeared on screen as early as 1894, in a short documentary directed by William K. L. Dickson entitled *Annie Oakley*. Later, Barbara Stanwyck memorably played the main role in director George Stevens's 1935 film, also titled *Annie Oakley*. Most accounts about the legendary Oakley and her years performing with the Wild West shows balance the tale of heterosexual romance with a story about the protofeminist possibilities of Oakley's sharpshooting skills. In the 1950 film, the conflict between savagery and civilization appears as the main character struggles between her desire for a heterosexual mate and her skills as a sharpshooter and outdoorswoman, the latter elements threatening to unsettle post–World War II ideologies of white female domesticity.

The Western's classic plot device of captivity and rescue makes a significant appearance in the story, and at times Annie Oakley herself must be "saved" from savagery through the civilizing love of Frank Butler. Although the story of captivity and rescue in frontier narratives is often linked to the mythic encounter with the Indian, a lesser-known element of the Wild West shows involved the use of Arab performers, who were frequently cast in the role of frontier captors. While William F. Cody's shows often featured Syrian riders, these performers tended to be more prevalent in other Wild West shows, including Pawnee Bill's Great Far East show. Gordon William Lillie, an Oklahoman also known as Pawnee Bill, had developed a popular show that rivaled Cody's Wild West performances at the time, and it even featured a female sharpshooter who allegedly matched Annie Oakley in skill: his wife,

May Manning Lillie.[13] Like his counterpart Cody, Gordon Lillie was memorialized in a number of dime novels over the years.[14] In the *New Buffalo Bill Weekly*, which published revisions of older stories, the character of Wild Bill Hickock was often replaced with that of Pawnee Bill as a companion to Buffalo Bill.[15] In 1908, as Cody faced financial problems stemming from a somewhat stale and predicable show with many aging performers, he decided to join forces with Lillie, a sometime scout who had been a teacher at the Pawnee Agency Indian school and had previously worked for Cody as an interpreter for the Pawnee performers in Cody's first Wild West show.[16]

Pawnee Bill's shows featured more circus-type acts by performers who allegedly hailed from the "Far East." Such figures included "Hindu magicians, Singhalese dancers, Madagascar oxen cavalry, Australian Aborigines with boomerangs, Boers, 'Kaffirs,' and 'Hottentots' (Bantu-speaking South Africans), Zulus, Abyssinians, Chinese and Japanese cavalry, Cossacks, gauchos, and Arabian horsemen."[17] One such circus performer, the Syrian tumbler George Hamid, remembered meeting Annie Oakley while on tour. Although he recalled enjoying the attention of the crowds at the shows, Hamid also had vivid memories of bodily suffering as a performer. In his autobiography, the performer recalls an evening when he curled up in a corner and began crying because of his hunger. A shadow came over him. He wrote that "I looked up to see who was standing near us and saw the first real smile of friendliness since leaving home. The smiler was a woman who started to speak to us in foreign words we did not understand. I stood up, shook my head, and pointed to my mouth and stomach." Hamid then notes that the woman, whose "eyes were pleasant . . . knew what I meant, for she knew the circus. She called to an attendant who was passing and ordered him to bring food to her tent. Then she beckoned, smiled, and we followed wonderingly. Our benefactress was Annie Oakley."[18] Hamid recounts the friendship that developed between the two performers and later credits Oakley for her help in learning a new language: "It was Annie Oakley who first taught me English, who kept helping me until I learned to read and write a little. She started with ABC's, patiently teaching me the strange new letters. She bought primers and helped me figure out the first easy words, told me how to pronounce them correctly."[19]

As a member of Pawnee Bill's show, George Hamid and other circus performers added an important element of Eastern spectacle that Cody hoped would attract new audiences to what was then advertised as the "Two Bills show."[20] The 1909 program for the show announces, for instance, that in "one arena the onlooker witnesses varied exhibitions of horsemanship, wherein the dusky-skinned Arabian vies with the American cowboy in displays of equestrian expertness; the camp life of the native American Indian is shown in contrast to the nomadic domiciles of the desert-born Bedouin."[21] Later the program announces that the section on the "Great Far East" features a tale of captivity. The drama's first scene begins with a desert caravan resting as a group of Bedouins prepare their camp near the Giza pyramids. A courier soon arrives with news that a "party of tourists" has arrived in the area to visit the Sphinx and pyramids: "Mounted upon his beautiful Arabian charger, the Sheik of the tribe arrives at this juncture and directs that the tourists be captured and held for ransom." As the captives are held hostage, the sheikh commands that the entertainment begin.[22] Audiences at the Wild West show were then treated to a spectacle of wild dancing and celebration in the Egyptian desert as members of the group of frightened tourists remain in captivity on stage.

Savagery and civilization also appear as central themes in *Annie Get Your Gun*, with Oakley herself portrayed as a near savage woodswoman in need of love, a job, and a good cleaning up. In order to claim these elements as a Consensus-era American heroine, Oakley must first engage in a number of competitions with other characters. When William F. Cody's Wild West show arrives in Cincinnati, the famed marksman Frank Butler announces a challenge to the local townspeople and arranges a shooting match in order to garner publicity for the show. When a wild, unwashed, and scruffy young Oakley arrives and eventually wins the bet against Butler, she falls in love with the marksman and asks him if he likes her too. Butler breaks out in song ("The Girl That I Marry"), explaining that he prefers a more civilized and refined woman who wears "satin" and "cologne." His comment unsettles the talented heroine, who becomes concerned about the status of her whiteness and femininity, elements she needs to develop in order to win her man.

When audiences first meet Oakley, she appears as the embodiment of the Western's stereotypical racial Other, the Indian. The scene shows her emerging from the woods dressed in buckskin, covered in dirt, her hair in disarray, and her face tanned and freckled by days spent out of doors. In order to enter the desired heterosexual relationship with Butler, the heroine's unruliness must be contained and she in turn must become civilized, a process that entails cultivating elements of whiteness and proper femininity. After Frank explains to her what he regards as his ideal female love object, the film shows Oakley attempting to emulate this figure, rubbing lemon on her face in order to lighten her skin and hide her freckles. "All I want to be is a pink and white lady," she tells Butler, who reassures Oakley that she's indeed becoming "pinker and whiter every day." The narrative eventually centers on her struggle to balance the extremes of savagery and civilization, her hard-fought shooting skills with her newfound efforts to embody proper white womanhood.

Jeffrey Magee argues that while *Annie Get Your Gun* may be remembered as a key Western musical from the era of *Oklahoma!*—a text I address in more detail in the next chapter—it is primarily a "show about show business."[23] One could extend this argument, however, by indicating how the two storylines come together in the film and by pointing to the ways the genre of the Western itself and shows about the American West—especially the Buffalo Bill shows—are indeed all about performance. These productions are typically about staging identity, particularly U.S. identity. They likewise highlight the meanings of U.S. landscapes, primarily the freedoms and possibilities of reclaiming the promises of the mythic American frontier. The show-stopping song, "Anything You Can Do," a duet in which Oakley and Butler question and challenge each other's talents, is significant beyond the typical "battle of the

On Savagery and Civilization

sexes" contest often found in Hollywood film and particularly in musicals of the era. Instead, the song also draws attention to the larger competition between nations as staged in the Wild West shows and between Buffalo Bill's performances and Pawnee Bill's Far East shows. In the story, Oakley must place herself against individuals from other nations as an example of a "civilized" U.S. citizen in order to prove her worth to Butler as a desirable object of romantic affection.

In an important way then, Oakley's efforts to become a "civilized" white lady take place against the backdrop of the Wild West show, whose global cast of performers embodies a savagery against which she can define herself. These multiracial performers, however, function largely as a spectral presence in the film, appearing only in what others say about them or in an advertisement for their show. In one scene, for instance, a program for the performance posted outside the tent announces Pawnee Bill's Far East show, the appearance of which disturbs the enterprising Cody, whose Wild West acts must compete with another group of exotic, foreign performers. Robert Rydell examines many of the posters produced for these shows and their uses of racial categories as a means of containing a modern "world in motion."[24] In several of these posters, Buffalo Bill and Annie Oakley are shown leading a group of international horsemen, their honored place at the front as the first in a long line of riders becoming significant to the racial logic of the procession. The posters specifically designate the show's other horsemen as embodying different racial types, a classification system that becomes important to various additional acts in the show. One scene in particular features "the Race of Races, the Show of Shows," which stages moments of violence—including attacks on Deadwood, as well as "menacing" Middle Eastern horsemen who threaten to cut off the other riders—only to eventually rein them in with the arrival of Buffalo Bill.[25] As Rydell notes, the scene offers assurances to audiences, reinforcing notions about "the modern world as a 'race of races' requiring the vigilance" of an American leader such as Buffalo Bill, arriving on the scene "astride his horse with his gun at the ready."[26]

Fig. 5. Buffalo Bill reacts to the arrival of Pawnee Bill's Far East show in *Annie Get Your Gun* (directed by George Sidney, 1950), from the DVD.

While the horsemen of the Far East may be an intriguing and exotic population for the showgoers featured in the film, they are also part of a group that threatens to disrupt the calm life of the town. In another scene, Wilson, the owner of a local hotel, expresses his annoyance at the behavior of these performers when they move to locations offstage. He is so upset by their actions that he vehemently refuses to allow Butler to set up the shooting competition near his hotel. In the film version, he says, "I don't want any actors. I just had Pawnee Bill and his Far East show here and some of them chased my guests up and down stairs on horseback." In the stage play, however, he complains about something different, claiming that the Far East performers "chased *women* up and down the stairs."[27] Thus in the stage play, the performers in Pawnee Bill's show, presumably various Syrian riders, along with other horsemen from the Far East, become cast in the role commonly assigned to Native Americans in the Western, emerging as danger-

On Savagery and Civilization

ous racial Others intent on capturing and violating white women while disrupting the "civilized" rules of the local hotel. In both versions of the story, performers from the Far East become menacing Indians, who, as Armando Prats points out, often appear only as spectral presences in the Western, where they are alluded to merely through sounds or partial signs as a way of both dehumanizing and removing them from the land. As Prats notes, the Hollywood Western makes the Indian *"present"* in this partial manner, "so that it may render him *absent*."[28] Just as Oakley undergoes a new racialization in the musical, so the American West and the Western itself become whitewashed, the transnational elements and the vast international influences from the East that helped shape the genre, the region, and the western hero often being erased from history.

The failure of Pawnee Bill's Far East performers to contain their violence and savagery is not shown directly on-screen. These figures thus become a spectral element of savagery against which Oakley may be measured, their lack of discipline contrasting with her efforts to be orderly and civilized. In an effort to achieve a desired entrance into respectable white culture and the norms of heterosexuality, the character must leave behind her frontier history of violence and savagery, elements she cultivated as a child long before the story began. As a gifted sharpshooter who is a key attraction for Buffalo Bill's audiences, however, she may keep hold of some of her well-honed skills, but only if they are safely expressed onstage in the Wild West performances and only if they remain there. By the end of the musical, Oakley's successful achievement of whiteness and civilization appears in stark contrast to the Far East performers in Pawnee Bill's show, who as menacing, would-be captors terrorize Wilson's hotel customers. Such figures are clearly not ready for life outside the show and thus remain located in a place of savagery onstage. According to the racial logic of the story, Pawnee Bill's performers may not be trusted outside the Wild West show in the civilized world, as they are unable to keep the drama of captivity and racial violence where it belongs—safely contained on the stage.

The film *Hidalgo* (2004) also revisits the era of the Wild West shows, in this instance in order to stage U.S. encounters with the Arab Middle East in the context of America's war on terror. *Hidalgo* appeared in theaters one year after the U.S. invasion of Iraq; it may come as no surprise that the movie stages generic Arabs as savage enemies of freedom, as potential threats to the cowboy hero, and as a force that needs to be defeated and contained.[29] The film features Viggo Mortensen in his first starring role since *The Lord of the Rings* trilogy (2001–3) and was directed by Joe Johnston, who also directed action/adventure films such as *Jurassic Park III* (2001) and *Jumanji* (1995) and who earlier served as art director for *Raiders of the Lost Ark* (1981). With a screenplay by John Fusco, *Hidalgo* is based on the much-contested and controversial autobiography of Frank T. Hopkins, who allegedly spent part of his life as a long-distance horse racer and whose travels took him from the American West to the Middle East in the late nineteenth century.[30] The horse race itself is coded as a kind of survival of the fittest, with the region's future imperial rule showcased in the form of the American hero, Frank T. Hopkins. In staging the race between cowboys and Arabs, *Hidalgo* enters discussions about American national identity and foreign policy, particularly the nation's twenty-first-century role in the Middle East as Americans struggled to make sense of the nation's new mission in the world.

Hidalgo begins as the main character, Hopkins, experiences the massacre of Lakota Indians by troops of the U.S. Seventh Cavalry at Wounded Knee in 1890. In dealing with the trauma of witnessing the event, he turns to alcohol and joins the Buffalo Bill show. Known as a gifted horseman by other entertainers in the show, Hopkins is invited to join the "Ocean of Fire," a three-thousand-mile horse race across the Arabian Desert, which allegedly had been held annually for centuries. During the horse race, Hopkins faces challenges from treacherous opponents, thwarts the sexual demands of a female British horse owner, and woos the daughter of an overcontrolling father played by the Egyptian actor Omar

Fig. 6. Sheikh Riyadh enjoys a dime novel about Buffalo Bill's adventures in *Hidalgo* (directed by Joe Johnston, 2004), from the DVD.

Sharif, whom audiences may remember as the real-life Michel Shalhoub, the childhood bully known for his painful arm twists and other brutal punishments as described by Edward Said in his memoir, *Out of Place*.[31]

Born in Alexandria, Egypt, in 1932, Omar Sharif began appearing in films during his early twenties, when he was cast by the well-known Egyptian director Youssef Chahine. While the actor went on to appear in a number of Egyptian movies from 1954 to 1961, he first gained international recognition in 1962 for his work in David Lean's film, *Lawrence of Arabia*, for which he received an Oscar nomination for Best Supporting Actor. The film later encouraged generations of moviegoers outside North Africa and the Middle East to imagine Sharif as the "archetypal Arab" on-screen, even though he was cast in such roles only a few times after his early work in Egyptian cinema. In watching his performance in *Hidalgo*, audiences may experience a certain degree of intertextual interference, as his role in the 2004 Western is similar to the character he played in *Lawrence of Arabia*. In both films, Sharif's character serves initially as the hero's enemy but is converted to his ally, and his friendship with the westerner—whether T. E. Lawrence or Frank T. Hopkins—grants approval to the colonial presence in the region.[32]

After *Lawrence of Arabia*, Sharif frequently appeared on-screen as a generic Mediterranean type. He once told an interviewer that his identity made him a "foreigner in every film industry in the world" except Egypt's.[33] Sharif went on to play a surprisingly wide variety of types; in addition to appearing as a German in more than one film, he was also cast as an Armenian, Yugoslavian, Mexican, Austrian, Italian, Greek, and Russian.[34] Sharif's role as Yuri in David Lean's *Doctor Zhivago* (1965) solidified his star appeal, with the film's popularity due in part to his strong performance and to the ways the movie screened U.S. Cold War myths of and fantasies for a pre-Soviet Russian past. Richard Fleischer's *Ashanti* (1979) was one of the few non-Egyptian movies in which Sharif played an Arab character. His appearance in the film earned him negative press, however, and later led to a general boycott of his work because of his role as an oil-rich Arab caught up in a kidnapping scheme involving an American woman. Sharif's earlier performance as the Jewish American card player Nick Arnstein in William Wyler's 1968 musical comedy *Funny Girl*, with Barbra Streisand as his love interest, also sparked controversy as filming took place during the Six-Day War, which led to strong criticism of Sharif for appearing on-screen with a Jewish actress.[35] In 2003, the French director François Dupeyron's *Monsieur Ibrahim* brought him more positive attention for his performance as an elderly Muslim shopkeeper who becomes a mentor to a young Jewish boy from his neighborhood in 1960s Paris.

For an actor seeking broad international appeal, one's screen name can help or hinder the process, and film stars often take great care in understanding the nuances and subtle meanings a name can have in different national contexts. Over the years, the actor has explained his transformation from "Michel Shalhoub" to "Omar Sharif," offering two versions of the story. In a 1989 interview, the actor explained the circumstances around his choice of names, noting that he wanted a name that would be easy for the Americans, the British, and the Europeans. He considered the famous Omars of history, including Omar Khayyam and the U.S. general Omar Bradley. Later the actor explains, "I thought of the sheriffs, the ones in the Westerns, and I decided Omar Sharif was

On Savagery and Civilization

a good combination."[36] Aware of how these meanings needed to travel globally with a maximum of ease, he chose a name whose broad significance played into his larger star persona.

However, in his autobiography, *The Eternal Male* (1977), the actor recounts a slightly different version of how he came upon his screen name as he deliberately considered how best to position himself for both Middle Eastern and international audiences: "I tried to come up with something that sounded Middle Eastern and could still be spelled in every language. . . . Next, I thought of combining Omar with the Arabic sheriff [i.e., a descendant of the Prophet and considered a high-born figure in most Muslim countries] but I realized that this would evoke the word 'sheriff,' which was a bit too cowboyish. So I opted for a variant—I became Omar Sharif."[37] In these competing versions of the name change, the actor at one time celebrates the popular associations with the mythic cowboy figure of the filmic Western; in the other version, he emphasizes the larger Arabic connections and a shift of spelling that enables him to bypass references to the law-bringing hero of the American West whose meanings might be received negatively in a global context.

Just as the actor faced the problems of competing and contradictory meanings in his adopted name, various conflicted elements also tug at the meanings of *Hidalgo* as a popular Western. In this way, the film is reminiscent of John Milius's *The Wind and the Lion* (1975), a Western captivity story that positions itself both for and against the American presence in the Middle East, often shifting allegiances in terms of which characters are cast as savages and civilizers.[38] By the time *Hidalgo* appeared in theaters, the Western had entered a revisionist cycle and could no longer easily demonize Native Americans as savage enemies. Like *Dances with Wolves* (1990), a film commonly cited as helping usher in the recent cycle of revisionist Westerns, *Hidalgo* is positioned as an "Indian sympathy film."[39] As such, the film avoids using broken English to signify the supposed racial and cultural inferiority of Native Americans, instead employing subtitles to translate the dialogue of Lakota- and Arabic-speaking characters. As a revisionist text with some pro-Indian sympathies, the film also divides its loyalties between whites and Native Americans as if to acknowledge the complexities of racial identity in contemporary multicultural U.S. society. This dual allegiance is explained in part by the bicultural identity of Hopkins, whose mother was Lakota and whose father was a white army scout. Much of the film is preoccupied with finding a usable American past for the divided hero, whose experiences at the Wounded Knee massacre are framed as both a personal and a national trauma. By the end of the film, the shameful experiences at Wounded Knee are alleviated by the successes Hopkins has in the horse race against his Arab rivals.

The complexities of racial identity complicate the cultural politics of the film. Throughout U.S. history, Arabs have been placed in a complex, ever-shifting racial category. In the pre-9/11 era, Arab Americans were granted status as "probationary whites," a term used by the philosopher Charles Mills for those groups whose cultural identity as whites remains conditional and uncertain as power relations expand and contract racial definitions in different historical periods.[40] At various moments, Arab Americans have experienced the privileges of whiteness, even as such privileges were often revoked in times of national crisis and racial anxiety. The war on terrorism certainly shifted the racial status of Arab Americans.[41] The complex redefinitions of race in America mirror the conditional multiculturalism of *Hidalgo*, as the encounter between the United States and the diverse Arab populations of the film is presented within the logics of benevolent supremacy. It is not an outright conflict like the Indian massacre at Wounded Knee but is framed as a more innocent venture, with the hero, a mixed-race American, not just winning a race but liberating Arab people along the way. Audiences have, however, noted the uneasy way in which *Hidalgo* operates as a revisionist text, with one film critic calling the movie "Viggo of Arabia," linking it to Lean's epic film, *Lawrence of Arabia*, which also received mixed reviews for its largely sympathetic treatment of Britain's colonial past in the Middle East. The phrase "Viggo of Arabia" also calls to mind the nickname given to Kevin Costner's attempts at making revisionist film

On Savagery and Civilization

in *Dances with Wolves*; the film likewise sparked controversy and was labeled "Lawrence of South Dakota" for its representations of racial conflict and nation-building in the nineteenth-century American West.[42]

"A horse of a most unusual color"

The film *Hidalgo* takes its title from the name of the horse that Frank Hopkins rides throughout the story, an animal whose purpose and function carry complicated meanings throughout the film. As a cultural text, the film is preoccupied with racial definitions and boundaries. When Hopkins first enters the competition, for instance, an opponent comments on the animal's pedigree, describing the animal as "a horse of a most unusual color." Hidalgo, we learn, is a mustang, a free-roaming horse of the American West, an animal whose freedom is meant to mirror that of the western American hero. The early Spanish explorers called the horses *mesteños*, which meant "wild," and later they became known as mustangs among the Anglos. Having descended from various breeds—most notably Arabian horses brought earlier to Spain and then to the Americas—mustangs were thought to possess endurance, strength, and speed.[43] Here the horse's name and pedigree are significant for a number of reasons. The wildness of the horse may reference aspects of the American West that are frequently lauded in the Western, particularly the possibilities of the wild and the celebration of nature that are central to the promises of the region. Yet, the name "Hidalgo" also references other moments of freedom and postcolonial possibility, particularly Miguel Hidalgo y Costilla, the Mexican priest who led the 1810 revolt that marked the beginning of what would become the Mexican War of Independence.[44]

As a Spanish term, the name "Hidalgo" is also a reminder that one of the central icons of the American West—the horse—is not indigenous to the region but instead arrived from someplace else, just as the Western itself has a complicated transnational history as an offshoot of colonial adventure narratives. Even tumbleweed, that ubiquitous symbol of the formidable challenges facing the cowboy hero in the archetypical Western landscape, is not indigenous to the American West but is believed to have migrated from Russia on burlap bags that traveled with the railroads.[45] Cowboys, as pointed out earlier in this study, also cannot claim their origins in the U.S. West but serve as the offspring of the vaqueros, who themselves borrowed from the earlier horse traditions of the Moors.[46] Even the cowboy boot, with its pointed toe and distinctive stitching reminiscent of intricate Arabic patterns, may have been originally designed by Muslims in Andalusia.[47]

One is reminded too of the un-American origins of another icon of U.S. identity, the Statue of Liberty, which Hopkins gazes at with ambivalence when he boards the ship that will take him to the Middle East. With this scene, the film contributes to a long history of complicated meanings associated with Lady Liberty. Sometimes understood as a symbol of the American national values of freedom, independence, and emancipation, while at other times positioned ironically by marginalized populations in the United States, the Statue of Liberty has accrued both national and global meanings. One such transformation from national to global meaning emerged in the instance of the Lady Liberty statue known as *The Goddess of Democracy*, famously erected in Beijing's Tiananmen Square for different national purposes.[48] While in the United States the statue is often thought of as the "Mother of Exiles," who maternally welcomes millions of immigrants to the land of freedom, the Statue of Liberty has also acquired less positive associations. The late nineteenth century saw rising nativism and increased efforts to restrict immigration across the nation. In 1882, for instance, the Chinese Exclusion Act barred entry to Chinese laborers and denied citizenship to the Chinese already in residence. Critics have thus noted the irony that, just as Lady Liberty was rising in New York Harbor, opportunities to enter the United States were increasingly being foreclosed for some populations.[49]

The Statue of Liberty also carries with it a transnational history that has been overlooked by Americans and that has unintended meanings for *Hidalgo* as a whole. Those who are familiar with Egypt's history, particularly its struggles over the control of the Suez Canal, will remember that the Statue of Liberty was initially

On Savagery and Civilization

designed for display in the Middle East and was originally modeled after an Egyptian peasant rather than a European woman. The person who designed Lady Liberty was the French artist Frédéric Bartholdi, who was primarily known for his sculpture but who also contributed to the larger body of nineteenth-century European orientalist painting. During a visit to Egypt in 1855, Bartholdi was awed by his tour of the Sphinx and Giza pyramids. "Their kindly and impassive glance seems to ignore the present and to be fixed upon an unlimited future," he wrote.[50]

While in Egypt, Bartholdi was a productive orientalist artist, creating more than two hundred drawings and more than two dozen oil studies, some of which he displayed in salons upon his return to France. Influenced by the Suez Canal project, he was inspired in 1867 to design a giant lighthouse that would stand at the entrance of the canal. His plans for this project included a figure in the tradition of the Roman goddess Libertas, this time modeled to represent an Egyptian peasant, or *fellah*, who would carry a light that beamed through a headband and a torch that was directed to the skies. The plans were presented to Ismaïl Pasha, Egypt's ruler from 1863 to 1879, who eventually rejected the commission. Beginning first as clay models based on watercolor drawings of women that Bartholdi encountered during his travels to Egypt, the images eventually shifted in their later form. In Lady Liberty's transition to New York Harbor landmark, the figure lost her Egyptian features and instead became what the art historian Darcy Grimaldo Grigsby calls a "remote, abstractly chastened and generalized" female icon.[51]

In a similar way, Egypt—the initial national site for the statue— has experienced a shifting identity between East and West throughout history. As a contested geography and terrain located between various worlds, Egypt has at times been claimed as African, Mediterranean, Middle Eastern, and European. When the Suez Canal opened in 1869, the leader Ismaïl Pasha famously declared, "My country is no longer in Africa; we are now part of Europe. It is therefore natural for us to abandon our former ways and to adopt a new system adapted to our social conditions."[52] In doing so, the

Fig. 7. Frédéric Bartholdi, *Egypt Carrying the Light into Asia* (1867).
Reprinted with permission from Musée Bartholdi, Colmar, France.
Reproduction by C. Kempf.

leader underscored how Egypt's identity was provisional rather than fixed or determined, an understanding that continues to shape how the nation is regarded by Egyptians themselves, as well as by others outside the country.[53]

A similar concern about shifting understandings of identity appears in *Hidalgo* through discussions of Hopkins's horse, an animal of "impure" origins. In the film, much is made of the thoroughbred horses in the race, which are compared to the mustang, with its mixed pedigree and travels through the Arabian Peninsula and Spain to the Americas. On the one hand, the mixed-breed mustang with its impure past can be regarded as a celebration of multicultural America, a nation made up of diverse populations from all over the world. On the other hand, the "impure" past of the animal parallels the hero's own troubled identity as a biracial American as well as the hybrid cultural origins of the cowboy hero

On Savagery and Civilization

and the Western. Yet, it is through both the mixed-breed animal and the multicultural American hero that the film is able to heal the wounds of the nation's past. In winning the race against the Arabs, both Hopkins and the horse recast the American nation, with all of its diversity and complexity, as a force to be reckoned with on the international stage. With the prize money from the race, Hopkins buys back land that was stolen from the survivors of Wounded Knee. He also frees his beloved horse, who runs off with a herd of wild mustangs at the film's end.

Gender is also mobilized in the narrative as a means of defining American national identity through Hopkins's female counterpart, the British aristocrat Lady Anne Davenport, who has designs not just on the race and the right to breed her horses with the thoroughbreds but also on the possibilities of capturing the Wild West hero. Davenport figures as an imperial competitor, a symbol of British power in the region, even though, as one Egyptian film reviewer pointed out, there are problems in the film's staging of British presence in an era when the region was still under Ottoman rule.[54] Nevertheless, Lady Davenport figures as a powerful threat to be reckoned with in the film. She makes much of the fact that she is "looking for a breed apart," as she puts it, in reference to both the horses and the western hero. In the classic Western, the frontier hero is often positioned in a triangulated relationship between eastern American civilization and western American savagery. The Anglo hero must constantly negotiate between the two forces, avoiding the domesticity and exhaustion of the urban American East while also not succumbing to the temptations of "going native" in the Wild West.[55]

In the genre, the West is represented as wild space, the domain of savage nature and unruly racial Others, both of which much be tamed by the hero. Meanwhile, the American East is often feminized and likewise racialized, sometimes a force to be contained or controlled and at other times represented in the figure of the white woman who is the hero's love interest. Jane Tompkins makes a case for the ways the Western emerged as a means of countering female cultural power in the domestic sphere in the nineteenth century and that the qualities devalued in the Western are often those associated with white women.⁵⁶ Like the typical Anglo hero in the Western, Hopkins struggles to liberate himself from the corruptions of an overly modernized world, represented here in the form of Lady Davenport. Her sexual as well as political competitiveness make her a poor choice for the hero. Here Lady Davenport serves as the feminized symbol of hypermodernity—the domestic, urbanized Other in the classic Western—a figure who tries to tame and conquer the hero. In addition, Davenport serves anachronistically as a stand-in for British colonial order, a force that has to be defeated—if only symbolically—in order for the American to assert his own national interests.

"Remember, you're the good guy"

Early in *Hidalgo*, the character Annie Oakley, played by Elizabeth Berridge, yells out to Hopkins just as he is entering the Wild West arena, "Remember, you're the good guy." Such assurances on the part of the sharpshooting female character are reinforced in the film through Hopkins's relationship with Sheikh Riyadh's daughter, Jazira, played by Zuleikha Robinson, a British actress of Burmese, Iranian, Scottish, and Indian heritage. Like Omar Sharif, Robinson has portrayed characters from diverse ethnic backgrounds in her films.⁵⁷ The love plot between Hopkins and the sheikh's daughter operates within an orientalist logic as it features the "woman of cover" uncovering and thus apparently gaining agency and independence from patriarchy and Islam in this line of thinking. "Woman of cover" is a term Pres. George W. Bush used in a speech he gave one month after 9/11.⁵⁸ The term "woman of cover" connotes difference by playing on and appropriating the multicultural concept of "woman of color." At the same time, it suggests, especially in the U.S. culture of security and surveillance, a kind of suspicious behavior, as if Muslim women who cover have something to hide.

As the free-thinking and brave Jazira becomes interested in Hopkins and he with her, the film borrows from what Ella Shohat describes as the "colonial rescue fantasy," which relies on the imperial trope of the dark woman "trapped in brutal retrograde

On Savagery and Civilization

societies" in need of rescue.[59] Within the context of what Richard Goldstein calls Bush's "stealth misogyny," the chivalrous imperative to emancipate the nonwestern woman takes place within a colonial framework.[60] The orientalist rescue narrative of the film becomes linked to the frontier captivity narrative, with an Arab Muslim replacing the Anglo Puritan female, as Hopkins struggles to free Jazira from her restrictive clothing, family, and community. Jazira eventually uncovers in front of the western hero, defying her father's power and rejecting her role as the so-called oppressed Muslim woman. The uncovering is presented as a feminist move toward liberation and freedom that also prompts Hopkins's own delayed racial self-reflection. Having kept his identity as an American Indian secret throughout the film, he is now free to uncover and liberate himself racially as a multicultural American, a true Western hero who rescues not only himself but others.

Jazira's liberation of Hopkins occurs in other instances throughout the film; far from being a passive or submissive character in the film, she willingly participates in her own uncovering and continually expresses her desires to participate as an active agent in the race. Although Hopkins tracks down her kidnappers and eventually restores her to her family, Jazira turns the tables on Hopkins in a postfeminist move in which she "rescues her rescuer" by helping him escape. The film's gender politics follow the complicated and contradictory postfeminism of the Bush administration, the logic being that certain women need help to free themselves and, in doing so, will return the favor by casting their lot with their liberators.

Both Jazira's name and that of her father, "Sheikh Riyadh," are also obvious allusions to contemporary geopolitical issues in the Middle East that serve as strong American touchstones, with Al Jazeera being the television network based in Qatar and Riyadh being a reference to the capital of Saudi Arabia.[61] Both references call to mind recent American efforts at bringing democracy and modernization to the region, as debates about Al Jazeera in the western media circulate around issues of press censorship, freedom of speech, and the transparency of the media, while Saudi Arabia

Fig. 8. Jazira's uncovering in *Hidalgo* (directed by Joe Johnston, 2004), from the DVD.

Fig. 9. Jazira "freed" by her cowboy/savior in *Hidalgo* (directed by Joe Johnston, 2004), from the DVD.

figures as a key ally for the United States in the region, albeit one that American officials believe must open up more fully to U.S. views and lifestyles. Other significant references also abound in the film. As the updated Tonto figure and subordinate figure to the Anglo hero in *Hidalgo*, Sharif's character gives his grudging respect to the cowboy hero after the latter proves his worthiness as a male competitor to the sheikh, even before the race officially begins. The first test comes after Hopkins downs a cup of coffee in the middle of a warning from the sheikh. "Most foreigners find our coffee to be too potent," he tells Hopkins, who surprises the sheikh by finishing the drink in one gulp. "Back home, we toss a

On Savagery and Civilization

horseshoe in the pot. Stands up straight, coffee's ready," the laconic cowboy replies.

Hopkins also earns respect from the sheikh when he displays his Colt pistol, in the film a symbol both of the hero's strength on the American frontier and of U.S. global power, past and present. The sheikh's fascination with Western technology functions as an orientalist cliché, an age-old expression of the West's alleged superiority and power over the East. The Colt pistol brings further into focus the theme of modernization and the West's civilizing mission in the region, elements that one reviewer in the Middle East has addressed at some length. Pointing to the ways that Arab history is dismissed throughout the film, the Egyptian critic Emad El-Din Aysha highlights what he calls "the satirizing of all things non-American" within *Hidalgo*, as audiences are "constantly presented with symbols of decay, of relics and archaeological remains, of long-gone civilizations, swallowed up by time and the desert." The reviewer goes on to note that in the film the "general idea is that the Arabs (may have) had a great past . . . their present is awful; they are lagging behind the rest of the world and the only way to get ahead is to turn their backs on the past." He points out that they "have to throw themselves wholeheartedly into the hands of the West, with the most Western of all being the Americans." Ultimately, the film advances the idea of Arabs throughout the world as bereft or "having no future" unless they have the foresight to "work hand in hand with the West, America."[62]

As played out in *Hidalgo*, however, this notion of modernization proves to be complicated. On the one hand, an irony that may be lost involves the use of the Western to impart themes of modernization. As one of the most nostalgic of all film genres, the Western usually expresses ambivalence toward modernization and typically operates as an antimodern response to the changes the rest of the world is experiencing. A central plot element in the genre involves escape, with the hero retreating from an overly developed and modernized world to the wild, untamed, and celebrated *premodern* landscapes of the American West. The popular Western may thus be somewhat out of place here in its role as modernizing force in the Middle East. Yet critics such as T. J. Jackson Lears have also indicated that modernism itself always contained a large element of nostalgia and melancholia, frequently referring back to a previous world and mourning its loss, as this post-9/11 Western does.[63]

Ultimately, *Hidalgo* operates not so much as a historical document of the past but as an instance of "benevolent supremacy," with the American hero appropriately besting what turns out to be an anachronistic British presence in order to take its place in the region. In fact, the source material guiding the plot has been largely discredited, as critics have uncovered various deceptions in Hopkins's version of these events.[64] It becomes clear that the movie is not just about defeating ghosts of the nineteenth-century past. Instead, the film is less about nineteenth-century Indians and more about twenty-first century U.S. encounters with the Arab Middle East. In this context, it is not difficult to see the horse race itself as a contest between nations that has global consequences, as the American rider Frank T. Hopkins represents the race that should rightfully win the race and the nation that figures as an appropriate heroic model and standard for others to emulate.

On Savagery and Civilization

FOUR

The Persian Peddler and the Egyptian Elixir

Racial Intimacies in *Oklahoma!*

The term *Arab* is often figurative. *Arab* could and did indicate
an intermediary position between foreigner and citizen, black
and white, primitive and civilized. Literate black slaves on
the Southern plantation, American Indians on the western
frontier, and new immigrants in the urban slum were all,
at one time or another, referred to as Arabs.

—JACOB RAMA BERMAN

Immigrants as other have a productive function in national
culture, for they simultaneously shore up the mythical view
of the United States as a cradle of democracy and the
view of it as a threatened asylum.

—ALI BEHDAD

Set in Indian Territory near the town of Claremore during the
early years of the twentieth century, the Rodgers and Hammerstein musical *Oklahoma!* and its source material are the product of
a complicated history of shifting racial ideology as well as notions
of citizenship and belonging. These texts situate Arabs and Persians
as a menacing presence in the American West, as outsiders who are
provisionally white and thus only marginally qualified for citizenship. Based on the 1931 play *Green Grow the Lilacs* by the Cherokee
poet and playwright Lynn Riggs, *Oklahoma!* is also the product of a

complicated history of adaptation and revision that highlights these racial and national politics. First produced on Broadway in 1943, *Oklahoma!* went on to receive a special Pulitzer Prize for Drama in 1944.[1] Setting records as the longest-running play in its time, the show has been considered a "landmark event," with histories of Broadway often being divided into "pre- and post-*Oklahoma!* phases," according to the theatre critic Tim Carter.[2] The Broadway show was later made into an Oscar-winning 1955 movie featuring Gordon Mac-Rae, Shirley Jones, and Gloria Grahame. The film was directed by Fred Zinnemann, who had gained success in Hollywood, particularly with his 1952 Western, *High Noon*. The musical remains popular today, with theatres across the country and the world staging more than six hundred productions of the show each year.[3]

While some critics celebrate the achievements of the musical, noting that *Oklahoma!*'s successful merging of music, dance, and story made it the "first real phenomenon in modern Broadway history," thus dramatically changing the development of the American musical on stage and screen, other critics remain vexed by its treatment of race and national belonging.[4] As a musical Western, *Oklahoma!* employs the genre's racialized struggle between savagery and civilization and its tale of establishing order and defeating chaos on the mythic American frontier.[5] The musical tells the story of Laurey Williams, a young orphaned woman who is left to care for her family's farm with her widowed Aunt Eller and who has to decide which suitor should accompany her to the town's box lunch social. Courted by two quite different men—the cheerful singing cowboy Curly McClain and the "scowling" and "burly" hired hand Jud Fry—Laurey's task involves more than just finding a proper male companion for the event.[6] While the central drama of the musical involves the task of locating an appropriate mate for Laurey and the other young people in the territory, it does so in an effort to ensure a successful future for Oklahoma as it petitions for statehood in 1907. The romance plot of the musical thus links the story's heterosexual pairings to the fate of the nation itself, a struggle that involves managing the boundaries of whiteness in order to secure an appropriate racial future for an expanding America.[7]

Persian Peddler, Egyptian Elixir

A point of criticism about *Oklahoma!* often centers on its treatment of racial logics, particularly the manner in which Native Americans are removed from the stage and written out of the region's past, a rather perplexing absence considering that the musical takes place in Indian Territory in the beginning of the twentieth century and that its source material was written by the Cherokee author Lynn Riggs. This absence has prompted critics such as Raymond Knapp to comment on the "deep ironies" of the drama, particularly the ways it "colludes" in whitewashing the nation's violence toward its Indigenous populations and overlooking a bloody "chapter in American history" through celebrations of Oklahoma's statehood.[8] The Creek-Cherokee scholar Craig Womack also notes problems with the story's treatment of racial histories, focusing primarily on Riggs's 1931 play. Like other critics, Womack is unsettled by the political meanings of the drama, arguing that the "golden-age nostalgia" at the center of Riggs's story "fails to account for what happened to Indian people" at the hand of its "hardy settlers."[9] He also accuses "the oppressed pioneers" who have relocated to Indian Territory of not considering "their own role as oppressors."[10] While he recognizes the difficulties Riggs faced as a closeted gay writer who frequently guarded his personal life from his family and community and who, as a result, often wrote in code about controversial topics, Womack is nevertheless critical about the larger political meanings of the drama. He remains especially unsettled by the ways Riggs's story "celebrates one of the biggest land rip-offs in history" and how it turns "physical and cultural genocide" into a series of light-hearted "song-and-dance numbers."[11]

More recently, director Molly Smith's 2010 revival of *Oklahoma!* at Arena Stage in the nation's capital received positive response for her casting choices and particularly for bringing issues of race to center stage in the musical. Hilton Als's review in the *New Yorker* applauds Smith's production for breaking with tradition by featuring African American actresses E. Faye Butler and Eleasha Gamble in the roles of Laurey and Aunt Eller and for casting Latinx actor Nicholas Rodriguez in the role of the cowboy suitor Curly.

The reviewer likewise praises the production for excavating the racial histories of Oklahoma, depicting the territory around the turn of the twentieth century as inhabited by white settlers from other regions of the country, as well as populations of freed slaves and forcibly resettled Indians, thus more accurately showing "how characters might have looked if they were actual Oklahomans of the period."[12]

Examining the adaptations and revivals of *Oklahoma!* and its source material, I am interested in assessing how the 1955 Western enacts such erasures while also complicating other issues concerning national belonging and citizenship. Struggles over the category of whiteness, for instance, become a central conflict in the story, with determinations over which characters are worthy of membership in the community—and by extension American citizenship after statehood—operating as a primary theme of the musical. Richard Dyer's observations about the racial logics of the Western are useful to note in this context. While the Western as a foundational myth of the United States typically entails a story about national "destiny" that embraces movement through the land "in the name of race," "breeding," and "heterosexual reproduction," Dyer argues that the Western is not entirely about "white exhilaration and glorification."[13] Instead, he contends that the genre often "has elements that challenge optimism, that drag at the sense of energy and freedom, that complicate any idea of the white man as the citadel of right."[14] Dyer attends to the genre's treatment of whiteness, arguing that "the greatest threat in most Westerns comes not from the native peoples or Mexicans but from within, from bad whites. This does not however tarnish the white project." Instead, the genre often acknowledges "the variation in white people" and "the ways in which some white people fail to attain whiteness." In Westerns, bad whites "are often associated with darkness," and the genre typically "expunges such darkly coded bad apples the better to celebrate the struggle for whiteness."[15]

Building on these observations, I argue that Native Americans and African Americans are erased from the story in order for certain "bad whites"—presented here as not-quite-white Arab and Per-

Persian Peddler, Egyptian Elixir

sian characters—to come into racial relief and that such absences enable the drama to avoid acknowledging the region's past and its unresolved territorial conflicts. Because *Oklahoma!* celebrates the possibilities of the expanding nation, reminders of the brutal conflicts over land tenure and national belonging among European Americans, Native Americans, and African Americans must be repressed. Furthermore, *Oklahoma!* and its source materials rely on a complicated and shifting understanding of whiteness to which Native Americans and African Americans are denied access and to which they cannot be assimilated. In the drama, Dyer's "bad whites" are depicted as racially ambiguous immigrants—in earlier versions, the nameless Syrian peddler and, in later versions, Ali Hakim, the Persian merchant. While the peddler in both cases introduces an orientalist threat into the rural West—a racialized and sexualized danger that must be contained so that the territory of Oklahoma can properly achieve a civilized status and thus statehood—the figure undergoes transformations in the musical that settle, at least temporarily, contested definitions of race as well as concerns about citizenship in the early twentieth century.[16] Attention to *Oklahoma!* and its source materials helps restore to memory histories of racial intimacy, conflicted regional identities, and ideas about national belonging, transformations that can be read in microcosm in the story's treatment of the peddler. In examining how elements of a specific American orientalism function in the story, I also locate traces of a global history that has shaped the Western more generally.

By restoring the region to a larger transnational context, studies of the American West are able to trace new routes of influence, alternative contact zones, and different boundary crossings, as well as underexamined sites of meaning and cultural production. Analyzing what he calls the "rhizomatic West," Neil Campbell points out that the American West "has always had a global dimension as a geographical, cultural, and economic crossroads defined by complex connectivity, multidimensionality, and imagination, even if these have often been elided in favor of a more inward-looking . . . vision." He thus calls for a scholarship that views the region in a more worldly perspective and that enables the West to be "detached from its isolation as pure American."[17] Campbell notes that western spaces "are always far more complex than the East-West frontiers" as defined by the historian Frederick Jackson Turner. In studying the historical and cultural elements that often do not align themselves "with the official, mythic images," critics may be able to "produce a different and more sophisticated understanding of the region."[18]

The project of locating the region in a larger global setting also enables critics to recognize and address the many Wests that have emerged in American history—from the Pacific Northwest to the Southwest borderlands, from Alaska to the Great Plains, and so on—as well as the many Easts that come into play in mapping the boundaries and borders of the region.[19] While scholarship tends to locate and rely on a binary logic involving a U.S. East and a U.S. West, a globalized perspective helps direct critics to an alternative geography whereby a different eastern spatial imaginary—not the American East but an oriental East—operates in the production of U.S. regional identities. Here I attend to the racial politics brought to the fore by the figure of the orientalist peddler who brings with him various exotic objects from the Middle East to sell to residents of the rural farm communities of the Great Plains. These products, which include face whitener, perfume, and Egyptian elixir, carry significant meanings in struggles over citizenship and identity, even as they remind us of one of the primary themes of the story, that of "selling" a particular idea of whiteness and national belonging to American audiences in the first half of the twentieth century.

Racial Histories of *Oklahoma!*

A number of critics have noted how Lynn Riggs drew on experiences from his childhood in Oklahoma in writing his plays. The author was born in 1899 in a small town near Claremore. His mother, Rose Ella Riggs, was one-eighth Cherokee and his father, William Grant Riggs, was a cattleman and banker who became a Cherokee citizen upon his marriage to Rose. Before Riggs reached his first birthday, his mother enrolled herself and her children on the Cherokee rolls, which enabled them to receive an allotment of 160 acres. She died in 1901, after which Riggs's father married a woman who was also Cherokee. After enduring a lonely childhood, Riggs left home in 1912 to attend college in nearby Claremore, where he became interested in drama.[20]

After he graduated from college in 1917, Riggs tried his hand at various jobs. A somewhat restless young artist, Riggs traveled frequently, living and working in a number of cities, including Santa Fe, Chicago, New York, and Hollywood. In New York he worked as an extra in the many cowboy movies that were being produced in Astoria and the Bronx. Later he was employed as a bookseller in Macy's department store and also as a proofreader for the *Wall Street Journal*.[21] In 1923, on the advice of a doctor, Riggs moved to Santa Fe to recover from tuberculosis; there he developed his talents as a poet and a playwright.[22] Riggs ended up completing his most famous play, *Green Grow the Lilacs*, in 1929 with the help of a Guggenheim Fellowship during an extended stay in France.[23] After returning to the United States, Riggs continued to move around, at one point hopping a train for Hollywood, where he landed a position as an extra in the movies and a job working on various film scripts. In Hollywood, Riggs joined the ranks of other Native Americans who were involved in the film industry, primarily in the many Westerns that were being produced in the early twentieth century. At this time, a number of Native Americans who had previously been involved in the Wild West shows had moved into the film industry, such that by midcentury there existed a small but thriving community of American Indians living and working in Hollywood.[24] During his stay in California, Riggs was employed by Paramount and Universal Studios, earning a script credit for the Cecil B. DeMille Western *The Plainsman*, starring Gary Cooper as Wild Bill Hickok, as well as a writing credit for a 1936 film, *The Garden of Allah*, an orientalist fable set in the Libyan desert and featuring Marlene Dietrich and Charles Boyer.[25]

While most critics writing about *Oklahoma!* tend to address local and regional concerns while also focusing on the 1931 play *Green Grow the Lilacs* as the source for the 1943 musical, I wish to engage larger transnational developments by attending to the figure of the peddler and an earlier play by Riggs. His prior one-act drama, *Knives from Syria*, from 1928, may be examined for how it places the region in global contexts, introducing character types included in later versions of the story. The 1928 play addresses conflicts surrounding a Syrian peddler whose entry into the world of a rural family in Oklahoma raises fears about racial difference and intimacy. Appearing across a variety of novels, memoirs, and plays, the Syrian peddler was a familiar figure in American literature beginning in the 1870s, when the first large wave of immigrants from Greater Syria arrived in the United States.[26] Peddling was one of the earliest forms of employment available to Arabic-speaking immigrants upon their arrival in the United States. It was a job that enabled them to learn English and gain economic stability, both of which became routes to assimilation.[27] Peddlers soon found employment all across the country, from the coal mines of Appalachia to the gold fields of Alaska. Many of them also traveled and worked in large metropolitan areas such as New York and San Francisco, as well as in small communities across the rural West.[28] Traveling from one home to another selling their wares, peddlers had close contact with various households as they traveled, bringing items and ideas from faraway places into rural homes. In Riggs's drama, the Syrian peddler is assigned a crucial role in the drama as he introduces cosmopolitan possibilities into the lives of the isolated residents he encounters on the Great Plains.

Riggs's *Knives from Syria* features a widow, Mrs. Buster, who resides on an Oklahoma farm with her young daughter. Like *Green Grow the Lilacs*, Riggs's one-act play also features two competing suitors: the hired hand Charley and a character known only as the Syrian "pedler." Riggs's drama primarily concerns the fate of the young daughter, Rhodie Buster, an aptly named character who dreams of taking to the road for life beyond the confines of her small town and who resists her mother's plans to marry her off to the much older Charley. The play opens with the women worrying about the safety of the hired hand Charley, whom they fear has been waylaid by a violent gang of outlaws that has been threatening the community. Mrs. Buster uses the occasion to remind her daughter about the urgency of marrying Charley, believing the union will ensure their safety. The younger woman protests marriage to the farmhand, telling her mother how "unfair" it would be, given the fifteen-year gap in their ages.[29] Mrs. Buster points out to her daughter that there are few options open to her, unless Rhodie wishes to end up with the Syrian peddler, who is sure to "beat" her "every day" and is likely to "never have no home" for his future family.[30] She reminds her daughter of the peddler's strange ways, elements she noted the first time they met: "He was twirlin' his mustache, awful smart-alec, and he starts talkin' a blue streak, tellin' jokes and actin' up. . . . It's one thing to have him make ye forgit yer troubles, and it's another t'marry him. Besides, he's a foreigner who goes traipsin' all over the world."[31] According to Mrs. Buster, the peddler would make an unsuitable match for Rhodie because not only does he introduce violence into the domestic sphere as a would-be wife beater, but his odd manner and dress also mark him as racially and culturally Other. In addition, his job requires endless mobility, with no possibility of settling down, thus likely ensuring that the peddler will remain an outsider who will never find a place in their community.

When Charley returns home, he explains that he was attacked by a mysterious man. When the outlaw tried to steal his horse, Charley resisted and, in the struggle, was slashed by a knife. Suspicions immediately center on the Syrian peddler, who has already been cast as a menacing outsider, a belief that takes on greater power when he returns to the farmhouse to hawk his wares. These items include a variety of knives that the peddler claims will appeal to farmers and bandits alike. "Knives! Knives from Syria! Pearl-handled, ten inches long. Blades of the very fine steel. Made to cut a hair—or a throat. In my country, the robbers carry them in their belts," the peddler tells the two women. "Many a throat is cut, many a good woman widowed by blades like these! They are *so very* sharp. See! And not only the bandits find them of use, Mrs. Buster. The husband who does not trust his wife, the son mistreated by his father, the lover crossed in his love—When there's two men who want the same girl, Mrs. Buster, it is knives they use to see who gets her."[32] The peddler's comments indicate that he may have something more to sell the family than just a set of cutlery. His self-exoticizing sales pitch combines orientalist discourses with codes of the Western, playing off images of the enticing East that would be familiar to audiences from reading the *Arabian Nights* tales, as well as the popular dime novel Westerns of the period.[33] Combined, these elements of danger and intrigue work to spark Rhodie's interest. What appears to be a frightening and menacing possibility for the mother serves as a point of attraction for the daughter.

Facing resistance from Mrs. Buster, the Syrian peddler steps up his sales pitch, offering additional items intended to appeal to the farmwomen and to gain their approval. He entices them with his exotic wares—"Syrian table-cloths, drawn work from little villages of Mexico, Dutch caps, beads from the shops of Paris, Italian colognes . . . a jacket of many colors from the land of Egypt." The objects speak of faraway lands that promise adventure and possibilities not available in the rural West—a "Japanese lacquered box from the cities of Chong-Chong. Slant-eyed women patting around in lovely silks. Their hearts are on the sea, I think, with their lovers."[34] Eventually the peddler is able to engage Rhodie in private conversation. Understanding her concerns about the life he promises her, the peddler admits that his job is "hard—and lonesome. . . . But the people who love beautiful things are very kind. And there is always the sky, and the rich brown earth, and waters flowing, and sunlight everywhere. . . . It cannot be forever. And there are always more and more hills, and I am free to go to them—whenever I choose! . . . If only you could share it with me."[35] Still under the impression that the peddler is responsible for Charley's injuries and unsure about whether he intends to use his knives for similar purposes once more, the panicked Mrs. Buster changes her mind and agrees to allow the peddler and her daughter to wed. Later, she breaks down, confessing to her daughter that the peddler "made me swear you'd go with him. He made me, I tell you! I didn't mean to . . . He would 'a' killed Charley; he

Persian Peddler, Egyptian Elixir

would 'a' killed us all. I knowed he was the one when I seen the handkerchief, and then the knives."[36]

While Rhodie initially seems resigned to marrying the peddler, the play offers lingering doubts about her distress. The daughter's actual feelings become evident when Charley discovers that his assailant was not the Syrian peddler, as the two women had suspected, but a neighbor named Earl Baker, who was assisted by a "worthless" cousin, both of whom "were sittin' down by the old spring a-laughin' at the joke . . . played on me."[37] While this information provides a way out of the marriage agreement, the younger woman refuses to break off the engagement. Seeing the marriage as her ticket out of a restrictive, dead-end life, Rhodie confesses her desire to leave the farm. "I won't even think of you," she tells her mother. "I won't even remember you and Charley a-slavin' here together. I'll be on the hills *he* told me about. I'll be with *him*! We won't never come back!"[38]

Riggs once noted what drew him to the characters he created, many of which were based on people he knew growing up in the region. "I wanted to give voice and a dignified existence to people who found themselves, most pitiably, without a voice, when there was so much to be cried out against," he explained. In writing the lives of the community he knew back home, he confessed, "it so happens that I knew mostly the dark ones, the unprivileged ones, the ones with the most desolate fields, the most dismal skies." Raised in a rural town that faced numerous hardships and traumas, Riggs noted, "it isn't surprising that my plays concern themselves with poor farmers, forlorn wives, tortured youth, plow hands, peddlers, criminals, slaveys—with all the range of folk victimized by brutality, ignorance, superstition, and dread."[39] Critics have observed that the conflicts facing Rhodie echo a theme running throughout Riggs's work, which often involves a young character who breaks away from a stifling and economically depressed existence in the rural West in order to experience the possibilities of life elsewhere.[40] The Cherokee scholar Daniel Heath Justice notes that Riggs's writings often highlight his desires for escape and his own struggles as a gay artist living in a homophobic community and feeling forced to hide his sexual identity from family and the public. Riggs's plays hint at his longing for acceptance as a self-exiled writer who relocated to various artistic communities in an effort to find a more supportive and productive environment.[41] In a similar way, Craig Womack notes how Riggs's work is often haunted by a "fear of recognition by others and by oneself" and by anxieties about being rejected for his sexuality.[42] Womack argues that Riggs's works may be read as coded narratives that offer glimpses into the "internal terrain" of an artist forced to live undercover and who wrote plays depicting his yearnings for freedom from a life marked by a fear of public disclosure and self-recognition.[43]

Other critics have located in Riggs's writing various concerns about the political and racialized world the author experienced growing up. Albert Borowitz examines violence and lawlessness in Riggs's work, noting the playwright's attention to both the "exuberant optimism" of the characters on the eve of Oklahoma's statehood, as well as the "threats of violence" that mar their enthusiasm.[44] In his letters and interviews, Riggs indicated how his writing often alluded to outbreaks of racial violence and other conflicts witnessed in his youth.[45] The Tulsa race riots of 1921, for instance, had a large impact on his portrait of Oklahoma, with elements of racial unrest and the threat of violence often woven into his plays.[46] Riggs also spoke in an interview about a childhood acquaintance named Jeter Davis whom he used as the basis for Jeeter Fry in *Green Grow the Lilacs* and who, like Riggs, was part Cherokee. Borowitz argues that, in *Green Grow the Lilacs*, Jeeter may be regarded as a stand-in for the larger marginalized Cherokee presence in the region, a racially ambiguous outsider who represents the alienated world and denigration of the Cherokee in Riggs's life.[47]

Jace Weaver likewise regards *Green Grow the Lilacs* as a coded play about Indians in the early twentieth century, building his case on the character of Curly McLain. He notes that, at the time in which the play was set, it would have been more likely that Indians would have been the cattlemen and white settlers, the farmers.[48] Weaver draws attention to various understated comments

Persian Peddler, Egyptian Elixir

in the play concerning race, particularly when Aunt Eller criticizes the territory folks for siding with the marshal. "Whut's the United States?" she asks her neighbors. "It's jist a furrin country to me." Other characters chime in with their protests: "We hain't furriners. My pappy and mammy was both borned in Indian Territory! Why I'm jist plumb full of Indian blood myself."[49] Critics suggest extending such readings to other characters in Rodgers and Hammerstein's 1943 musical, such as Jud Fry and the Persian peddler, noting how they operate as coded figures whose struggles lay bare concerns about assimilation and national belonging. Roger Cushing Aikin makes a case for reading Jud Fry as Jewish in the musical, noting that the character's name is Jud, not Judd, the word *Jude* meaning "Jew" in German.[50] In a story concerned with the success of proper racial and heterosexual unions, Jud threatens the stability of the community as a rival suitor and outsider; he also functions as the only "remotely evil person" in the story.[51] For Aikin, the conflict in *Oklahoma!* involves making sure the cowboys and the farmers may be friends so that the free-roaming European American cowboy embodied in Curly may be united with the European American land-owning farmer represented by Laurey. After this point, the two white characters can go forth to "make the land 'fertile' . . . and exorcise or banish the dangerous, lustful, and 'un-American' elements in themselves represented by Jud."[52] As a racially ambiguous man with a violent past, Jud operates as a stock figure in the Western, a character who represents dangerous elements of savagery that must be neutralized in order to ensure the future of the nation.

Andrea Most also examines the racial logics of Rodgers and Hammerstein's musical, following critics who read *Oklahoma!* as a tale about struggles for citizenship. An outsider figure, Jud often appears as "perpetually unshaven and smeared with dirt," a "bullet-colored man" whose home is a dark and filthy smokehouse and thus a sharp contrast to the comfortable and welcoming farm home of Laurey and Aunt Eller.[53] As Most argues, Jud is treated as the sexually menacing "dark" man in the musical, with his pornographic postcards and inappropriate sexual behavior making him a social outsider. His status as a racial threat erupts in the smoke-house scene when Curly, seeking to eliminate his romantic rival, tries to convince the other man to use his own rope to lynch himself. The sequence provides an occasion for the song, "Pore Jud Is Daid," in which Curly encourages his rival to imagine the pity inspired in others if he were to kill himself with his own rope.[54] The scene links Jud to the racial terrorism of the twentieth century, when African American males who were perceived to have gained too much economic power after emancipation were lynched by white mobs under the pretext that they had sexually violated white women. In the musical, Jud is portrayed as a menacing threat for having sexual designs on a white woman who owns a substantial amount of land that another character also desires.

While Jud is figured as a social threat, Most argues that his ambiguous identity also enables him to serve another purpose in the story—that of portraying the "bad Jew" in relation to the "good Jew," who is represented by the peddler Ali Hakim. As the "bad Jew," Jud is a dangerous force that cannot be assimilated into the community in the way that Ali Hakim can. In Rodgers and Hammerstein's adaptation, the peddler is no longer Syrian but Persian, an affable if slightly quirky merchant who is given the name "Ali Hakim." Most argues that the peddler's efforts to gain acceptance in the western rural community make him a stand-in for American Jews whose struggles for assimilation were often negotiated in theatrical performances, in which the stage and the film studio provided places for creating images of an "idealized America" and to imagine scripts that featured Jews as accepted members of the larger community.[55] She points out that Ali Hakim's name is "probably derived from the Yiddish and Hebrew word *hacham*, a popular term that Rodgers and Hammerstein would have known means 'clever man.'"[56] Although the character is portrayed as a cultural outsider, Ali's humor and light-hearted presence make him a relatively nonthreatening figure compared to Jud and thus a character who can be incorporated into the frontier community.[57]

Responding to the story's complicated treatment of race and national belonging, critics have located numerous possibilities for more inclusive readings of the play's revisions and revivals, directing their attention to the racial ambiguities in the texts and the ways the many adaptations may be read as statements about the struggles of other cultural groups. Although such recupera- tive efforts provide understandings for how difference has been staged in American theatre and film, in many ways these read- ings unwittingly replicate the problem of exclusion they seek to resolve. The process of uncovering hidden histories in the story— while an important and worthy task in its own right—is often con- ducted at the expense of the Arab and Persian peddler. In making sense of why these characters become underappreciated in schol- arship about *Oklahoma!* and its sources, I argue that critics must account for how the presence of these two groups works along- side the treatment of Native Americans, African Americans, and Jewish Americans in the story. What is needed is an approach that simultaneously examines the disappearance of Native Americans, African Americans, and Jewish Americans and that accounts for the contested emergence of the Arab and Persian, while explaining how certain racialized groups may be extended citizenship at one point in U.S. history but deemed unacceptable and marginalized at other moments. What is needed too is an understanding of how orientalism plays out in these moments of absence and presence in the Western, relying on ideas about civilization and savagery, as well as sexual deviancy and heteronormativity, in determining the basis for national belonging.

Ali Behdad's observations about the United States as a "forget- ful nation" are useful for this discussion. He argues that the "cele- bratory narrative of immigrant America" that appears frequently in U.S. culture relies on myths of the nation as a place of "hospital- ity, liberty, and democracy."[58] The discourse of American benevo- lence and openness rests on a collective amnesia about the nation's violent foundation, or what he describes as a "cultural disavowal that simultaneously denies certain historical facts and produces a pseudo-historical consciousness of the present."[59] For Behdad, the "pretense that the United States is a hospitable nation eclipses not only the economic dimensions of immigration but also the disciplining of its aliens" through a multitude of immigration laws, as well as various state institutions, from the FBI and the INS to the Border Patrol and the Department of Homeland Security.[60] *Oklahoma!* works in a similar manner by removing the troubling presence of racialized groups that challenge visions of American hospitality and inclusiveness, while allowing other groups a presence only once they have been properly contained and managed and are thus no longer regarded as a threat.

In revealing the stagings of a forgetful and disciplining nation, *Oklahoma!* likewise foregrounds how racial formations often relegate changing populations to the role of cultural outsider. As Behdad reminds us, "America's 'other'" constantly undergoes recasting, as each historical period "demands a new representation of the seditious foreigner," a transformation that always emerges out of changing "cultural conditions, economic needs, political exigencies, and social conflicts."[61] By examining the adaptations of the story, I foreground an archive of the American West and the United States that reveals lesser-known racial formations and intimacies in the cultural production of the region and the Western. In particular, the many revisions of the story offer insights into changing understandings of whiteness throughout the twentieth century and the manner in which Arabs and Persians have experienced, in different ways and times, a shifting racial classification that has frequently complicated their claims to citizenship.

Orientalist Archives and Western American Literature

In the 1870s Arabic-speaking populations from Greater Syria began to immigrate to the United States in substantial numbers, a movement that was eventually brought to a near close with the passage of the Immigrant Act of 1924, which imposed a quota system based on national origin.[62] While many of the first Syrian immigrants planned to work in the United States only long enough to earn money for their return home, a majority ended up staying in the country.[63] In the process, they established communities across the United States, the oldest and most famous of which is the Little Syria located on New York City's Washington Street.[64] Among the early

Syrian immigrants, peddling emerged as a popular form of employ-ment, with men, women, and children finding jobs selling wares to communities across the United States.[65] Networks that linked sales people to suppliers and distributors eventually developed, enabling individuals and groups of peddlers to work in diverse and distant regions. Some peddlers found a steady source of income in the iso-lated communities of the rural West, selling their wares to families that faced difficulties traveling into town to purchase needed house-hold supplies.[66] Many of these peddlers went on to become estab-lished merchants, later opening their own dry-goods stores near the small towns and rural communities they once visited.

In one of the few known autobiographies written by a Syrian peddler in the American West, Ed Aryain details his experiences working in the early twentieth century.[67] Having left his home near Damascus in 1913 during one of the peak years of immigra-tion, when more than nine thousand Syrians arrived in the United States, Aryain first lived in New York but later left for work in the rural West.[68] In his autobiography, Aryain chronicles his experi-ences with new people and places, often questioning myths of the West as an exceptional terrain of opportunity and adventure. In Cheyenne, Wyoming, for instance, the peddler describes find-ing a town "too thinly populated for my kind of business," with its ranches located too "few and far between," a place with few opportunities for forging successful business, friendships, or com-munity. The author expresses his dismay at confronting the dan-gers of life for a peddler working on the open range. He writes,

> Many times on this lonely journey in Wyoming I was afraid that my horse and I would both be killed by the wild cattle which roamed the open range. These enormous animals had long, sharp horns and shaggy, matted fur, and they would come dangerously close to my buggy and then bellow and snort and stomp the ground until the air was so thick with dust that I could scarcely see what I was doing. My greatest fear was that one of these animals would hook his long horn into the wheels of my buggy, for I knew that if he did he could easily turn it over.[69]

For Aryain, the western range he encounters in Wyoming is not necessarily a place of possibility or freedom. Instead, for the young peddler, the landscape offers a certain loneliness; its physical dangers and hardship make his labors as an itinerant merchant difficult at best. The description offers a reversal of orientalist discourse by depicting the Eastern subject as an intrepid explorer of the American West and the West that is encountered, a dangerous and deadly land itself, much like the Orient in European or U.S. travel narratives.

While traveling through Nebraska, Aryain goes to his first motion picture show at the invitation of a friend. The young peddler is hesitant to enter the theater, remembering that his father in Damascus had once warned him that movies should be avoided as "indecent" forms of entertainment. He soon overcomes his resistance, however, and agrees to watch a silent Western that is playing at the theater. Aryain writes,

> I thought to heck with it and went inside feeling very daring. It so happened that the movie showing was about an Indian and American war, and I noticed how the Americans used their guns against the Indians and how the Indians made direct hits on the Americans with their bows and arrows. This puzzled me until later when Charlie Amer explained that the Indians had owned this land until the Americans pushed them off of it and moved in themselves. I found the history part very interesting, but my sympathy lay with the Indians. As far back as I could remember I had heard how my own people had been pushed from their homes and land by the powerful Turks.[70]

Locating similarities between the plight of American Indians in U.S. history as depicted in Western film and his experiences of repression under Ottoman rule, Aryain finds affinities between Arabs and Native Americans, both of whom suffer under military occupation and yearn for different outcomes for their homelands. In his autobiography, American Indians are recast as the heroes of the national conflict featured on-screen and underpinning American history, their land struggles and acts of resistance

Persian Peddler, Egyptian Elixir

immediately recognizable to Aryain because of his similar experiences living under colonial occupation back home.

Later the author follows oil booms across Oklahoma and Texas, where he hopes better business opportunities exist for pack peddlers. The labor involved in selling his wares is often difficult and requires endless "traveling on foot and carrying the two heavy suitcases of goods on my back," leaving deep scars across his shoulders.[71] Arriving in strange places and often overcome with homesickness, he and his companions encounter rejection rather than hospitality: "I remember one night I had been refused shelter everywhere I went. Finally quite late I stopped at a farmhouse where the woman told me very sharply that she did not have room. Then she slammed the door in my face angrily."[72] Aryain describes instances of further mistreatment in the West: "Sometimes as I approached a house someone would step out on the porch and shake his fist at me angrily. 'Go away!' he would shout. 'Go away! We don't want your kind on our place!'"[73] On another occasion, he is grateful for a welcome extended by a farmer's wife and offers the woman a special gift as a way of thanking her for providing him shelter during the night.[74]

Syrian peddlers could not anticipate how they would be treated by potential clients; sometimes they were regarded as little more than beggars, while at other times they were welcomed into homes. One farmer remembers his experiences greeting a peddler who used to visit farm homes in the part of North Dakota heavily settled by Norwegians: "How excited [we] would get when Tofik came here with his buggy, pulled by a brown horse called Ruby. And how anxious we were to see what he had for sale in his trunks, and what a nice, clean smell the various cloths, tablecloths, scarves, and other wares had when he brought them out for inspection."[75] In some cases, peddlers were valued not only for the goods they sold but also because they provided information about the outside world, passing along gossip about neighbors and the local community, as well as news about national events.[76] As important sources of domestic goods and information about the lives of others, peddlers crossed into the private spaces of the rural West, gaining intimate access to and knowledge about the lives of small-town residents.

Lisa Lowe examines the forgotten intimacies embedded in histories of global labor, noting how accounts of nation formation frequently ignore and repress the "links and interdependencies" that shaped the lives of racial groups working in the world's colonial settings.[77] In addition to operating as instances of "spatial proximity or adjacent connection," racial intimacy typically involved private and domestic associations, the "conjugal and familial relations in the bourgeois home, distinguished from the public realm of work, society, and politics."[78] The experiences of intimacy Lowe locates often entailed contested forms of contact that emerged among "slaves, indentured persons, and mixed-blood free peoples living together"—encounters that were often volatile and conflicted.[79] In making sense of these forgotten histories of racial intimacy, Lowe notes that moral panics about cultural proximity frequently arose in contexts of "mixture and unstable boundaries," with dominant groups often working diligently to manage and control such experiences of closeness. "The repeated injunctions that different groups must be divided and boundaries kept distinct indicate that colonial administrators imagined as dangerous the sexual, laboring, and intellectual contacts" among different groups, she explains. As a result, racial classifications often emerged as a means of preventing and erasing from memory the "unspoken intimacies" found in colonial contexts.[80]

A similar task involving the regulation and management of racial intimacy operates as a central preoccupation of *Oklahoma!* While the musical is set in Indian Territory, the story unfolds as if Native Americans had never inhabited or worked the land. Likewise, in Riggs's 1931 version, Indian presence is downplayed so that audiences are given only brief comments about this history, such as Aunt Eller's claims about being one of the "territory folk" rather than an "American," and some of the cowboys' assertions about having Cherokee "blood." While Indian presence is also erased in the later versions of the story, elements of racial difference and intimacy are reintroduced through the figures of the Syrian peddler and the Persian, Ali Hakim. Both characters represent immigrant groups whose identities were contested in the twentieth century and who often faced negative treatment in the United States as a result. Since 1790, when the earliest immigration code in the United States legalized naturalization for "free white persons," racial discourses have defined the nature of immigration, as well as determinations about who may be granted citizenship in the United States.[81]

In the case of Syrian immigrants, various difficulties arose concerning the categorization and naming of the group. As a result, Arabic-speaking populations in the United States often experienced what Lisa Majaj calls "a history of inconsistent racialization," or an ambiguous and changing relationship to whiteness that affected their chances for citizenship.[82] Waïl Hassan notes too that Syrian immigrants posed problems for U.S. customs and courts, as their legal classification as "white persons" often contradicted how they were regarded in public opinion. While they were initially considered "Orientals," the term was not useful in legal contexts as it included Asians in general, a problem given that the Chinese had been banned from immigration in the Chinese Exclusion Act of 1882.[83] Likewise, while they arrived in the United States with Ottoman passports, they themselves did not identify as such, largely because of their history of struggle and oppression under Ottoman rule. Most Arabic-speaking immigrants resisted the term "Turk" as well, because for many Americans it was associated with Islam and Muslim identity, while most of the early Arabic-speaking immigrants in the United States were Christian. As Hassan explains, immigrants from Greater Syria also "had no sense of racial or national identity. Race and nationality, the two paradigms of identity and citizenship used to determine the legal status of immigrants, were not the operative ones in the Arab newcomers' culture of origin, where they identified by family, clan, sect, and region." Notions of race circulating in the United States thus did not carry meaning in the "ancient and thoroughly hybridized cultures of the Middle East." As Hassan notes, the term "Syrian" eventually emerged as a "default label" that was largely accepted "because the alternatives ('Turks,' 'Other Asians') were objectionable."[84]

Determinations about who was white and could therefore be granted U.S. citizenship were inconsistent in the late nineteenth and early twentieth centuries, with two main approaches emerging as the means of defining identity. Ian F. Haney López explains that the process of deciding who was white tended to involve commonsense appeals and arguments based on scientific evidence.[85] As long as the two approaches aligned, few problems emerged for customs officials and immigration courts. By 1909, however, changing demographics and new scientific findings had led to contradictions between common knowledge and science, thus indicating how whiteness functioned as a "highly unstable legal category, subject to contestation, expansion, and contradiction."[86] Haney López argues that most of the conflicts appeared in cases concerning immigrants from western and southern Asia, including Syrians and Asian Indians, groups that had been "uniformly classified as Caucasians by the leading anthropologists of the times."[87] The failure of science to counter commonsense beliefs about whiteness could have led the courts to question whether race was a natural category. Haney López notes, however, that officials instead often resorted to disparaging science as a means of resolving conflicts about whiteness in public opinion.[88]

As a result, between 1909 and 1923, court decisions frequently had contradictory results and competing rationales, with U.S. judges qualifying Syrians as "white persons" in 1909, 1910, and 1915 but not qualifying them as such in cases from 1913 or 1914.[89] Haney López notes the famous case from 1914 of George Dow, who was granted a rehearing on an earlier immigration decision. Dow's legal arguments about racial categorization and whiteness detailed how "the history and position of the Syrians, their connection through all times with the peoples to whom the Jewish and Christian peoples owe their religion, make it inconceivable that the statute could have intended to exclude them."[90] The judge's dismissal of the racial argument in Dow's case is noteworthy in part because white supremacist arguments have historically relied on Christianity for establishing their authority. Also, by ruling against Dow, the court unwittingly determined that, by extension, Jesus

Christ would have been racially ineligible for U.S. citizenship in the first half of the twentieth century.[91]

In the case of Ali Hakim, the transformation of the Syrian peddler into the Persian salesman may have made sense by midcentury. His recasting would have been feasible due to the fact that the state of Oklahoma is home to one of the nation's largest populations of Iranian Americans.[92] He may have also appealed to larger U.S. audiences captivated by notions they had about the ancient land of Persia. Unlike Syrian immigrants, who initially came in large numbers during the late nineteenth century, Iranians did not immigrate in large numbers until the early 1950s, arriving mostly after American immigration laws linking citizenship to whiteness had been overturned. Iranian immigration to the United States first arose out of an economic downturn Iran experienced following the oil nationalization movement from 1951 to 1953 and the subsequent American boycott of Iranian oil. After the nationalization of the Iranian oil industry, the CIA funded and staged a coup that removed the democratically elected prime minister, Mohammad Mosaddegh, from office and placed Reza Pahlavi in power as the shah. The second large wave of immigration came after the Iranian revolution in 1979 and continued until 1986.[93]

Like Syrian Americans, Iranian Americans have been officially classified as white in government data, yet the popular microrankings of whiteness in the United States often marginalize them as a group.[94] In addition, Iranian Americans have frequently faced conflicts about identity and belonging that stem from a long history of distrust and hostility between Iran and the United States, as well as a rising Islamophobia and religious prejudice that targets the group as a whole, even though not all Iranian Americans are Muslim.[95] Iranian Americans have also faced continuing negative responses to events such as the nationalization of Iranian oil in 1951, the CIA overthrow of the Iranian prime minister in 1953, the 1973 oil crisis, the Iranian revolution of 1979, and the hostage crisis a year later, as well as the second Bush administration's war on terror, which declared hostility toward the nation as part of the infamous "axis of evil." While Persia became officially known as

Iran in official government documents in 1935, many Iranians in the United States still prefer to call themselves Persians as a way of avoiding the negative views directed toward Iran. For many Americans, the land of Persia conjures up images of an exotic world and a mythical past that seems more attractive and enticing as well as far removed from the conflicts that currently divide the two countries.[96]

The figure of the peddler in Riggs's source materials and in Rodgers and Hammerstein's musical adaptation highlights an often overlooked history of struggle that Arabs and Iranians have faced in the United States. This history has been frequently set aside in scholarly readings that position the figure of the peddler as a stand-in for other marginalized groups in America. Critical attention to the role of the Syrian and Persian peddler in these dramas, however, enables critics to attend to the forgotten and neglected conflicts concerning race, citizenship, and national belonging that other racially ambiguous immigrant groups such as Arabs and Iranians have faced upon their arrival in the United States.

The Peddler's Goods

In all versions of the drama under discussion, the peddler serves an important function in highlighting the activity of salesmanship—the skill and craft needed to persuade others to buy what one has for sale. Indeed, a great deal is up for sale in *Oklahoma!*, with many of the characters besides the peddler occupying themselves with the task of persuading people in the community to buy what they have to sell. The territory folks take great care in positioning themselves as civilized people and in arguing that the savage aspects of the frontier have been properly managed and contained so that Oklahoma's petition for statehood can be successful. The selling of box lunches at the town social entails more than just raising money for the local schools; it also involves setting up heterosexual pairings that will create new citizens for the growing nation. In this way, Aunt Eller spends the first scene trying to sell Laurey on the idea of marriage with the cowboy Curly. She goes so far as to flirt with the much younger man and agrees to ride in his buggy in the hopes that Laurey will become jealous and fight to win back the cowboy. Curly meanwhile tries to eradicate his rival Jud by suggesting that he hang himself with his own rope in the smokehouse. Ado Annie is also involved in sales efforts, spending much of the play positioning herself as a desirable commodity on the marriage market. The peddler plays an important role in much of this activity as well, offering up not only consumer items but also carefully crafted arguments that enable each community member to achieve his or her goals.

In Riggs's *Green Grow the Lilacs*, the Syrian peddler enters the western community hawking commodities to isolated farmers, selling them consumer goods that promise to bring modernity to the rural West. On an earlier trip to Laurey's farm, the peddler had sold a legendary eggbeater to Aunt Eller, a kitchen item he claimed held unrivaled domestic possibilities. After finding that it failed to "wring out dish rags," "turn the ice cream freezer," and accomplish "I don't know whut all," she demands a refund from the peddler, giving him a tongue lashing for trying to cheat her.[97] Laurey too harbors suspicions about the peddler's motives and tries to warn her friend Ado Annie about her concerns. "They got wives in ever' state in the union . . . and other places besides," she tells her friend. "Why, Alaska's jist full of women a-livin' in icehouses, and freezing to death 'cause of peddlers runnin' off and leavin' 'em 'thout no kindlin' er nothing.'"[98] Laurey, however, finds herself interested in the peddler's wares, particularly in items that will enable her to achieve social status. Laurey confesses that she wants things to make her "purty," including hairpins, a special fine-tooth comb, a shiny silver buckle, and a lacy dress. She also asks for perfume to make her "smell like a honeysuckle vine" and soon inquires if the peddler has any face whitener in his cart.[99] Indeed he does; "the best they is," the peddler tells her. "Put it on you, they cain't no one stay away from you. Reg'ler love drops!" the man promises.[100]

Critics have pointed out that the history of makeup for Europeans and European Americans is linked to racialized notions of beauty that often entailed efforts to whiten the face.[101] The American cosmetics industry, for instance, typically sold products to women interested in obtaining an ideal "white, genteel beauty" by promising to remove unwanted freckles or lighten skin that was deemed to be too dark.[102] As Kathy Peiss explains, the "white face, purged of the exertions of labor," signified a certain race and class standing; it "simultaneously asserted bourgeois refinement and racial privilege."[103] In Riggs's play, Laurey applies the whitener to Ado Annie's face, promising to help her "hide them freckles" even if she has "to put it on" an "inch thick."[104] When her aunt sees the results of these efforts, she bursts into laughter and describes the outcome in racially degrading terms: "Mercy! She's plum whitewashed you! Look like a nigger angel turned all white and shinin'."[105] In the play, Ado Annie fails to achieve idealized whiteness after using the skin cream. Perhaps in so generously applying the whitener to Ado Annie's face and doing such a bad job in the process, Laurey is shown trying to thwart her competition by preventing her from achieving whiteness. The musical adaptation omits the sequence in which Laurey paints Ado Annie's face "an inch thick," as well as Aunt Eller's racist remarks, but hints at the face whitener when the peddler arrives with a sign on his cart advertising "Miss Toliver's complexion cream," the meanings of which would likely not have gone unnoticed by audiences at the time. In the musical, the Persian peddler offers other items to the farm women, including silk garters and Parisian undergarments, or what Aunt Eller bluntly describes as "fancy drawers." He entices Laurey with some "Egyptian elixir" he claims contains a "secret formula" used long ago by "Pharaoh's daughter" when she was deciding which man to love. As a signifier of female beauty and exotic power that nearly reached cult status in the twentieth century, Cleopatra was commonly used in American cosmetic ads and positioned as a historical icon whose identity as either European or African was itself contested.[106] Just as Ado Annie's failed attempts to lighten her complexion make her the butt of jokes, other American women who purchased these cosmetics were at times ridiculed for being "vain and foolish."[107] Some of this response likely stemmed too from public health scares that emerged when it was discovered that some cosmetics contained harmful ingredients, including mercury, lead, and arsenic.[108]

Persian Peddler, Egyptian Elixir

Fig. 10. The Persian peddler, Ali Hakim, with his cart in *Oklahoma!*
(directed by Fred Zinnemann, 1955), from the DVD.

Fig. 11. Ali Hakim peddling the "Egyptian elixir" in *Oklahoma!*
(directed by Fred Zinnemann, 1955), from the DVD.

The Egyptian elixir comes to play a significant role in the story. In the first half of the twentieth century, Egyptomania became a cultural obsession in the United States, often involving a fixation with tombs and temples, mummies and sheikhs. The mania played into an already evolving American orientalism that traded on ideas about hypersexual Eastern males who menace white women.[109] One evening, after sniffing the bottle's contents—what Aunt Eller identifies as common smelling salts—Laurey has a dream that highlights her sexual feelings for the socially unacceptable laborer, Jud Fry. The dream involves an aggressive, sexualized dance scene with Jud, who holds her captive in a roadhouse brothel where she is forced to share the stage with other showgirls. The scene operates through a stream of orientalist signifiers conjured up by the

Egyptian elixir, including Laurey's fantasies of sexual captivity at the hands of a racially ambiguous male. In foregrounding the captivity narrative, the scene also plays on dime novels and Western films about white women kidnapped by Native Americans.

Like Ali Hakim does with the elixir, peddlers themselves sometimes employed orientalist discourses to increase their sales. Often peddlers exoticized their wares, claiming that these goods had been made in the "mystery of the Holy Land."[110] While some peddlers told their customers that the tablecloths, doilies, and pillowcases they sold were fashioned in the old country, most of these items were actually crafted in their own homes.[111] Religious objects, including rosary beads and crosses, were often lucrative items for peddlers, and in the late nineteenth century various Syrian shops in New York were manufacturing rosaries that were marketed as "imports'" from the Holy Land.[112] These items carried meaning for American consumers who were attracted to consumer goods that hailed from the faraway lands of the East. In *The Innocents Abroad*, Mark Twain complained about similar Holy Land scams he encountered during his trip to the region, lamenting the hoaxes that advertised several improbable sites as once having been visited by Jesus, Joseph, and Mary.[113] The American tourists he traveled with were often so taken by the region that they frequently looted and plundered the ancient sites they encountered, taking pieces of the architectural structures they visited. Twain relates one instance when members of his tour group collected "fragments of sculptured marbles" and broke "ornaments from the interior work of the Mosques." They transported these items "at a cost of infinite trouble and fatigue, five miles on muleback to the railway depot," before a government official who had been warned about the group ordered them to surrender their stolen goods.[114]

In *Oklahoma!* Ali traffics in orientalist discourse himself as a means of gaining sexual favors from the young women he encounters on the job. When he first appears on-screen, audiences learn that he has already made inappropriate gestures to Ado Annie during a ride in his buggy, playing on his worldly knowledge and cosmopolitan experiences by promising to take her "all the way to paradise." When she asks how far away he means to take her, Ali confesses that he was aiming for a hotel room in nearby Claremore. She later boasts to her father that the peddler paid her a compliment, likening her to a "Persian cat with a soft round tail." The comment angers the older man, who tells the peddler, "In this part of the country that better be a marriage proposal." Later we learn that Ali does not just trade in kitchen goods and women's cosmetics but also peddles pornography. In a scene in the smokehouse, Ali offers to resupply Jud with postcards of naked women after learning that he is getting bored with his old pictures. When Jud tells the peddler that he no longer wants postcards but real women, Ali suggests that the postcard may be a better option. As he explains, if "you get tired of the picture, you give it away." On the other hand, if you get tired of the real thing, "what can you do" with her?

Through Ali's hypersexual presence, Rodgers and Hammerstein also incorporate queer elements in the story, drawing on what Jack Halberstam describes as a long history of "masculine love and homoerotic posturing" in the Western.[115] In doing so, the writers gesture toward a kind of sexual inclusiveness that the playwright Riggs himself was unable to achieve in his lifetime, an inclusiveness that operates through orientalist discourses. Joseph Boone's arguments about colonial erotics involving the Middle East and North Africa may be extended to *Oklahoma!*, whereby the "displaced or discovered homoeroticism" of Europeans or Americans emerging in "imagined or actual encounter with exotic otherness" is frequently mediated and managed through an orientalist imaginary.[116] The sexual exoticism represented by the East unfixes what seem to be stable categories of identity and desire in the musical, a shift that becomes simultaneously disturbing and exciting to the characters. When the peddler tries to get rid of the overeager Ado Annie, he does so by convincing her of the virtues of her cowboy suitor, Will Parker. He does such a good job describing the merits of Parker's beautiful "blue eyes" that Ado Annie is prompted to ask, "Do you love him too?" When the peddler later tries to make his exit, he offers a good-bye to Ado Annie, kissing her in what he calls the "Persian style." After Will encounters them kissing, Ali tries to distract him with a Persian good-bye as well. The peddler moves in for an embrace with the other man, but the cowboy moves back, refusing the gesture after noting that he already witnessed the previous good-bye.

In an effort to free himself from the excessive affections of Ado Annie, the peddler unites her with her cowboy suitor. After learning that Will can't marry Annie until he comes up with fifty dollars that he promised her father, Ali offers to buy the items Will has previously purchased for their wedding night. When the cowboy shows the peddler the woman's nightgown he bought for their honeymoon, holding it up for Ali to see, the peddler makes a joke that it doesn't look like it will be large enough to fit the cowboy on his wedding night. Later the peddler describes the joys of marriage awaiting the couple, relating to them some of the alleged rituals back home:

PEDDLER: Uh, it's a wonderful thing to be married. I got a brother in Persia, got six wife.

ADO ANNIE: Six wives all at once?

WILL: Why sure. That's the way they do it in them countries.

PEDDLER: Not always. I got another brother in Persia only got one wife. He's a bachelor.

Positioning the peddler as a threat that needs to be contained, Rodgers and Hammerstein draw on orientalist notions of the East's alleged deviant desires and passions, represented here by Ali Hakim's stories of nonmonogamous marriage practices in Persia.

Ultimately, the prospect of his own marriage is something the peddler is not buying. While the logic of the Western musical positions heterosexual union as a means of gaining access to citizenship, Ali Hakim, the marginalized and racially ambiguous Persian peddler, does all he can to resist marrying the young women in town. By the end of the story, he is caught taking liberties with a merchant's daughter named Gertie and is finally corralled by her father into marriage. The forms of intimacy he experiences as a peddler entering the private domestic worlds of the western farmers are finally managed and contained in an acceptable marriage to the merchant's daughter. Joseph Massad notes the ways orientalism often links sexual desire to a person's "civilizational worth," with deviant or excessive desire a sign of the primitive or the savage.[117] Here the alleged savagery of the licentious Persian is neutralized, and he is made civilized by his entry into the institutions of marriage and work. David Roediger likewise argues that labor itself was often a route to belonging and acceptance for recent immigrants, enabling some groups of racially ambiguous newcomers a means of working toward whiteness.[118] Many peddlers in the United States became shop owners like Ali Hakim, once they had saved enough money to make the transition to merchant, thus gaining economic status and the means for assimilation. The famous lyrics of the musical, which insist that "the farmer and the cowman" should be friends, point to this possibility. The song continues, adding that the farmer, the cowboy, and *"the merchant"* should put aside their differences and "be like brothers."[119] By giving up his itinerant labors as a peddler and moving into monogamous heterosexuality and the settled life of a shopkeeper, Ali Hakim gains access to assimilation and civilization.

Ultimately, *Oklahoma!* manages racial conflicts by reducing Native Americans and African Americans to a marginal presence while extending conditional whiteness to the Eastern Other.[120] Following traditions of orientalism that position an imagined East as a dreamlike space of escapism and sexual fantasy, the Western positions the peddler as a figure offering mobility and cosmopolitanism, as well as new sexual and racial intimacies, to the rural West.[121] Weaving orientalist tropes into the conventions of the genre, the story foregrounds the vast geographical horizons that have often shaped the Western. In reaching across regional, national, and global terrain for its settings, characters, and conflicts, the Western has not only employed the imagined spaces of many Wests but has also relied on various Easts in its development, resolving certain racial conflicts only to repress and elide the existence of others. What should be noted here is that a Cherokee author provided the first drafts of this complicated story of intimacy and national belonging, initially offering a racially ambiguous figure in the form of the Syrian peddler who introduces difference and diversity into the rural West. Arriving from an exotic, faraway world with his cart full of foreign consumer goods, from Parisian undergarments to magical Egyptian potions, the peddler represents intriguing promises of life elsewhere, a figure who hails from the East and who experiences mobility and cosmopolitan possibilities that the playwright Riggs remained drawn to and fascinated by all his life.

FIVE

Specters of Loss

Violence and the National Mission in Post-9/11 Westerns

You have to remember . . . Baghdad was the Wild West.
—MARK BOAL

War always returns home, even when it seems safely exported.
—CATHERINE LUTZ

Situated as a cultural terrain of struggle on the post-9/11 battle-ground, the cinematic Western has often been deployed in efforts to shape discourse about American democracy and the scope of U.S. foreign policy in an age of terror. As I argue throughout this study, sometimes the Western plot has been used to embody an unreflective cowboy diplomacy and unquestioned patriotism that justifies extreme means for ensuring national safety and defense. The scripts deployed in this manner have not figured as diverse or open narratives but have been recuperated as narrowly defined texts that work to control speech and language, constrain public discourse, and limit the possible meanings ascribed to these events. While some uses of the Western narrow the genre's scope and power in defending an exceptionalist America, restrict the diverse ideolog-ical possibilities that have historically operated in the form, and shut down the genre's multivocal possibilities, the Western has also been employed for other purposes: as a critique of these nation-alist sentiments and as a counternarrative that expresses uncertainty about the war on terror and misgivings about the project of advancing U.S.-style democracy and freedom across the world.

As a genre shaped by competing impulses and desires, the Western has often emerged during moments of national crisis as a useful narrative for mediating larger political uncertainties. Addressing the genre's ability to "thrive" in so many different "guises," Neil Campbell emphasizes the multiple meanings often expressed in Westerns. As he explains, the form has always been an immensely "flexible vehicle" for showcasing a number of "conflicting desires, tensions, and struggles," especially around questions concerning national identity, the writing of history, and the possibilities of creating successful and thriving communities. The post-9/11 era has provided abundant instances in which the Western has functioned as an important cultural form, deployed in some instances as a discursive weapon in the U.S. war on terror, while in other cases used to reassess the triumphalist and exceptionalist beliefs that became prevalent during this period.[1] This chapter examines the cinematic Western as it encountered the world outside national borders in the twenty-first century, focusing on the diverse role it played in framing American identity and U.S. foreign policy across the Middle East.

In his influential essay, "The Problem of the Popular in the New Western History," Stephen Tatum points to a tendency among scholars to overlook the genre's scope of critique and its history of development across the political spectrum.[2] Noting how scholarly discussions often fail to regard the Western as an "evolving" rather than a "frozen" cultural form, he argues for recognizing the ideological diversity of the genre.[3] In doing so, Tatum draws attention to the endless "fluidity of audience identification . . . in the presence of popular culture texts," particularly the "potential ability" of audiences to identify as much with the genre's "outlaws" as with its traditional "agents of civilization."[4] Because Westerns "are not seamless texts promoting one political perspective," it is crucial to realize how "ambivalences and ambiguities about, and counterstatements to, dominant class beliefs and meanings circulate at the level of both the production and reception" of these texts.[5] He cautions against monolithic or totalizing readings of the genre, noting that even as there exists a "powerfully homogenizing force" located in the "dominant culture's constant effort to enclose and confine the popular in accordance with its own values and needs," there are always "a multiplicity of points or locations at which one can gauge both accommodation to and resistance against a dominant patriarchal bourgeois ideology."[6]

Meanwhile, Forrest G. Robinson describes a pattern of recognition and denial in popular Westerns that displays a critical awareness of social or political issues only to then subvert or deny that knowledge.[7] While Westerns frequently "reinforce our sense of the heroic, they also challenge it," he explains. If Westerns sometimes celebrate the exploits of European American male heroes, Robinson argues that they also explore the underside of "a dominant self-image" while showing a keen awareness about the "grave injustices of the social order they portray, especially as those injustices bear on people of color and women."[8] Focusing on similar complexities shaping the genre, Hannah McGill centers on the cowboy hero, a character whose cultural meanings have been debated with particular frequency in the post-9/11 period. She examines how the Western helped create a "potent American creation myth," in part through its portrayal of this figure. Understood as "emblems of an uncomplicated, effective masculinity," cowboys became symbols of an "unpretentious frankness" and the embodiment of "down-home" patriotic ideas. Echoing the arguments of Tatum and Robinson, she notes that a "strange doublethink" emerges in Westerns, one that expresses both "American innocence" and "American corruption," seemingly opposite sentiments that function as "two sides of the same coin." McGill draws attention to the iconic black or white cowboy hat as a reminder of the multiple and complex politics of the Western, tracing how the cowboy hat manages to capture both the stereotypical heroism of the American hero and the buried history of the cowboy himself. In particular, she examines the overlooked role the cowhand played in the "establishment of the earliest European settlements on US soil." Her reminder that the term "cowboy" during the American Revolution served as "a slang term for a supporter of the British side against independence" and her observations concerning "the powerful association of cowboys not just with rough-hewn individualism but with black marketeering, smuggling and theft" are useful in reassessing dominant uses of this iconic western figure in recent years.[9]

John Ford's *The Searchers* (1956), with its divided protagonist Ethan Edwards portrayed by John Wayne, has played an important role in post-9/11 cultural production, where it serves as the ur-text for understanding American power and identity in the age of terror. In an interesting way, the film has been used in making arguments about often very different and competing ideas concerning America in the world. In some instances, Wayne's character is featured as the embodiment of an exceptional American, one who is able to restore safety and security to Americans facing terror and violence on a new global frontier. Susan Faludi's study, *The Terror Dream*, outlines recent treatments of Ford's film, providing an important reading of the often not-so-patriotic historical materials out of which the American "captivity-and-rescue metaphor" has appeared. This reading includes a much more complicated account of the actual captivity experience upon which Alan Le May based his 1954 novel *The Searchers*, as well as a detailed analysis of the elaborate lies and cover-up involved in recent rescue missions, such as the infamous case of POW/MIA Jessica Lynch.[10]

In *The Searchers*, Ethan Edwards is a former Confederate soldier, a figure burdened by history and a fighter who hasn't left the war behind. A self-avowed Indian hater who is often regarded as Ford's most famous cinematic racist, Edwards seeks to rescue his captive niece Debbie from her fate at the hands of the Comanche leader Scar but actually plots to annihilate her because of anxieties about miscegenation and fears that she has passed from a state of civilization to one of irredeemable savagery through her years in captivity. The famous closing scene reveals how his devotion to a life of retribution and violence leaves him outside the community and beyond the frame of the white frontier family, banished from the people and life he previously sought to restore. In the post-9/11 period, various Westerns borrow from the film to express a deep ambivalence about U.S. projects of rescue, recovery, and vengeance. These cautionary sentiments shape the work of such filmmakers as Paul Haggis and Kathryn Bigelow, as well as Ethan and Joel Coen, whose recent Westerns use Wayne's conflicted role in *The Searchers* to reexamine the interplay between innocence and corruption and to question the uses of the genre in advancing exceptionalist projects on a global frontier.

Searching beyond *The Searchers*

Both Paul Haggis's *In the Valley of Elah* (2007) and Kathryn Bigelow's *The Hurt Locker* (2008) examine the plight of U.S. rescuers in Iraq and their failed missions of recovery across an international war zone, addressing the problems of militarized masculinity and the ways in which the war on terror also comes to have unintended, troubling consequences for life on the home front. The screenplay for *The Hurt Locker* and the story for *In the Valley of Elah* were written by the journalist Mark Boal, who drew on his experiences as an embedded reporter covering U.S. troops in Iraq during the early years of the invasion.[11] The films revisit a plotline shaping the Western that may be traced back to the dime novels of the nineteenth century. The action sequence structuring many Westerns, as Christine Bold notes, frequently contains elements of "capture, chase, and rescue." She explains that in the genre the hero is often tasked with the job of pursuing enemies who "threaten settlement by abducting helpless maidens or attacking townspeople."[12] As it has developed throughout literary history and across various forms of writing, the project of rescue and recovery has also been complicated. Russ Castronovo observes that, in many American narratives of captivity and recovery, "men and women often return only to find that they themselves bear the taint of their foreign interludes, or else that foreignness is lodged at home."[13] In recent Westerns, savagery likewise becomes located within the rescuers themselves, who are damaged by their violence, hatred, and desires for revenge. Both *In the Valley of Elah* and *The Hurt Locker* foreground limitations in the search-and-recovery narrative, extending a similar critique expressed in *The Searchers* by offering what Amy Taubin calls glimpses into Ethan Edwards as a character "split open," a process that reveals the important "fissures in the masculine ideal he monumentalized" and the problems that plague an American who "can't accept" the terms of his "defeat."[14]

In the Valley of Elah is based on events Boal reported in a magazine article entitled "Death and Dishonor," which tells of the 2003 murder of U.S. soldier Richard Davis.[15] The film features Tommy Lee Jones as Hank Deerfield, a desperate father searching for his missing son, Mike (Jonathan Tucker), a soldier who has gone AWOL upon his return from an eighteen-month tour in Iraq. The story opens with a voice-over from a distressed soldier captured on a cell phone recording found on Mike's computer. "What are you doing?" an unknown man asks as grainy, fragmented images provide incomplete clues about the young man's disappearance. The question carries significance not only for the soldiers in battle but also for the nation and its mission in Iraq, highlighting unsettling issues about U.S. liberators and the problems of framing the invasion as a rescue mission. Hank's growing ambivalence about the war emerges after he recovers a digital movie implicating his son in less-than-heroic behavior during combat. The images capture horrifying scenes of Mike tormenting an Iraqi prisoner by sticking his hand into a wound while taunting his captive. The act of torture becomes a defining experience for Mike, earning him his nickname: "Doc." A haunting photograph of a war-torn street and an abandoned military vehicle recovered from the computer reveal further disturbing truths about the war. As Hank learns, his son was responsible for the death of a young Iraqi boy when he failed to stop the vehicle he was driving and it ran over the boy while he played in the street with his friends. The event torments Mike, who calls Hank one evening from Iraq and pleads with his father to bring him home.

Other soldiers suffering from their combat experiences highlight the ways war itself always returns home, with the issue of untreated post–traumatic stress disorder serving as a major concern in the film. Hank discovers that Mike's murder came at the

Specters of Loss

hands of a soldier who suffered from PTSD and whose peers help him cover up the crime. At first, the army blames the death on a drug deal gone bad. As Hank learns, recent gang activity along the border has brought increased violence to the region, with three U.S. soldiers arrested after being caught trying to smuggle heroin from Kuwait to sell to a local Mexican gang. For the U.S. military, the long-standing war on drugs intersects with the new war on terror, calling attention to what Stephen Tatum aptly describes as a "contagious violence" whose route links the U.S.-Mexico borderlands to the Middle East, a collective and chaotic savagery that unsettles the meanings assigned to nations and regions, as well as the fantasy of security across geopolitical boundaries.[16] It is a violence that appears in the form of racial profiling and prejudice, a violence Hank participates in when he falsely accuses a Latinx soldier of murdering his son. Pvt. Robert Ortiez (Roman Arabia), calls him on his racial hatred: "Wouldn't it be funny if the devil looked just like you?" he yells at Hank while being taken away for questioning. It turns out that Private Ortiez is innocent and eventually helps Hank understand the photograph found on Mike's computer depicting the events surrounding the death of the Iraqi boy.

In the Valley of Elah addresses a failed act of recovery and the difficulties of comprehending truths about war. In the process, the film centers on generational divides, which emerge in conflicts between fathers and sons, the problems of understanding the different meanings and lessons of Vietnam and Iraq, and the vast changes in technologies used to represent history, as well as in military conflict itself. An updated embodiment of the veteran Ethan Edwards, Hank is a warrior diminished by violence and a man left behind by history. As he discovers, there are no military colleagues left from his generation who can help him find out about Mike's fate. Likewise, the rules he learned in the service no longer apply, and the new regulations seem to be no improvement. Even the advances in new media that might be of help are beyond his capacities, and at one point Hank finds he must hire a younger soldier to access corrupt files on Mike's computer for clues about his disappearance. The world Hank moves through

Fig. 12. The Frontier Restaurant in a scene from *In the Valley of Elah* (directed by Paul Haggis, 2007), from the DVD.

also has not weathered changes well. Both Hank's hometown in Tennessee and the New Mexico army post where his son has gone missing are less-than-heroic or promising landscapes, filled with worn-down truck lots, seedy motels, and modest homes with peeling paint and unkempt lawns, as well as bleak parking lots outside even bleaker strip malls and strip joints. At one point, he drives by a local eatery that's seen better days. Its out-of-date storefront sign reads "Frontier Restaurant," the declining establishment a clear indication that this Western will end up screening very little of the mythic "geography of hope" often associated with the popular genre and the American West.[17]

In the Valley of Elah features Hank as a diminished and exhausted veteran no longer employed by the military and now hauling dirt for a living in an economically depressed town. His marriage is strained because he is preoccupied by the past and has not fully returned from the war in Vietnam. Audiences see glimpses of Hank's continuing ties to military life through the regimented world he creates as a civilian: he still makes his bed and polishes his shoes according to regulation and conducts daily life with a hyper-vigilance that frames his interactions with others. Wound tightly and always on alert, he is warned by a shopkeeper, "You gotta trust somebody sometime, Hank." As he drives through town in one scene, Hank sees an employee outside a public school raising an American flag in an upside-down position, which he recognizes as a signal of distress. Stopping to assist the worker, Hank learns the man is originally from El Salvador and offers him impromptu training in proper flag display. Warning him not to let it touch the ground, Hank explains that a U.S. flag displayed upside down is an ominous sign: "It means we're in a whole lot of trouble, so come save our asses. We don't have a prayer in hell to save ourselves."

The flag's multiple meanings become significant in the film, reflecting the knowledge Hank uncovers as he tries to make sense of his son's plight, the problems of the American mission in the Middle East, and the corruption of various U.S. institutions he encounters in his search for Mike. The film turns upside down the popular rescue-and-recovery narrative, becoming a tale about national distress and the anguish of losing traditional belief systems. While the movie initially may seem to hold out promise for a heroic or redemptive closure on Vietnam, it does not offer such deliverance in the end. At one point during the investigation, a concerned military police officer reminds Hank, "This is not Saigon. This is not 1967." The invasion of Iraq will not serve as a corrective experience for previous U.S. failures. In fact, the inability to recover from the previous conflict and the certainty of the national mission serve as impediments to the characters and a form of collateral damage in their own right. Hank's son, for instance, signs up for the service in order to gain his father's approval and respect. Mike shares stories about his father's experiences in Vietnam with his fellow soldiers and carries Hank's duffel bag from Vietnam instead of the one he was issued for Iraq. The son also brings with him to Iraq an engraved watch that Hank's father had given him during his tour in Vietnam; that object links three generations of men through history, masculinity, and war. Mike's mother, Joanie (Susan Sarandon), is distraught over her son's disappearance. Both of her boys followed in their father's footsteps by joining up, with the elder son, David, having been killed ten years previously in a helicopter crash at Fort Bragg. Upon learning about the death of her remaining son, she lashes out at her husband, accusing him of setting impossible standards for their boys while growing up and lamenting the lessons he taught them about patriotism, gender, and war. "Living in this house he never could have felt like a man if he hadn't gone," she bitterly tells him.

The title of the film takes up these issues as well, with the Valley of Elah serving as the ancient setting for the biblical story of David and Goliath, the allegorical struggle between two mismatched fighters who meet in a legendary battle. Armed with only a rock and a slingshot, young David is sent to fight a formidable foe when no one else in his community volunteers. Often recounted as a parable about an underdog's unexpected victory against a menacing superpower, the meanings of the David and Goliath tale shift in this retelling, becoming instead a story about fathers and sons and the reproduction of patriarchy and militarized masculinity across the generations, as well as the personal and social costs involved in sending sons to war.[18] The David and Goliath story unfolds as Hank befriends the son of Detective Emily Sanders (Charlize Theron), a military police officer who has been assigned to the case and who is a single mother making her way in a male-dominated world. Sanders's son is named David, which links him not only to Hank's deceased first-born son but also to the young fighter in the Bible. In the film, Sanders's son is a somewhat fearful boy who sleeps with the lights on, who lacks athletic talent or interest, and whose thoughtfulness and sensitivity embody a different kind of masculinity than what is celebrated around him. For his mother, however, the boy shows great promise as one of those "oddballs and misfits" she claims are usually the people who go on to live interesting lives. Sanders embraces her son's personality and doesn't pressure him to conform to gender norms. Later in the film, he asks why the biblical David was sent by his elders to battle the giant, why of all people he was the one chosen to fight. "He was just a boy," the son reminds his mother.

In the Valley of Elah meditates on this question as well, foregrounding the dilemma of young men who are sent into battle and sacrificed by their communities. In doing so, the film references a scene in *The Searchers* involving conflicts between fathers

and sons and the reproduction of masculinity across the generations. Martin Pawley (Jeffrey Hunter) is an adopted, part-Cherokee
brother of Debbie in Ford's film. As Ethan Edwards's long-suffering
companion and a mixed-race male who does not embody proper
Anglo masculinity, Pawley is belittled, abused, and mistreated
by the older man throughout the film. Martin shares this unfortunate fate with another male character in the story, Lieutenant
Greenhill, who is played by John Wayne's own son—the tender-
faced, seventeen-year-old Patrick Wayne. Lieutenant Greenhill,
an inexperienced and tongue-tied Yankee soldier, almost decap-
itates Captain Clayton (Ward Bond) in his enthusiasm to fight a
Comanche. The younger Wayne's performance in the role of the
inept but eager warrior injects humor into a movie that remains
largely somber in nature, a humor, however, that comes at the
character's own expense.

In his major scene of the film, for instance, Patrick Wayne's
character becomes flustered after being hazed by a group of older
men, which includes Ethan Edwards, who is played by his own
father and who interrupts the character as he tries to relay an official message, making him the butt of jokes between the other soldiers. Both Patrick Wayne and his character Lieutenant Greenhill
are consigned to subordinate positions, belittled, and ridiculed by
more powerful male figures due to their lack of status and experience. In these scenes, the reproduction of masculinity appears
through coercive means, what the critic Michael Kimmel describes
as a code of behavior that "extracts compliance" through fear,
whereby boys and young men are pressured into a kind of gender
conformity that requires them to "shut down emotionally" and
"suppress compassion" in order to "inflate" their own status, power,
and ambition.[19] Younger men fall in line with older men out of a
fear of humiliation and concerns about becoming the object of
male scorn. Such compliance comes with certain rewards, however, enabling younger men to eventually gain entry into established circles of male power and privilege.

Daniel Worden analyzes the operations of masculinity in the
context of popular Western fiction. "Masculinity is not a thing but

a history," he argues. "Actions, bodies, styles, texts, images, publics, and politics compose this history." As he explains, masculinity is not an object one might possess but an ongoing activity that "involves negotiation of a complex set of signs" and "a series of performative gestures and public presentations."[20] Throughout *In the Valley of Elah* masculinity is also an active defense, a means of covering up and ensuring protection against threatening Others. Detective Sanders is familiar with the army's forms of masculine presentation, having been raised by a veteran father who, like Hank and Ethan Edwards, never left the war or fully recovered from his combat experiences. Throughout her own military career, Sanders is forced to confront an old-boy network that isolates her at work and erects roadblocks that thwart her success on the job. She is often assigned to what the other men regard as insignificant or minor crimes and is then ridiculed for her diligence in pursuing those cases.

The male-centered world of the army becomes a space needing to be shored up and protected against threatening outsiders, particularly the intrusion of women, who bring with them unsettling reminders of human vulnerability and interdependence. At one point, a distraught army wife reports that her husband has been abusing the family dog and expresses concerns about his untreated PTSD. Sanders's male coworkers belittle these complaints, interrupting the detective's efforts to conduct an interview with the army wife by making barking noises and erupting into loud laughter. In dismissing the woman's reports about her husband's suffering, the men brush aside disturbing reminders of male weakness and dependence on others. Near the end of the film, the detectives arrive at a late-night crime scene on the army post where a homicide has taken place. A soldier waits in handcuffs at the back of a police car as Sanders finds the woman she interviewed earlier dead in the bathtub, the body of the family dog nearby. Although the war itself is conducted in a faraway geography, here its effects come back to haunt the home front, the war's violence and brutality having dire effects on the domestic lives of returning soldiers and their families.[21]

At the end of the film, Hank opens a package containing a tattered American flag that his son had mailed from Fort Bragg before his death. Hank decides to display it upside down in an act that signals national distress and his recognition of the ways U.S. liberators themselves may be in need of saving. As a critical examination of the American mission in the Middle East, *In the Valley of Elah* did not perform well at the box office for a number of reasons that I address later in this chapter. The writer Mark Boal would return to elements of this plot with his script for *The Hurt Locker* (2008), a film that faired better, both commercially and critically, but at the time of its nomination was the lowest-grossing movie contending for the Best Picture Oscar.[22] Directed by Kathryn Bigelow, *The Hurt Locker* won several Oscars, including awards for Best Film, Best Director, and Best Original Screenplay. Like *In the Valley of Elah*, the film interrogates the rescue-and-recovery plot structuring the Western while reexamining the tensions between American innocence and corruption. In doing so, *The Hurt Locker* unsettles divisions between savagery and civilization, a duality that has provided meaning for yet continually troubles the genre throughout its historical development.

"I can't help you, I'm sorry"

The Wild West discourses appearing after the September 11 attacks served as a useful shorthand for projects of defending national honor and laying claim to the American values of freedom and democracy. In her essay, "The Intimacy of Four Continents," the critic Lisa Lowe examines how notions of freedom often operate centrally, not only in dominant American self-concepts but also in those of other modern European nations, thus indicating how exceptionalist ideologies of national identity may not be exceptional to the United States. Examining how self-understandings about freedom and democracy have emerged through a series of displacements and elisions, Lowe explains that "modern humanism is a formalism that translates the world through an economy of affirmation and forgetting within a regime of desiring freedom. The affirmation of the desire for freedom is so inhabited by the

forgetting of its condition of possibility, that every narrative artic-
ulation of freedom is haunted by its burial, by the violence of forgetting."[23] Such amnesia appeared after 9/11 in efforts to position
the United States as a freedom-loving nation under savage attack
from terrorists and to rhetorically frame U.S. military responses
as just another instance in the heroic saga of bringing democracy
to struggling regions of the world.

In the war on terror, such amnesia shaped the Bush administration's narrow uses of the Western in efforts to control the official narrative about terror and security, violence and revenge, as
well as the United States' global mission. These efforts culminated
in what Richard Crockatt describes as a restricted re-articulation
of the meanings and contours of "Americanness."[24] The administration worked diligently to manage and direct knowledge about
the terrorist attacks, with efforts to command and influence cultural and collective acts of storytelling a central part of this project. In *Cinema Wars: Hollywood Film and Politics in the Bush-Cheney
Era*, Douglas Kellner recounts how Karl Rove, in a meeting with
American film producers, called upon Hollywood moviemakers
to help the country by making "patriotic" films that would inspire
Americans.[25] In *Firestorm: American Film in the Age of Terrorism*, Stephen Prince also details how the White House sought the help of
the film and television industries in promoting U.S. foreign policy. Prince recounts a story by the *Washington Post* reporter Sharon
Waxman, who describes a meeting with a roomful of "television
power brokers" in which a White House representative urged the
production of more "patriotic, pro-American" films and television shows.[26] Hollywood producers also ended up restricting the
types of stories appearing in the weeks and months after 9/11, initially delaying the release and production of certain action films
that were deemed too violent and thematically connected to the
trauma of terrorism to be well received by American audiences.[27]
Christiane Amanpour reported that news organizations such as
CNN engaged in their own acts of self-censorship following intim-
idation by the Bush administration and Fox News.[28] Finally, the
Bush administration's efforts to cast any criticism of U.S. foreign

Specters of Loss

policy as dangerous and unpatriotic, as well as its projects to shut down competing discussions of 9/11, serve as yet another reminder of the stakes involved in controlling and directing the flow of stories and information in this period.[29]

Hollywood films in the early twenty-first century that depicted the events of 9/11 tended to receive mixed reactions. Michael Atkinson argues that, historically, war films have required some "distance and acclimation," what he calls a "cool-down period." Building on Paul Virilio's concept of "pure war," he argues that the "cultural pause" that typically allows some time to unfold between the military events themselves and their cinematic representation did not exist after 9/11. In fact, because of Virilio's "pure war," such a time period may no longer exist in our era of "anywhere-anytime conflict, the post-9/11 'forever war' world" where conflict is a constant presence and accords "no such breathing room."[30] Unlike the Vietnam War, which generally saw a lag time between the end of conflict and Hollywood productions about the event, recent U.S. filmmakers released their productions about 9/11 and terrorism during wartime itself. While several Hollywood films about Vietnam went on to become commercial successes, American movies about the war on terror and combat in Iraq and Afghanistan did not perform as well at the box office.[31] Many of the dramatic productions that directly addressed 9/11, such as *United 93* (2006) and *World Trade Center* (2006), failed to become commercial successes, even with well-respected, award-winning directors and A-list stars. Likewise, films about the war on terror and the U.S. invasions of Afghanistan and Iraq, including *Lions for Lambs* (2007), *Rendition* (2007), *Redacted* (2007), and *The Kingdom* (2007), also underperformed at the box office, the exceptions being Bigelow's *The Hurt Locker*, which made a respectable profit only after being nominated for and winning several Oscars, and Bigelow's other war film, *Zero Dark Thirty* (2012), which gained a wide audience but was criticized for its treatment of torture and was subsequently shut out in the Oscar nominations by the Academy of Motion Picture Arts and Sciences.[32]

The Hurt Locker is not a particularly patriotic film, although it features a main character in the quintessential role of the cowboy, whose job involves bringing order to a chaotic and unlawful frontier. Like *In the Valley of Elah*, the film employs codes and conventions of the Western in examining the borders erected between savagery and civilization and in acknowledging that such divisions are not always clearly discernible. In a departure from other Westerns of the period, *The Hurt Locker* returns less to *The Searchers* than it does to the revisionist movies made two decades later in the 1970s, which reference Ford's 1956 Western in launching critiques of the genre. In an influential 1979 article, the critic Stuart Byron notes how a number of films, such as *Taxi Driver* (1976), *Close Encounters of the Third Kind* (1977), *The Deer Hunter* (1978), and *Hardcore* (1979), focus on the limitations of rescue missions whereby an obsessed American searches for a loved one who has been taken by alien or outside forces. When they are finally recovered, it turns out that these captives resist recuperation by the searcher and often do not wish to be rescued or returned home.[33] In *The Hurt Locker*, the U.S. mission in the Middle East encounters a similar conflict as American soldiers face an occupied nation that staunchly resists their liberation and rescue efforts.

The Hurt Locker pits American techno-warfare against under-armed yet deadly Iraqi insurgents, with main character Sgt. William James (Jeremy Renner) leading a U.S. explosive ordnance disposal squad charged with dismantling improvised explosive devices (IEDs), or roadside bombs. At one point, James is initiated into the band of brothers when a soldier welcomes him to "Camp Victory." James corrects him—"Camp Liberty"—but is told of a name change that "sounds better" and that occurred the previous week. These men have a mission in Iraq, albeit one whose goal may shift abruptly, with no prior warning. In an interview, Boal described Baghdad in the early years of the invasion as the "Wild West," and his screenplay thus incorporates elements of the Western in depicting the war. James appears in the film as the quintessential lone Westerner, a rugged individual who follows his own protocol even in battle zones and is described by other soldiers as "restless," "rowdy," and "wild." In an early scene, his predecessor,

Specters of Loss

Sergeant Thompson (Guy Pearce), gears up for the job as Sergeant Sanborn (Anthony Mackie) wishes him "Happy Trails." The film proceeds by juxtaposing scenes of combat with the squad members sweeping the city in order to defuse hidden IEDs. The men counter the tense situation with forms of male banter, exchanging penis jokes and calling each other "cowboy."

The opening soundtrack for *The Hurt Locker* features a muezzin's call for prayer in Arabic as the film screens images of chaos and violence. A subtitle appears in the frame, indicating the setting is Baghdad, 2004. Sounds of Arabic spoken on the streets and in the announcements from the mosque provide an immediate sense of everyday life in the city. The film in turn marks a shift in the writer's focus on how to represent the war and its victims.[34] Boal's earlier work on *In the Valley of Elah* centered on the plight of returning American veterans and their experiences on the home front. While his script for *The Hurt Locker* also focuses on U.S. soldiers, it addresses in greater detail the violence and suffering experienced by Iraqi citizens, whose homeland is now a war zone. In both stories, Boal uses the figure of a young boy to explore tensions between savagery and civilization, and between corruption and innocence. As noted before, *In the Valley of Elah* references the biblical David in his battle against the enemy Goliath, features Detective Sanders's son as the embodiment of nonnormative masculinity and as a counterpoint to the hypermale world of the military, and showcases an unnamed Iraqi boy whose death is captured on a cell phone recording and whose fate haunts Mike and his fellow soldiers, as well as his father, Hank. *The Hurt Locker* features an Iraqi boy whose fate plays a significant role in the film. The young Iraqi in *The Hurt Locker* goes by the name "Beckham," after the British soccer player, and makes a living selling pirated DVDs on the black market. Even in the early years of the invasion, Beckham has already forged ties with various U.S. troops. His English is peppered with American slang and profanity that was not likely learned in primary school. He also seems adept at connecting with soldiers in a fairly short time. Sergeant James develops a fondness for Beckham; he buys the boy's damaged goods at outrageous prices and loses a soccer bet that he pays back many times over. Beckham's untimely death later in the film profoundly affects the soldier, who realizes that the murder likely came at the hands of Iraqi insurgents concerned about the boy's potentially dangerous relationship with enemy soldiers.

Sergeant James eventually combines his job dismantling explosive devices with the mission of finding out how Beckham died. His obsession puts other soldiers at risk as he veers off course to find the person responsible for the boy's death. James's mission takes him to side streets and neighborhoods throughout Baghdad. At one point, he breaks into the home of an Iraqi man, who is caught off guard but quickly regains his composure. When asked if he speaks English, the man (played by Nabil Koni) introduces himself as a professor and explains that he indeed speaks English, as well as French and Arabic. With great manners and equally impeccable English, he invites the intruder to sit down and feel welcome. "This is my home . . . you are a guest," he says, then tells James, albeit cautiously, "I'm very pleased to see CIA in my home." As the professor prepares a tray of tea for his guest, his wife (Nibras Qassem) emerges from another room, taken aback by the intrusion of American military personnel in her home late at night. The woman doesn't miss a beat in responding to the appearance of this soldier/savior. She immediately begins yelling at him, waving him away from her home, her arms hitting the tea service as the tray spills its contents on James while her husband tries to intervene. Flustered and confused, James realizes that his informants have given him faulty intelligence and that he has been sent to the wrong family. He manages to leave quickly through a side door.

The scene is significant in that it counters stereotypes of Arab or Muslim women as being in need of rescue. Here the American soldier meets formidable resistance from an Iraqi woman who neither wishes to be liberated nor feels the need to extend Arab hospitality to such invaders. The limits of the rescue narrative become clear once again toward the end of the film, when Sergeant James is sent to help an Iraqi man with numerous bombs chained to his body. The American soldier realizes that the wiring system is too intricate for him to defuse the bombs before they explode. The Iraqi man pleads with him through an interpreter, explaining that he is not an insurgent trying to draw them closer to a scene of violence but a peaceful person with a family. James continually apologizes to the man for his inability to free him. "I can't help you, I'm sorry," he cries, as time runs out and the bombs explode.

In another scene, a fellow soldier wounded in a battle alongside Sergeant James is airlifted out of Iraq for medical treatment. As James approaches him in the helicopter, the man resists his offer of help, indicating again the other soldier's failures as a rescuer. In this context, it is useful to return to Boal's description of Iraq as the mythic "Wild West." Typically, such a comparison is used to reference a world of chaos, anarchy, and violence and thus the need for a law-bringer to restore order and sanity to that terrain. *The Hurt Locker*, however, questions the logic of the Wild West analogy, asking whether the chaos of war and suffering of Iraqis is instead the result of the liberators themselves, the consequences of American cowboy diplomacy and the violence unleashed by the so-called "humanitarian warfare" of western law-bringers in the region.[35]

"What a girl's gotta do ..."

While *The Hurt Locker* did well both critically and commercially, the Hollywood movies that had the most success in addressing terrorism and the wars that followed tended to be productions that *indirectly* referenced these events. Joel and Ethan Coen's *True Grit* (2010) falls into this category. Winner of Academy Awards for Best Director and Best Picture, *True Grit* became the filmmakers' highest-earning movie to date, bringing in nearly three times what either of their previous high-grossing films, *O Brother, Where Art Thou?* (2000) and *No Country for Old Men* (2007), earned.[36] Foregrounding problems of restricted speech and narrowly defined uses of the genre in the Bush era, as well as the pitfalls of small-minded or closed-off understandings of morality, justice, and revenge in the war on terror, the Coen brothers' allegorical film offers insights into how dominant uses of Western plots often limited the diversity of the genre in the post-9/11 era. These texts frequently treated the Western as a monolithic form that can tell only one story about how to ensure justice in the world. With its critique of monomaniacal acts of vengeance and retribution, *True Grit* evaluates the unintended consequences unleashed by a young girl's efforts to hunt down the violent outlaw who killed her father. The film highlights the failures in efforts to control the meaning of events or to determine the significance of the stories the characters tell about themselves and their communities. As such, the movie foregrounds the ambivalence and ambiguity at the center of the Western, offering a critical take on the ways dominant national discourses after 9/11 likewise fixed the official meanings and values assigned to the United States' civilizing mission and its ongoing wars against terror.

Unlike recent Westerns that revisit *The Searchers*, the Coen brothers' film returns to a different John Wayne vehicle, director Henry Hathaway's 1969 adaptation of Charles Portis's novel of 1968. Their remake of *True Grit* intervenes in discussions of post-9/11 America by more directly referencing violence and restricted storytelling in the Western. The film tells the tale of young Mattie Ross (Hailee Steinfeld), a fourteen-year-old girl from Yell County, Arkansas, whose single-minded determination to hunt down her father's murderer unleashes a chain of violence that diminishes her life and future, as well as the lives and futures of the people around her.[37] The events of the film unfold through a voice-over narration by the protagonist, who proves that she's mentally and physically up to the task of extraordinary rendition. She embarks on a mission to bring in her father's murderer, Tom Chaney (Josh Brolin), a former hired hand who has terrorized a community by taking a man's life, his horse, and $150 in cash, along with two California gold pieces, and who appears to go unpunished after law enforcement refuses to go after him. Mattie leaves her home and family in Arkansas to track down the outlaw, who has fled "across the river in Choctaw Nation," where local sheriffs have "no authority" to capture him, as we learn in the film. Mattie's success stems in part through the control she asserts in determining the flow of information and the means by which she secures her narrative authority. The film in turn speaks to concerns in the post-9/11 era, indicating what is at stake in controlling how political events may be narrated, understood, and remembered and by addressing what may be at risk in undertaking such single-minded, monomaniacal projects of violence and retribution.

Learning that Chaney is hiding out in Indian Territory with a gang of outlaws run by the notorious Lucky Ned Pepper (Barry Pepper), Mattie hires the former marshal, Reuben J. "Rooster" Cogburn (Jeff Bridges), to help bring him in. The film opens with the voice of Mattie, now an older woman (Elizabeth Marvel), reflecting on her past as she describes the extraordinary circumstances surrounding the events of her youth. "People do not give it credence that a fourteen-year-old girl could leave home and go off in the wintertime to avenge her father's blood. But it did happen," she explains. The voice-over at the beginning of the film establishes one of the central struggles of the movie—Mattie's efforts to exert control over the narrative and limit the meanings of the past. Such efforts entail more than determining how the story will be told; they also involve her attempts to dictate a code of morality for herself and the community. Throughout the film, Mattie counters other characters' acts of storytelling, makes efforts to rewrite the past according to her own interpretations, and cuts off or silences folks whose speech threatens to undermine her version of the events. The girl continually voices what she considers to be the proper, ethical forms of behavior that the rest of the community should follow, showing disapproval when others do not abide by her strict moral code. As in the Bush/Cheney years, Mattie's belief system entails drawing stark divisions between victims and perpetrators, and between savagery and civilization. "Not a soul in that city could be bothered to give chase," she complains. "No doubt Chaney fancied himself scot free, but he was wrong. You must pay for everything in this world one way or another. There is nothing free except the grace of God."

Alongside the older Mattie's voice, *True Grit* opens with the sounds of a nineteenth-century hymn, "Leaning in the Everlasting Arms," music that is also featured in Charles Laughton's memorable 1955 noir-thriller *The Night of the Hunter* and that is repeated in the final credits of the Coens' film, providing particularly unsettling effects. Laughton's noir offering featured Robert Mitchum as the ex-con Harry Powell, who pretends to be a small-town southern preacher in order to locate money that a dead bank robber has buried near his home. *The Night of the Hunter* offers a disturbing tale about a sinister predator who poses as a man of faith, hoping to win over the children of the dead bank robber, young John (Billy Chapin) and his sister Pearl (Sally Jane Bruce), who have knowledge of their father's buried money. The hymn used in the two films has its thematic origins in the book of Deuteronomy, its lyrics offering encouragement and assurance to believers as they struggle with difficulties, temptation, and doubt in their daily lives:

> What a fellowship, what a joy divine
> Leaning on the everlasting arms
> What a blessedness, what a peace is mine
> Leaning on the everlasting arms.

In both films, the lyrics lend an eerie quality to the narrative, foregrounding the hypocrisy and corruption involved in efforts to cloak violence and corruption in the language of religious faith. In *True Grit*, Mattie's code of honor is tied to Bible passages ranging from Ezekiel to Psalms, all of which are meant to justify her acts of vengeance and violence. In a letter she writes to her mother back home in Arkansas, Mattie explains that "though I walk in the valley of death, I shall fear no evil," her certainty about the rightfulness of her vengeful acts stemming from her belief that "the author of all things watches over me." As dead bodies pile up across the landscape, the film begins to question the moral system that authorizes such violence. The movie reveals the costs of retribution and problems in the girl's obsession with taking justice into her own hands—even though unquestionably a crime has been committed and the murderer has indeed gone free.

Mattie's efforts to seek revenge in the film are accompanied by instances of censored speech or restricted opportunities for language. Whose words carry meaning and which version of the story may claim authority operate as central concerns of the narrative and serve as a foundation for the film's larger critique of similar post-9/11 restrictions. At one point, Mattie makes inquiries in town about a man to hire for the task of hunting down Chaney. As she moves through the streets of the community, she comes upon prisoners who are about to be hanged for the crimes they have committed. The first man is repentant and offers a lengthy apology to the crowd gathered at the gallows before he is condemned to death. The second man is unrepentant, claiming his only crime is that he killed the wrong man, while the third—a Native American—is not even given a chance to speak his last words. Instead, a black hood descends over his head as the floor drops below him, cutting off his speech and silencing what he had prepared to tell the crowd. While the image is also featured in the 1969 version of the film, the black hood tied around his head calls forth different associations in the 2010 remake, bringing to mind the human rights violations of prisoners at Abu Ghraib, as captured in the series of disturbing photographs that were made public in early 2004.

Mattie's command of language appears again in a scene when she manages to out-haggle the seasoned and experienced auctioneer, Colonel Stonehill (Dakin Matthews), who had sold her father several mustang ponies before Chaney killed him. Through verbal wit and sheer tenacity, Mattie convinces the older man to buy back the horses her father had purchased and then insists that he sell her one of the animals at a reduced cost and pay for her father's saddle, which had been stolen from the colonel's stable. Stonehill employs every form of argument he can muster in order to avoid entering into the transaction with Mattie, insisting that the earlier deal with her father should be respected and upheld. Stonehill tries to rely on biblical authority in asserting the fairness of the previous horse sale. "I am looking at it in the light of God's eternal truth," he insists to the girl, only to find himself defeated at language, wiping bullets of sweat off his forehead as he gives in to Mattie's clever persuasions.

Critics have noted how efforts to control speech and language serve as central elements in the Western. In her study of the genre, *West of Everything*, Jane Tompkins suggests that "the hunger West-

Fig. 13. A condemned prisoner's speech is silenced as he is denied his last words in *True Grit* (directed by Ethan Coen and Joel Coen, 2010), from the DVD.

Fig. 14. Condemned prisoners in black hoods in *True Grit* (directed by Ethan Coen and Joel Coen, 2010) recall the hooded prisoners photographed at Abu Ghraib in Iraq. From the DVD.

erns satisfy is a hunger not for adventure but for meaning."[38] She argues that, as a vehicle for meaning, however, language itself is typically distrusted in the genre, associated as it is with the corrupted realms of domesticity and the hypermodern world of the urban industrial East. As she points out, Westerns are frequently "full of contrasts between people who spout words and people who act."[39] While Tompkins observes that language in the Western functions as a source of conflict and struggle, such battles over speech may be more complicated than she acknowledges. Lee Clark Mitchell

Specters of Loss

points out how "wordsmiths" often prevail over "gunslingers" in the genre, noting several instances in which a character's speech is elevated over and celebrated at the expense of action.[40] As a way of complicating Tompkins's argument about language and speech, he offers a reading of Owen Wister's *The Virginian* (1902), the novel typically credited with making the "restrained, soft-spoken, sure-shooting cowboy into a figure worthy of sustained popular interest." Instead of providing a character of "quiet violence" whose actions speak louder than words, Wister's tale offers a loquacious hero who "celebrates language at the expense of action."[41] The novel becomes a story of "quick wit" triumphing over "quick draws," as the main character defeats the outlaws and prevails over Molly Stark Wood through his mastery of the art of talking.[42]

As Mitchell goes on to note, in later instances of the Western, linguistic struggle often functions as a form of action in its own right. In his reading of Zane Grey's *Riders of the Purple Sage* (1912), he notes that many of the struggles over the fate of captive white women and even captive western lands center around the main character's efforts to verbally best powerful Mormons who exert control over both entities. Appearing in the novel as a shadowy, unknown Other and long-standing enemy of the main character, Lassiter, the Mormon community carries powerful secrets that enable its members to determine the fate of the region and its inhabitants. According to Mitchell, the Mormons' use of language and their "master claim to narrative power" in Grey's novel often occur through the restriction of speech and words, through their larger efforts at "locking narrative itself away." Such attempts to control and even silence language, however, come to have the opposite effect, as the non-Mormon characters are frequently compelled to take part in extensive debate and conversations with one another in order to make sense of the inner workings of the Mormon rulers and the community. "Through their own obsession with silence," the Mormons "paradoxically induce a narrative proclivity in others," Mitchell argues. "The complete lack of information" about Mormon plots and practices has the reverse "effect of sparking the melodramatic expectations they had hoped to silence."[43]

Such interplay between silence and speech appears at important moments in the Coen brothers' film. While Mattie struggles to control words and language in the story, other characters likewise try to claim power through speech. Early in the movie, Mattie's quest to hunt down her father's murderer is complicated by the arrival of the Texas Ranger, LaBoeuf, played by Matt Damon, who is also looking for the outlaw Chaney because he is wanted for killing a state senator in Waco, Texas. LaBoeuf thinks highly of himself and his skills as a gunman, an opinion he often voices to others. Throughout the film, the ranger wears a buckskin jacket and pants, an outfit that sets him apart from the other characters and that subjects him to various jokes from his fellow travelers. Mattie calls LaBoeuf a "rodeo clown," warning that his "Texas trappings" are sure to make him an "object of fun" in this part of the country. She later goes on to accuse him of being "eluded the winter long by a halfwit" while "ineffectually chasing" down Chaney. LaBoeuf counters with a comment that she is "headstrong" and "saucy" and goes on to accuse her of rudeness toward him as a man of the law. "You give out very little sugar with your pronouncements," he complains to the girl.

Yet, if Mattie fails to be careful with words, LaBoeuf also abuses language. Over a campfire one night, the marshal tries to shut him up after hearing one too many "tall tales" about his prior life and adventures with the Texas Rangers. Cogburn calls it "women's talk," dismissing the younger man for his lack of properly regulated speech. He accuses LaBoeuf of not only exaggerating the past but also telling a tale that has circulated in the region so long that it has now become a cliché. Near the end of the film, when LaBoeuf manages to survive the shoot-out with Chaney and the Ned Pepper gang, Cogburn complains that "even a blow to the head could silence him for only a few short minutes." LaBoeuf proves the marshal right as he rides off on his horse to return home, still championing his skills as a gunman even though he is now gravely injured. Yelling out to Mattie, he gets the last word, assuring her, "Never doubt the Texas Ranger. Ever stalwart."

While Cogburn tires of LaBoeuf's incessant speech, the marshal frequently fails to censor himself, his heavy drinking each night loosening his tongue and making him verbally abusive toward his companions. While they are raiding a cabin in their search for Chaney, for instance, LaBoeuf is injured under questionable circumstances that become a source of conflict among the characters. LaBoeuf believes he was hit by friendly fire, while the marshal disparages the ranger's injuries, announcing that even though the ranger "has been shot, trampled, and nearly severed his tongue," he not only fails to cease talking but "spills the banks of English." As the argument continues, with the marshal claiming that LaBoeuf is himself at fault for being a "man who walks in front of bullets," Mattie tries to intervene, telling the marshal "it is unfair to indict a man when his jaw is swollen and tongue mangled and who is therefore unable to rise to his own defense." LaBoeuf does not appreciate the girl's interference. Asserting himself angrily, he announces, "I can speak for myself." That evening, as the two men continue to spar with each other over the ranger's injuries, Mattie responds again with efforts to redirect the narrative. She declares that she will stage for the two men a play that she knows well and characteristically offers to perform "all the parts" herself, noting that the men are unlikely to be familiar with the roles in her story and thus are in need of her verbal abilities.

Throughout the film, the control of language emerges in other moments when the characters use simple, direct statements as if to establish their own truth and reality, as if to convince themselves and others of the authority or rightfulness of their actions. One outlaw named Moon (Domhnall Gleeson) "jabbers on" about the whereabouts of Ned Pepper's gang and is eventually killed by his partner, Quincy (Paul Rae), for failing to curtail his speech. Immediately after being shot by Quincy, Moon announces the obvious, "Oh Lord, I am dying." Likewise, when the outlaw Ned Pepper is injured in gunfire, he tells Rooster in a matter-of-fact way, "Well, I am shot to pieces." After the Texas Ranger is wounded during an attempted ambush of the outlaws, he notes simply, "I am severely injured." Later, when the mission of finding Chaney is over and LaBoeuf's task as a ranger is completed, he explains his decision to ride back home to Texas to Mattie and the marshal. Pointing to his many injuries, LaBoeuf succinctly declares, "I am considerably diminished." Finally, throughout the film, the murderer Chaney utters what are perhaps some of the most puzzling and humorous statements of the film. When Mattie finally catches up with him, Chaney laments his misfortune, repeatedly complaining that "nothing's gone right for me," "nothing's going my way," "everything's against me," and "you're all against me." Chaney's simple declarations do not reflect the situation he finds himself in but reveal in a telling way how the outlaw misconstrues reality in an effort to appear innocent and blameless. Mattie herself responds to such events and characters with her own direct statements that counter the comments of others. At one point, she dismisses a character, asking him, "How can you sit there and tell such a big story?"

Mattie's desire to determine the conditions and meaning of narrative and her effort to serve as the authorizing force of the story shape her quest for vengeance. Much of the conflict arising between the girl and LaBoeuf centers on his plans to arrest Chaney for the murder of a Texas state senator. Mattie resents such interference, wanting not only to control the circumstances in which Chaney is caught and punished but also to determine the meaning of the crime itself, which situates her as the sole wronged party. For Mattie, it is not enough to punish Chaney for the murder in Texas; instead, she wants him to be brought in explicitly for the crime of killing her father and wants to reserve for herself the role of victim. After the marshal finally challenges her on this point, she responds, "When I have bought and paid for something, I will have it my way." Later, once the quest to find Chaney seems to be thwarted and the only solution appears to involve giving up the search, Mattie announces firmly to Rooster, "I will not go back. Not without Chaney, dead or alive."

Mattie's line about bringing in Chaney does not appear in Charles Portis's novel, but does uncannily appear in the 1969 film version with John Wayne. The "dead or alive" comment in the Coens' adaptation references more recent sentiments about retribution and violence in the post-9/11 era. Rooster's full response to Mattie also does not appear in the source material. Instead, the Coen brothers' script has the marshal calling Mattie on her bloodlust, sarcastically assuring the girl that he will not let her desires for revenge be thwarted. "You can spit on him and make him eat sand out of the road. I will hold him down," Rooster assures her. "If you want, I'll flay the flesh off the soles of his feet and find you an Indian pepper you can rub into the wound." Even for a corrupt alcoholic marshal who previously served in the Confederate army and who once hooked up with William Clarke Quantrill's gang, which was responsible for the Lawrence, Kansas, massacre, this moment provides rather strong and unsettling words.

An earlier scene helps foreground the problems in Mattie's single-minded obsession with retribution and revenge when she explains why she insists on hiring Cogburn out of all the potential gunmen in town. She is told by a sheriff in Fort Smith that Cogburn is the "meanest" marshal available, a "pitiless man, double tough, and fear don't enter into his thinking." As Mattie explains to the marshal, "They told me you had grit and that is why I came for you." In this context, the word "grit" might refer to a person's determination or strength of character, to Cogburn's abilities to complete a job in a way that no one else seems capable of doing, and to Mattie's single-minded efforts to ensure that justice prevails after the death of her father. Yet, as at least one critic has pointed out, the word *grit* in some parts of the American South functions as a pejorative term that refers to "white trash."[44] The southern slang use of *grit* here comments negatively on Mattie's single-minded obsession, on her ability to serve as a trustworthy narrator of the story, and on her compromised morality in seeking retribution and revenge.[45]

The meanings entailed in her choice of a "trashy" man with "true grit" are evident too when we remember that Mattie had the opportunity to hire other gunmen but passed over them when she learned of the former marshal's capacity for violence, his ability to complete the task no matter what the cost. In the Coen brothers' remake, "grit" becomes a significant term in other ways as well—denoting something dirty, tenacious, ugly. What the filmmakers restore here is a commentary on the ugliness of violence, as well as the ugliness entailed in the Western revenge tale itself, all of which prove to be "ugly" in the southern uses of the term, meaning something morally offensive and vulgar. The Coens' film foregrounds what happens to Mattie and the other characters in the process of avenging the death of Frank Ross, the underlying qualities of their "true grit" proving to be complicated, ugly, and uncivilized.

Counter-Westerns of 9/11

Addressing what he calls the "arts" of 9/11, Jeffrey Melnick notes that much of the cultural response following the terrorist attacks aimed at reclaiming or renewing notions of manhood and fatherhood, both of which appeared damaged or diminished in the aftermath of the events. Following the terrorist attacks, Americans witnessed the production of a number of narratives about renewed masculinity that often appeared in tales about "redeemed dads."[46] Melnick argues that many of these responses function as a type of "father worship," a "collective national dream of the good father" that "necessitated, not surprisingly, a tacit agreement to render mothers absent or insignificant."[47] In *True Grit*, Mattie's mother appears as an ineffectual figure, described by her daughter as "indecisive and hobbled by grief," a woman with little common sense or intelligence who was "never any good at sums and . . . could hardly spell 'cat.'" It is therefore up to the more capable and exceptional daughter to get the job done by hiring a bounty hunter who can bring in her father's murderer.

Cynthia Weber examines how family narratives became popular in post-9/11 cinema, arguing that "it is possible to get indications of how the official moral character of the United States is drawn individually, nationally and internationally" through a cinematic "narration of the family." Weber notes that in these films, fathers, mothers, sons, and daughters all come to "figure predominantly" on the screen, their roles functioning allegorically for a nation coming to terms with the trauma of the attacks.[48] In celebrating Portis's mastery of voice in his depiction of the young female narrator, critics have used a similar familial language in analyzing the novel, describing Mattie as Huck Finn's little sister, her voice being as distinctive as Twain's boy hero from the previous century.[49] Donna Tartt, however, reads Mattie a different way, suggesting that Mattie's literary ancestry makes her "less Huck Finn's little sister than Captain Ahab's," a description that perhaps better captures the unappealing aspects of the girl's personality, helps explain her missing limb at the end of the story, and cuts across ideologies of exceptionalism central to American national identity.[50] Throughout literary history, numerous critics have noted how the youthful protagonist has appeared in American fiction to articulate ideas about the alleged innocence of the nation itself.[51] Likewise, in addressing cultural production following September 11, Melnick has noted how much of this work is shaped by a "rhetoric that emphasizes heroism, selflessness, and national purpose," with the arts of 9/11 helping to usher in an exceptionalist narrative, what he calls "the growing secular religion of total American innocence."[52] Such innocence is put to question in the Coen brothers' remake. Indeed, *True Grit* troubles the story of innocence and exceptionalism, with the young female protagonist at the center of the film proving to be not a blameless child but a perpetrator of violence, a figure who is driven by as much bloodlust as any of the male characters in the story.

The Coen brothers' film likewise takes a critical position on the popular narrative of the family and its elevation of heroic fathers. While Rooster Cogburn serves as a substitute father for the girl, he is quite clearly flawed as a model of morality and honor. It may come as no accident that, when viewers first encounter him, the marshal is caught inside an alley outhouse ambushed by the eager Mattie looking for her hired hand. Once on the job and in the midst of one of his drunken hangovers on horseback too, Rooster reveals his less than heroic paternal abilities. Here he reveals to his traveling companions details about his shady past, as well as his two failed marriages and estranged son, Horace, confessing that the boy never actually seemed to like him and that he in turn never quite knew how to connect with his son. The marshal also dismisses Mattie, telling her at one point, "You're no bigger than a corn nubbin," while referring to her as "little sister," a title that helps him better establish his power in the relationship even though, or perhaps because, she is the figure responsible for directing the action and for paying the marshal to do the task. LaBoeuf likewise treats Mattie as if she were a young sister, and he threatens to punish the girl with "five or six licks" with his belt if she gets out of hand or continues to talk back. Eventually, LaBoeuf delivers on his promise, bending Mattie over and spanking her as if she were a wayward child. "Now you will do as the grown-ups say or I will get myself a birch switch and stripe your leg," he tells her. Such instances indicate how Mattie is consigned to a lesser role in the action, that of the younger sister or daughter, a helpless female requiring strong male rescuers and capable heroes who can carry out the task of vengeance while keeping her in place.

As if understanding the need to break out of this gendered confinement, Mattie adopts the clothing and behavior of a man. Before she embarks on her quest, she is given a bundle containing her late father's belongings, including his pistol and some clothing. She finds his wool coat and puts it on, adding his belt and leather hat along with some newspaper tucked into the brim to make it fit better, and then leaves town to hunt down Chaney. Such moments of female cross-dressing recur in the Western, with films such as the classic *Johnny Guitar* (1954) or the more recent *Ballad of Little Jo* (1993) offering scenes of women dressing in men's clothes before embarking on their western adventures. Mattie's decision to dress as a man highlights the failure and inability of her male companions to play the part themselves. The "duded out" ranger in his "Texas trappings" and the aged and physically weak marshal who drinks himself into poor health do not appear to readily embody a competent and reliable masculinity that is capable of retribution and violence.[53] It is left to Mattie to cowboy up and "do what a man's gotta do."

In a similar way, Bonnie Mann reminds us that the Bush administration encouraged Americans to embark on a "strange and fated project of 'manning up'" in an effort to counter the feminizing losses of the earlier war in Vietnam, as well as the more recent humili-

Specters of Loss

ation following the terrorist attacks. Such projects of remasculin-
ization, however, came to have the opposite effect for the nation,
creating "more vulnerability, not less," and thus increasing "in a
global climate . . . intensified disgust for the world's one remaining superpower."[54] In *True Grit*, Mattie is a young girl angered by
the justice system that doesn't punish her father's killer, and she
sets it as her task to avenge his death, finding it necessary to play
the part of a man along the way. Because the gendered politics of
mobility in the nineteenth century do not allow fourteen-year-old
girls to ride off on horses by themselves across the country to bring
in their father's killer, Mattie undertakes the task of dressing differently for the journey, her project of manning up enabling her
to move from being a mere victim of a crime to being an instru-
ment of violence and vengeance.[55]

"Keep your seat, trash"

A number of feminist critics have examined the gendered logic
of the revenge fantasy fueling the war on terror. Angela Davis
addresses how the "victimized woman who has to be saved by US
democracy" has come to function as a "rallying call for state terrorism."[56] Tracing what she describes as the "fracturing of feminism"
and the proliferation of competing and contradictory notions of
democracy, Davis argues the need to rescue and revive a progressive gender politics, as well as a more rigorous understanding of
democratic processes. Such entities require a renewed commit-
ment in an era that has seen a number of human rights violations
conducted in their names.[57] Susan Faludi likewise examines gendered post-9/11 narratives, particularly the "fixation on restoring
an invincible manhood by saving little girls," which has resulted
in a feminization of victims and a masculinization of heroes. As
she argues, the war on terror has often deployed imagery that
hearkens back to the 1950s, with its "odd mix of national insecu-
rity and domestic containment." In turn, Faludi notes how John
Wayne's character from *The Searchers* has been used both to "rein-
state a social fiction" from the Consensus era of the Cold War as
well as to speak to "actual" terrorist threats in the present era.[58]

The Coen brothers' remake of *True Grit* complicates the rescue narrative and the masculine redemption story common in the arts of 9/11.[59] Mattie is rescued from her fate as a captive of the Ned Pepper gang but is also the figure responsible for hunting down her father's murderer, unleashing a horrifying chain of violence that thwarts both her status as feminized victim and the male redemption narrative. The film is thus less a captivity narrative than a revenge story, a tale that chronicles an act of extraordinary rendition in tracking down an outlaw across Indian country and that leaves audiences with a trail of maimed, mutilated, and murdered bodies. Mattie herself is left alone and bereft at the end of the story, unable to make contact with her former colleague Rooster Cogburn, who dies before she can see him perform with the Wild West show. Like the famous closing shot of *The Searchers*, she remains outside the life of the community and confines of the family. The final scene of *True Grit* features the much older Mattie Ross, now missing an arm, standing on the snow-covered hillside near the marshal's gravestone as the gospel song, "Leaning in the Everlasting Arms," is heard once again. The closing scenes make clear that Mattie hasn't changed or learned much from her previous experiences but still tries to change others' language and behavior. As an older woman, she travels to Memphis, hoping to meet up with Rooster, who has sent her an invitation to the show. "Brief though his note was, it was rife with misspellings," Mattie complains, acknowledging the poorly written language of his letter. She crosses paths with the former outlaws Cole Younger and Frank James, who once performed with the marshal. Reacting negatively to James's failure to stand up, take off his hat in her presence, and thus display proper manners to a "lady," Mattie barks to him, "Keep your seat, trash," before leaving the show. By the end of the film, Mattie still lives by a strict moral code and continues to judge others harshly for not abiding by the same rules.

While critics such as Faludi have noted the post-9/11 nostalgic appeal to the 1950s in the recent revival of the Western, the Coen brothers' remake is less a return to that era than a response to the culture of the 1960s, the era in which Portis's novel was published

Specters of Loss

and director Hathaway's adaptation appeared. In returning to cinematic traditions of that era, the Coens reference the revisionist
cycle of Westerns that emerged in the 1960s and led to the production of movies such as Sergio Leone's *The Good, the Bad, and
the Ugly* (1966), which helped popularize the Italian-made "spaghetti Westerns"; Sam Peckinpah's *The Wild Bunch* (1969), a brutal
narrative of aging outlaws wreaking havoc south of the border;
and John Schlesinger's *Midnight Cowboy* (1969), which transposed
the violence of the mythic frontier to the streets of contemporary
New York City.

The Coens' remake of *True Grit* also intervenes in the star persona of John Wayne, who often played the conservative, law-abiding
American in ways that have perhaps interfered with public understanding of the critical potential that Westerns in general may
carry. Indeed, the conflicts facing Wayne's character in *The Searchers* are frequently overlooked or disregarded in post-9/11 arts. While
Edwards is the classic Western hero who brings order to the mythic
frontier, he is also a man with a shadowy, savage past, a figure of
violence whose brutal acts prevent his successful return home and
thus leave him forever exiled from the community.[60] As William
Handley explains, the Western often "goes against itself in several
respects, undermining the very values it seems to affirm." Thus, even
when its hero "brings a demonstrated track record" to the story,
"something always seems to be in question." As Handley argues,
no matter who "wins or loses at its end, something has already
been lost before a Western begins that can never be recovered.
The genre survives as the search continues for both the searchers
and the sought, whether the object of the search is dead or alive."[61]

While the search for Frank Ross's murderer is successful by the
end of *True Grit*, audiences are also left with a similar sense of loss,
as all of the main characters become permanently marked by the
violence they've enacted. Rooster Cogburn has long ago lost his eye,
wears a patch throughout the film, and even confesses his diminished health. "I am grown old," he announces to his travel companions. Although he survives the journey to hunt down Chaney,
the marshal never manages to recover and instead spends the last

years of his life performing staged acts in the Wild West show with other aged and worn-out outlaws. The Texas Ranger LaBoeuf has also been wounded by friendly and not-so-friendly fire, and audiences do not learn much about him after these events. The older Mattie notes at the end of the film that she expects "some of the starch" has gone out of his "cowlick," a comment that serves as the film's only sexual innuendo. Mattie herself loses an arm when she is bitten by a poisonous snake after falling into a cave. She never marries and is left at the end of the film fending off the gossip of others who speculate about her solitary life and prior relationship with the much older Cogburn. Each of the primary figures is thus "considerably diminished" by the violence unleashed in the film. In this way, the Coen brothers' remake of *True Grit* captures aspects of the Western's ambivalence and dividedness toward larger acts of brutality, as well as the genre's frequent answer to questions about morality and the unexpected consequences of U.S. violence and retribution.

Scott Simmon examines the popularity of cinematic Westerns over the years and the renewed cycles of interest in the form, arguing that the genre may actually enjoy more rather than less freedom in expressing complex visions of America. Largely because of the distant time period in which they typically take place, cinematic Westerns may "have been permitted to speak" about controversial issues "in ways generally forbidden Hollywood genres set in the contemporary world."[62] In a certain manner, *True Grit* may appear to be the least "Coen-esque" of the many movies the Coen brothers have made. Their version of the film is devoid of the sometimes over-the-top campiness found in many of their works, while their remake is a surprisingly more faithful adaptation of the original novel. Ultimately, the Coen brothers' *True Grit* is a clever take on critical elements already present in the genre, even if or perhaps because audiences did not always recognize it as an allegory about the contemporary United States in an age of terror and as a cautionary tale about the costs of restricted speech, retribution, violence, and revenge in the post-9/11 era.

SIX

East of the Spaghetti Western

Global Travels of the Genre

I get stopped every time I try to cross the border,
but stories go wherever they please.
—THOMAS KING

What happens when texts move into new contexts, taken up by
audiences beyond the imagination of their producers, emerging
from radically different social and discursive spaces? . . . Should
we examine the function of texts within their new context . . .
how new readings of otherwise familiar texts expand our
sense of the capacious meanings of the original?
—BRIAN T. EDWARDS

In his novel *Censoring an Iranian Love Story* (2010), Shahriar Mandanipour tells the story of an Iranian writer who is frustrated by
his ongoing efforts to fight censorship of his work and decides
to assign himself the impossible task of producing a love story
set in modern-day Tehran. The book's narrator—a fiction writer
also named Shahriar—develops the characters Sara and Dara, two
young lovers who are forbidden under Islamic law to spend time
with each other and who agree to meet furtively in a variety of
public settings. At one point, they secretly conduct their romance
throughout the stacks of a library in Tehran where they exchange
notes about their favorite books and devise plans for future encoun-

ters across the city. Later, in front of an old movie theater that has been shut down by the state, the lovers encounter a bootlegger selling foreign items—mostly CDs and DVDs—on Tehran's black market. The meeting inspires the narrator to comment on some of the unexpected cultural freedoms currently enjoyed in his homeland. "Iran is one of the very few countries in the world that has music and films (especially Hollywood movies) favored by segments of its society produced overseas and delivered to its shores with no capital investment of its own, no shipping and insurance costs, and no copyright," he wryly notes.[1] Later in the novel, the narrator remarks on the particular types of film that seem to have a wide circulation in Iran, pointing out that the most popular movies tend to be of the "American anti-American" variety, which "these days," he argues, "are not hard to find."[2]

One of the items the street vendor offers is a pirated copy of *Brokeback Mountain* (2005), by the Taiwanese-born U.S. director Ang Lee. It is a film that carries particular significance in *Censoring an Iranian Love Story*, as the problems facing the characters in the Western turn out to be similar to the struggles Sara and Dara confront. Both narratives foreground the costs of forbidden love and the tremendous obstacles the protagonists encounter in pursuing their relationships. Both sets of characters face a common lack of freedom and numerous cultural restrictions that have a negative impact on their everyday lives. Lee's film, for instance, features the experiences of two Wyoming cowboys who struggle against a deeply entrenched homophobia that eventually dooms their relationship. Although the American West is often imagined as a land of freedom and independence, a mythic space that allows for big dreams and provides an important break with the social constraints limiting life elsewhere, in Lee's revisionist Western the region offers no such promise but is instead rife with restriction, censorship, and violence. In *Brokeback Mountain*, knowledge about the relationship between Jack and Ennis results in a gay panic, a savage beating, and death.

Meanwhile, in offering details about the struggles facing the two young lovers in Tehran, *Censoring an Iranian Love Story* pro-

East of the Spaghetti Western

vides insights into larger political restrictions that shape everyday life, particularly the dire consequences of being targeted since 2002 as a member of the "axis of evil," a term used in the United States to identify countries that were allegedly enemies of democracy and freedom. In doing so, the novel parts ways with the work of recent authors who are also Iranian by birth or heritage and who now reside in the United States, like Mandanipour. Contemporary best-selling memoirs, such as Azar Nafisi's *Reading Lolita in Tehran* (2003) and Azadeh Moaveni's *Lipstick Jihad* (2005), have been critiqued for the ways they profit from axis-of-evil discourse by offering one-sided and partial views of Iranian life that are appealing to mainstream American audiences. These autobiographies position U.S. culture as a timeless purveyor of democracy and freedom whose meanings and messages are easily translatable to other political contexts, national settings, and time periods. The texts frequently uphold rather than complicate stereotypes about Iran and Islam circulating during the war on terror, even as they are cloaked in the rhetoric of cosmopolitanism and multiculturalism.[3] As such, their arguments play into prevalent U.S. misunderstandings about Iran and Islam in ways that may account for the books' popularity among American readers.

Ali Behdad and Juliet Miller note how these texts function as neo-orientalist works whose modes of representation are indebted to older forms of orientalism but whose power in the present day lies in their ability to offer "new tropes of othering" for contemporary audiences while presenting "otherwise biased accounts of the region" as authoritative knowledge.[4] In claiming insider status for themselves, these authors capitalize on the nation's "post-9/11 thirst for knowledge about Muslim societies" through their position as self-appointed native informants about Iran and Islam.[5] While Behdad and Miller trace continuities between newer and classical forms of orientalist representation, they also highlight discursive breaks within the tradition that are important for understanding the memoirs. "Unlike traditional Orientalists who maintained at least the pretense of objectivity and scholarly disinterest in current affairs," they point out, "neo-Orientalists perceive of their discourses as political engagements aimed at liberating the region from tyrannical regimes."[6]

In sharp contrast to these texts, Mandanipour's novel avoids a narrowly defined vision, offering instead a critique of the restrictions impeding freedom in Iran and the United States. The novel in turn places various crises in contemporary Iranian life alongside problems stemming from the post-9/11 American exceptionalist mission, particularly its conflicted and compromised projects of spreading democracy, freedom, and capitalism across the globe. At one point, the narrator recalls the experiences of Dara's father, who is jailed after the 1979 revolution for supporting communist causes. While his sentence includes physical punishment, the narrator explains that prison conditions in his country are "not even comparable to Guantánamo," as the constitutional law of the Islamic Republic forbids any form of torture or even any form of censorship. Dara's father, however, is later given a jail sentence that effectively silences him, and he is eventually found guilty of lying to the authorities, a crime that in Iran carries the sentence of flogging.[7] Through references to the abuses reported at the U.S. military prison in Guantánamo, Mandanipour draws attention not to the alleged differences separating the two nations but to the comparable political corruptions that link Iran with the United States. Neither country is let off the hook; instead, the author demonstrates the ways both nations violate the civil liberties of their citizens through censorship and repression and shows how leaders in both nations find loopholes in their legal systems to justify and facilitate the abuse of state power and torture of political prisoners.

In *Censoring an Iranian Love Story*, the "American anti-American" film *Brokeback Mountain* circulates significantly in Iran because its themes resonate with conflicts and restrictions the characters face in their everyday lives. In this way, a popular Western reaches a new international audience through the particular meanings viewers assign to it because of their own national interests and concerns. As I have been arguing in this study, the popular Western has undergone numerous permutations throughout its cultural development, a process of adaptation and revision that continues in important ways across the Middle East. While the Western has made something of a comeback in the United States in the post-9/11 period, I am interested in tracing how the genre has also circulated transnationally, capturing the attention of populations beyond an American setting, in places like Iran, Libya, and Egypt, where fiction and film have reconfigured the possibilities of the form. Here I focus on recent transformations of the Western in global culture, particularly the ways the codes and conventions of the genre are revised and reshaped by audiences targeted as threatening or dangerous to the United States in an age of terror. As the genre circulates across the Middle East, it accrues new and often conflicted meanings, appealing to diverse audiences who adopt the form for specific motivations and purposes. In examining these new uses and meanings of the genre, I attend to the routes through which the Western travels before it appears in the Middle East. In many cases, the genre loops back to a European context, where it undergoes important permutations and revisions before it arrives in the Middle East.

Of course, to speak broadly of the recent travels of the Western across the Middle East risks erasing important national differences and producing a reductionist account of the significant differences between these texts. For example, while Iran is a Middle Eastern country whose population is largely Shiite Muslim, it is also made up of many other religious and ethnic groups. Although it was targeted as an enemy nation by the United States after 9/11, Iran is not an Arab nation, and the Iran/Iraq war from 1980 to 1988 further divided the country from its Arab neighbors in the region. Likewise, Libya and Egypt have experienced specific histories of colonialism and nationalism that shape their responses to the Western in different ways. For much of the first half of the twentieth century Libya was occupied by Italy (home of the spaghetti Western; more on that later), and it faced tremendous censorship and political repression from 1969 to 2011 under Gen. Muammar Qaddafi, one of the longest-standing rulers in the Middle East. Meanwhile, as the media capital of the Middle East, Egypt is the center of a well-established film tradition that has a large audience nationally and regionally. The country produces the most widely received popular music in the Middle East, while cinema is the nation's most successful cultural export. Egypt, however, faces tensions as efforts to establish a distinct national identity often carry more weight than its pan-Arab affiliations.[8] In my discussion of the Western's circulation in the contemporary Middle East, I foreground both connections and disturbances, taking into consideration how diverse audiences in specific national contexts may assign these texts distinct and at times contested meanings and how the Western's distribution routes may take decidedly different forms for specific and distinct purposes.

Screening the Western in Tehran

In a variety of ways, *Censoring an Iranian Love Story* links the political situations in Iran and the United States, opening up discussions about censorship and repression through references to the Western. At one point in Mandanipour's novel, Kevin Costner's *Dances with Wolves* (1990) becomes a topic of debate after it is recognized as an important "American anti-American" film, similar to the way that *Brokeback Mountain* is understood. In the text, Costner's movie becomes available to national audiences on state television only after it undergoes careful scrutiny by the Ministry of Culture and Islamic Guidance and is officially determined to be critical of U.S. foreign policy. Unlike neo-orientalist readings that predetermine possible interpretations of a cultural text, Mandanipour's novel highlights struggles over meanings in the genre, the heated intellectual discussions among Iranian officials indicating how the Western's significance may undergo important shifts from one context to another. *Dances with Wolves* was controversial for many American audiences as well, although for different reasons. Upon its release in the United States, some viewers thought the movie failed as an Indian sympathy film because it appeared to reify Anglo American power by centering on the importance and achievements of the white western hero and thus marginalized Native Americans once again. In *Censoring an Iranian Love Story*, the film is understood in a contrasting manner by the official censors—as a story that supports the American Indian cause and that operates as a succinct critique of U.S. military power and expansionist desires—a reading that departs from the critical reception it received in some quarters in the United States.

In the tradition of absurdist storytelling, the novel's Ministry of Culture and Islamic Guidance is directed by a blind supervisor known as Mr. X and his "group of seeing expert consultants," whose job involves describing the visual elements that the sight-impaired Mr. X misses during film screenings. During a showing of the film for Iranian officials, one expert on morality voices his objection to the word *dance* in the movie's title because it draws attention to cultural practices that may be "vulgar and obscene" for Iranian viewers.[9] "Dancing is dancing. Do you think Iranians will think of dancing with wolves when they see or hear the word 'dances'? They will immediately think of Arabic belly dancing. The Westernized ones will think of the tango, and the minute they think of dancing, they will start dancing," he contends. "The burden of their sin is on your shoulders, brother." In contrast to this argument, Dara, in his position as the ministry's expert on cinematic affairs, insists that the larger political messages of the Western may ultimately override such moral concerns. "There is nothing wrong with dancing with wolves," he points out. "In this film they show how wonderful and civilized the Indians were and how savage the Americans were. We have to broadcast this film so that the people of Iran realize that, without us, the Americans will either massacre them or banish them to parched wastelands in America."[10] Later in the meeting, another member of the committee raises objections to the display of Native American bodies in Costner's film; the figures are unclothed from the waist up and thus potentially offensive to Muslim viewers. His concerns are dismissed by the blind Mr. X himself, who draws on historical precedent, reminding the ministry officials that we "have broadcast several Italian westerns, and as far as I have been told the Italian Indians were also half naked, and no one has complained. So, it is not a problem."[11]

In Mandanipour's novel, the Western undergoes critical revision through its global travels before it arrives in Iran, a circulation that does not occur in a direct or straightforward fashion but in an important rerouting through Europe, in particular through the tradition of the Italian Westerns made famous by filmmakers such as Sergio Leone. The mid-1960s saw the emergence of spaghetti Western films produced initially by the Cinecittà studios in Italy, which sparked a subsequent international boom in the production of global Westerns.[12] As Louis Chude-Sokei cogently argues in assessing Jamaican reggae and its use of the Western genre a decade later, this earlier wave of international revisionist filmmaking "critiqued American culture and politics by reversing, rejecting, and revising its moral structures."[13] Many international artists and musicians found alternative inspiration in the form, he argues, claiming new "space within American allegories to navigate and explore the conceptual and economic meanings of the 'West,' the 'frontier,' the 'border.'"[14] Austin Fisher notes too that Italian filmmakers were attracted to the Western because it allowed them to "expose brutal mechanisms lying behind modernday Western society."[15] The cycle of Italian Westerns eventually became recognized as an emergent "critical cinema" that not only appropriated and redirected the meanings of the genre but also examined "how America imagined itself and how those on the fringes of its projections re-imagined it while simultaneously re-imagining themselves through it."[16] Like the reversals found in 1970s Jamaican reggae, Iranian recastings of the genre in Mandanipour's novel appear to be far more indebted to the spaghetti Western than they are to the American version.[17] In Iran, the Western's dominant form is Italian, not American, with the appropriation and revision engaging the concerns addressed by director Sergio Leone rather than John Ford.

The argument against restricting *Dances with Wolves* on Iranian television that becomes most convincing to state officials involves appeals to tradition. In this case, the appeals reference what Mr. X curiously calls the "Italian Indians," a term he invents to speak of the Native Americans featured in spaghetti Westerns, which were often read as pro-Indian films. As one official reminds his colleagues, because these Italian Westerns had already received approval and had been broadcast on state television for some time, they formed a respected tradition in their own right. For the official censors in Mandanipour's Iran, *Dances with Wolves* is appealing precisely because it follows this tradition—the Italian tradition of filmmaking and critical cinema. Costner's Western becomes recognizable, is interpreted, and thus circulates in this context as an anti-American allegory, the tale of an innocent people overtaken by a corrupt superpower intent on restricting their freedoms and way of life. The travels of the Western reveal the ways the genre arrives in Iran already reshaped, revised, and reconfigured by another nation's film tradition. Popular understandings of the Western as a quintessential U.S. genre are thus disrupted, its identity thoroughly altered and remade by its prior movement and reception in a different national setting, a process it undergoes again as Iranian audiences claim its possibilities for their own cultural narratives.

The director Asghar Farhadi's Academy Award–winning film, *A Separation* (2011), offers another take on Iranian appeals to Native Americans in the Western, this time as a means of debating abstract concepts such as censorship, freedom, and individual liberties in both Iran and the United States. In doing so, *A Separation* draws on the figure of the cinematic Indian in order to reference American histories of captivity, restriction, and mobility. The film comments not only on similar complexities shaping freedom and liberation in postrevolutionary Tehran but also on the hypocrisy of the United States as the national embodiment of these virtues. Farhadi notes in an interview that while filmmaking in Iran faces certain restrictions and challenges, censorship in one form or another may be found in every culture: "In Iran censorship is more ideological and political, but that doesn't mean there isn't censorship of a different kind in the West."[18] In a brief but significant scene in the film, the figure of the American Indian becomes a potent reminder of the ongoing presence of censorship, restriction, and lack of freedom in U.S. history, a figure who represents the imagined "separation" that divides the political realities of Iran from events in the rest of the world.

A Separation opens with a scene depicting the marital breakup of a secular, professional couple, Simin (Leila Hatami) and her husband, Nader (Peyman Moaadi). As the film indicates, the characters still have strong feelings for each other and are reluctant to end the marriage. Watching her young daughter Termeh (Sarina Farhadi) grow up in Tehran under the regime's religious and gender restrictions, Simin is anxious to leave the country for the possibilities of a better life elsewhere. Meanwhile, Nader has the responsibility of caring for his elderly father (Ali-Asghar Shahbazi), who suffers from Alzheimer's disease and whose health issues prevent him from leaving Tehran. Both spouses are in a difficult situation that has no simple or right answer. Simin wants what she believes is a better life for their daughter, while Nader feels an obligation toward his ailing father and thinks his wife is seeking the easy way out instead of staying and fighting for meaningful political change in their country. Nader hires a caregiver, Razieh (Sareh Bayat), a working-class, devout Muslim woman who is pregnant and faces family concerns of her own. At one point, she too finds herself in an impossible situation after Nader's father soils himself and needs her help changing his clothes. Razieh is forced to weigh her religious beliefs with the demands at hand, deciding if she should aid a man in this situation who is not related to her or leave him to suffer without help.

In a key scene that takes place after she decides to quit the job, Razieh has a confrontation with Nader, who in his anger and haste in making her leave his home, accidentally pushes her down the stairs. She ends up having a miscarriage, and Nader is brought to court, where he faces criminal charges. The film proceeds through investigations meant to determine the cause of the crime, which may not involve Nader after all. As the characters face judgment about their choices, each of them comes to have a believable story to tell, a convincing point of view, and a compelling motivation that make assigning guilt a difficult act. In his review of Farhadi's film, Massoud Hayoun suggests that there is much for U.S. audiences to learn about contemporary Iran and about themselves by watching the film. In particular, he draws connections between the crisis the family faces—especially the futility of efforts to "assign blame to a single character . . . for an explosive chain of events that threaten devastation"—and the growing political tensions between Washington and Tehran. Hayoun argues that the film features elements of the characters' struggles that are similar to events that may often lead to war, with the conflicts featured here "as a dizzying exchange of blame between a variety of painfully flawed parties."[19]

The figure of the American Indian makes a brief appearance in a scene with Nader and Razieh. As the camera moves through the family's living room and kitchen, audiences gain glimpses of items from European and U.S. culture that decorate the apartment. One such object includes a framed reproduction of Andrew Wyeth's *Christina's World*, which features a haunting image of young woman who is turned away from the foreground, gazing toward the horizon behind her, a painting that perhaps captures a similar desire for a world just beyond the frame and out of reach for these characters. Meanwhile, the kitchen wall features an image of a Native American in full feather headdress who gazes off to a world just outside the frame. The depiction of the Indian is fleeting and the camera doesn't linger long on it, yet the picture carries significant meanings for the story. In his review of *A Separation*, Hayoun suggests that these elements of kitsch displayed in various scenes throughout the film serve as a reminder of the European and U.S. presence that already permeates everyday life in the Middle East. Also, by avoiding abstract politics and instead featuring distinct people in their personal homes surrounded by everyday objects of life, the film may help bridge larger cultural and political separations, which "may make it a little harder" for the United States to "go to war with them."[20]

I would extend Hayoun's comments about the importance of such cultural exchanges—the appearance of European and American kitsch in the film and the travels of Iranian cinema across the United States—by lingering on the depiction of the Indian displayed on the kitchen wall. The image features a highly staged head shot of a Native American as he stoically faces west, frozen in a tableau shot, a composition that shares similarities with early U.S. motion pictures featuring Native American characters. As Scott Simmon argues, conventional introductory shots of individual Indians in the earliest Westerns often present a lone figure turned slightly away from the camera, looking off into a space that is out of the frame and thus unseen by audiences—the representative of a dying race and defeated people. "The iconography evoked here had evolved in American painting," he argues, "until this simple image of the Indian staring off into the middle distance was alone enough to imply an entire narrative of civilization's advance and the native's demise."[21] In the cinematic Western, the Indian rarely achieves freedom and is instead traditionally consigned on-screen to a fate of immobility, dispossession, disappearance, and death. The image of the American Indian becomes a potent sign of political protest here, with Iranians standing alongside Indigenous Americans as both populations historically face restrictions and even captivity in their position as enemies of a powerful nationalizing and globalizing force. Likewise, the image of the Indian becomes a haunting figure that reveals conflicts in Farhadi's film surrounding the possibilities of claiming freedom on a collective level against the ability to determine the course of one's own life.

A Separation thus gestures toward the Western and U.S. history by referencing the figure of the Indian and by complicating key concepts that often drive the genre and define the nation itself. In particular, the film disrupts simplistic understandings of freedom and individual liberty associated with deployments of the Western in the war on terror. As one critic suggests, *A Separation* undermines naïve understandings of these concepts by featuring a tale about "freedom and its discontents" and the ways "abstract ideas of justice or objective truth clash with human frailty and limits of understanding."[22] In the film, the quest for personal liberty always impinges on the lives of others and entails a difficult set of decisions that carry tremendous consequences for the community as a whole. Freedom, in other words, is neither a simple concern nor an individual matter. *A Separation* thus enters into dialogues about the war on terror by upsetting grand notions of

Fig. 15. Debating U.S.-style "freedom" with Razieh in *A Separation* (directed by Asghar Farhadi, 2011), from the DVD.

liberty, which are often presented as universal truths that may be exported across the world by the United States. In the film, freedom appears as a more complex set of concerns that have social and collective impacts and that cannot be debated abstractly. As such, the American Indian becomes a complex image in the film, a figure suggesting cultural restriction and the larger experience of separation itself. More importantly perhaps, the image of the American Indian is also a reminder of the costs certain populations have often had to pay for someone else's pursuit of individual liberties in the United States. It is the price Indigenous Americans paid throughout history as generations of white settlers sought the mythic promise and possibilities of "free" land in the American West. In Farhadi's film, it also the unexpected price that family and loved ones pay as they or others seek a life of freedom.

Sergio Leone in Tahrir Square

Although cowboy diplomacy has deployed the Western in efforts to position the American hyperpower on a global frontier while situating the nation as a model of freedom and democracy to be replicated across the world, this version of the Western has undergone an important critique in world culture through a counter-tradition that brings to the fore critical elements of the genre. Likewise, the tradition of the cinematic Western that previously achieved wide circulation across the Middle East—the Italian spaghetti Western—also has been transformed and altered in recent Arabic-language film and fiction. At times, the spaghetti Western is usefully deployed as a means of expressing popular resistance to repressive state power, while in other moments the Italian Western appears as a failed or simplistic means of explaining and resolving a complex political situation in the contemporary Middle East.

In 2011, for instance, during the early months of the Arab Spring in Egypt, the spaghetti Western became a means of critiquing political repression and the nation's regime. One effort at employing the genre for these ends appeared in a documentary detailing the early days of the pro-democracy movement and its efforts to oust the long-ruling leader, Hosni Mubarak. Ayten Amin, Tamer Ezzat, and Amr Samala's film about the early days of the Arab Spring, *Tahrir 2011: The Good, the Bad, and the Politician*, draws on and extends Leone's similarly titled spaghetti Western, playing on critical elements in the Italian director's 1966 revisionist take on the genre.[23] The documentary captures the Egyptian revolution from the three perspectives of its major players: "the good" refers to the pro-democracy protesters, "the bad," to the police forces, and "the ugly"—here reframed as "the politician"—to the Egyptian president, Mubarak. The documentary won the CICT-UNESCO prize at the Venice Film Festival, Best Documentary Award at the Oslo Film Festival, and Best Arabic Producer Award at the Abu Dhabi Film Festival; it was also the first documentary released commercially in Egyptian theaters in nearly thirty years.[24]

The poster for the documentary incorporates both Arabic and English text and thus hails an audience within and beyond national boundaries. In addition, the ad employs a retro style to signal the older world of the spaghetti Western and the Italian tradition of critical cinema from the 1960s. The poster itself incorporates a movie poster within its frame and is shown mounted on a concrete wall erected on the side of an urban street. The image borrows from the tradition of revolutionary graffiti art, with black spray

East of the Spaghetti Western

paint dripping down from the scene of political conflict above it. In red paint appear images of the various players involved in the uprising. Yet, if *Tahrir 2011: The Good, the Bad, and the Politician* references the Italian tradition of spaghetti Westerns, the documentary also incorporates elements of the war film, as blood seeps into the black graffiti and images of Egyptian protesters wounded in the streets during the uprising share space with the armed soldiers who supported the Mubarak regime.

In an important way, the poster for the documentary references the complex and hybrid forms of media through which the Arab Spring unfolded, what Helga Tawil-Souri calls the "shifting spatialities" of the contemporary pro-democracy movement.[25] While the wide-scale political protest across the Middle East has been called a "digital revolution" or "Revolution 2.0," demonstrations throughout the region took place, as she points out, across both old and new media, while also employing elements of local and global culture. Here the movie poster engages old and new as well as local and global elements by using the work of Sergio Leone to depict revolutionary activities unfolding in Tahrir Square. During the uprising in Egypt, protesters likewise relied on older means of communication such as political signs, posters, songs, and graffiti that often drew on elements of local culture. These forms of protest played alongside newer technologies of global culture, including Facebook, Twitter, blogs, and email.[26] As Brian T. Edwards notes, all of these forms of media intermixed; at the moment the Mubarak regime imposed a curfew on Egyptian protesters during the uprising, the pro-democracy activists left the streets only to turn their attention and efforts to cyberspace, thus bringing the movement back to the sphere of the Internet and global culture.[27]

Armando Salvatore notes that, well before the events of 2011, Egyptian society had already produced "a range of 'preparatory' contributions from literature, movies, and television serials" that circulated voices of opposition to Mubarak's government.[28] While it may seem as if the revolution came out of nowhere, Walid El Hamamsy and Mounira Soliman likewise point out that the protesters in the streets and across cyberspace had long been active

Fig. 16. Poster for *Tahrir 2011: The Good, the Bad, and the Politician* (2011).
Used with permission.

and vocal about their dissent. They argue that, in the case of Egypt, widespread discontent with the Mubarak government was in place by 2004, as seen in demonstrations by workers, university protests, the Kefaya ("Enough") movement, and the April 6 Youth Movement.[29] Later in this chapter, I examine instances of pre–Arab Spring cultural critique in Egyptian cinema, noting how it also engaged the Western and the cowboy, recoding elements of the genre for new political purposes. First, however, I turn my attention to the context of Libya and how the spaghetti Western was understood differently there, particularly how the European tradition of the Western was treated in literature about the pro-democracy movement in Italy's former colony. It is important to recognize that just as the pro-democracy movements in Tunisia, Egypt, Libya, Yemen, Syria, Bahrain, and Sudan unfolded in specific ways and were not all the same, so the popular Western has been referenced in different ways by various writers and artists in North Africa and the Middle East.[30]

Written a few years before the Arab Spring unfolded, Hisham Matar's semi-autobiographical novel, *In the Country of Men* (2006), incorporates the Italian Western as a means of examining possibilities for protest and the struggle for democracy in Libya. Shortlisted for the Man Booker Prize, the novel highlights the problems of freedom and costs of struggle for individuals and their families across the country. In doing so, the author reveals aspects about the problems of circulation—how various elements of global culture that may move across Libya offer only limited political solutions in a revolutionary context. Set in 1979 as the el-Dawani family from Tripoli struggles with life ten years after General Qaddafi came to power in a military coup, the novel details the problems faced by members of the country's underground pro-democracy movement. Suleiman is the nine-year-old protagonist of the novel who narrates the novel as an adult, reminiscing about his father who continually leaves home, traveling abroad for business reasons. One day, after Suleiman recognizes him at a bustling marketplace hidden behind dark sunglasses, his father disappears. It turns out his father was captured by the Revolutionary Committee,

Libya's secret police, after being involved in protests organized by the pro-democracy movement. Suleiman tries to survive the long wait for his father's return by hanging out at his friends' homes and watching popular Westerns on television or video in the afternoons. The young friends are amazed at the particular skills of one boy, Osama, who is always able to find the "latest cowboy films," which they view together with great enthusiasm.[31]

Throughout the story, Suleiman dreams of rescuing his missing father, as well as his long-suffering mother, who may be physically present in the novel but remains preoccupied by thoughts of her absent husband and is thus not emotionally present for her son. Suleiman's dreams involve elaborate rescue fantasies that have been spurred by all of the Westerns he's watched at the movies, on television, and on rented videos over the years:

> Perhaps it was all the cowboy films with their logic of happy endings that made me think this way . . . that just at the point when the hero had the rope around his neck, suddenly, and with the Majesty of God, a shot would come from nowhere and break the rope. The hero would kick the man beside him, and the rest of the mob—*the cowards*—would jump on their saddles and ride off, up and over the hill. Everyone at the cinema would jump and shout and clap and hug one another as if it was a football match.[32]

The scenes described here come straight out of the spaghetti Western, particularly Leone's *The Good, the Bad, and the Ugly*, with its over-the-top heroic antics and scenes of improbable, last-minute escape. Here the cowboy rescue films Suleiman and his friends watch are imported not from Hollywood but from Italy, which ruled Libya as a colony from 1911 until its independence in 1943. In the novel, Suleiman expresses his frustrations in trying to find a revolutionary Libyan cowboy hero who can single-handedly rescue his missing father and help his long-suffering mother. "Where were the heroes, the bullets, the scurrying mob, the happy endings that used to send us out of the dark cinema halls, rosy-cheeked with joy, slapping one another's backs, rejoicing that our man had won, that God was with him," the young boy wonders.[33]

East of the Spaghetti Western

In the postcolonial era, Libya's engagement with Italy occurs in part through the circulation of the former colonizing power's popular cinema. While spaghetti Westerns are widely considered an aspect of Italy's critical film tradition, they are subjected to critique in the novel as Suleiman becomes more deeply engaged in his country's specific pro-democracy movement. As the young protagonist discovers, the Italian Westerns are disappointing as revolutionary art and fail to be useful political tools because they largely favor what turn out to be simplistic visions of regime change. In some ways, they replicate the problems that emerge in creating political movements led by charismatic and powerful individuals, which was the case with General Qaddafi or Egypt's Hosni Mubarak. As Suleiman learns, such mythic rescuers like the Italian cowboys screened in Leone's spaghetti Westerns will not lead his country forward. The political movement in Libya will not achieve its goals through the individual heroics of a solitary Arab cowboy in one fortunate and elaborate act of bravery but will take many more years, much more collective struggle, and several generations of protesters and activists to achieve. As such, *In the Country of Men* reveals political differences in uses of the global Western and its rescuing hero, even in cases when they are created in the spirit of a critical cinema.

Texts about Westerns from the Middle East and North Africa appearing before and after the Arab Spring invoke the codes of the genre, countering recent uses of the form in justifying the war on terror and the invasion of Iraq. In these texts, the term "cowboy" appears as a broad insult in speaking of the U.S. military presence in the Middle East, so closely is the cowboy associated with military aggression across the region, thanks in part to the Lone Ranger diplomacy in the early twenty-first century. Thus, in *The Sirens of Baghdad*, by the Algerian novelist Yasmina Khadra, the cowboy takes on alternative meanings. Set in Iraq at the beginning of the U.S. invasion, the novel features a character who complains about the American military presence in the region. "They know nothing of our customs, our dreams, or our prayers. They're particularly ignorant of our heritage and our long memories," he notes. "What do these cowboys know about Mesopotamia? Do you think they have a clue about this fantastic Iraq they're trampling down?"[34] At another point, a character describes the U.S. soldiers as "bleating, dim-witted cowboys" that no one wants "to have anything more to do with."[35] In his recent 2013 collection, *The Corpse Exhibition and Other Stories of Iraq*, the author Hassan Blasim creates a character who also curses the American military presence. "What does that bunch of cowboys want? It's because of them I lost my legs in the Kuwait war. What do they want next?" he asks.[36]

"Stop Cowboy"

An Egyptian comedy, *The Night Baghdad Fell* (2005), offers another response to the circulation of the Western across the Middle East while complicating the genre's cowboy hero in a global context.[37] Written and directed by Mohamed Amin, the film is a political satire that highlights national fears about a potential U.S. invasion of Egypt after the fall of Baghdad in 2003. Although the film is a comedy and uses broad humor to critique American foreign policy, the movie also incorporates disturbing scenes of violence and abuse as a means of "awakening" Egypt from its political apathy in the years before the Arab Spring while laying bare the inadequacy of Egypt's stagnant government. The film incorporates footage from Arab television of the U.S. war in Iraq, photographs of dead Iraqi children, and images of torture from Abu Ghraib, as well as news stories about the U.S. kidnapping and rape of Arab women during the war in order to draw attention to the inadequacy of Egypt's response to the invasion.

With references to American cowboys, the film points to the colonial logic of the popular Western, countering recent uses of the genre in justifying the war on terror and the invasion of Iraq. As a result, the Western that often circulates in the Middle East becomes indistinguishable in director Amin's movie from the tradition of the war film. Although the Western and the war film have often overlapped (as in John Ford's cavalry Westerns), here the connections become visible in new ways. Examining circulations of global film culture, for instance, Barbara Klinger addresses

East of the Spaghetti Western

the emergence of what she calls "local genres" and the manner in which specific audiences may classify individual movies in ways that counter how they originally may have been envisioned by the industry.[38] In genre theory, film scholars typically offer overarching or "master" definitions that try to explain "affiliations between numerous and diverse films," identifying "formulas and conventions" in order to determine "the shared characteristics of a body of films," she argues. Hence, a film is confirmed as a Western "if its setting, characters, and iconography reflect the historical conflict between wilderness and civilization rooted in the latter half of the 19th century." In assessing how genres may undergo variation or change from one text to another, critics frequently point to the emergence of specific subgenres of film or cycles of production that appear at different historical moments. While these concepts are useful in understanding mutations in film genres over time, Klinger argues for the need to shift critical focus to the realm of circulation itself and the power specific audiences have in determining the status of a film text in a particular context. In doing so, she especially examines the role of audiences outside academic institutions in defining a text's genre status.[39]

Klinger argues that the importance of such nonacademic venues is that they "demonstrate how certain films were identified historically for popular consumption, helping us to assess the mechanisms behind the creation of a film's social image or meaning at particular moments."[40] By studying a broader range of viewer responses to individual films, critics may learn that what was frequently considered a Western for particular audiences in a particular moment was actually understood quite differently for audiences in other times and locations.[41] In noting these differences, scholars may better understand genres as "volatile" and "contingent phenomenon, conditioned by social, institutional, and historical circumstance."[42] Klinger suggests the term "local genres" to describe the ways a text may accrue different meanings to different people at different times and places.[43] In studying the complexities of global circulations of culture, the concept of local genres may be useful in understanding the circulation and reception of the Western in the post-9/11 era. While certain films might be classified as revisionist Westerns, in other contexts they circulate as "American anti-American" films, as extensions or revisions of Italian critical cinema, or as an instance of the American war film itself.

The Night Baghdad Fell opens with a political protest at a high school in Cairo as two students approach the headmaster, Shaker, about making a banner of support for Iraq. "Didn't we have one up for Afghanistan?" he asks them before devising a clever solution to the problem. Instead of having to make new banners, he tells them to just "move the parenthesis and add Iraq." As the film continues, the student protesters are forced to keep moving the parenthesis as new nations are targeted as enemies of the United States. While the demonstrators chant "no to American bullying," the headmaster tries to placate them and end their protests. "Kids," he promises somewhat ineffectually, "I'll send a telegram of condemnation in your name." Such efforts are underwhelming and unsatisfying to the student demonstrators. A conflict emerging in the film thus involves divisions between the generations in the years leading up to the Arab Spring. The older generation appears passive and cowed by the political events unfolding after 9/11. Some older Egyptians even seem to embrace American power in the region; at various points, for instance, the movie cuts to the response of an Egyptian man who spends a lot of time in cafés commenting on the benefits of a U.S. invasion. A devoted reader of *Newsweek* magazine, he cheers on the actions of the American soldiers. "Good," he proclaims. "Let them invade us all and raise us out of the gutter." The character goes on to predict that Egypt will likely suffer dearly for a decade or so, but then "we'll be part of the free world," he insists. Meanwhile, Shaker worries about his daughter's involvement in the antiwar movement but has no solutions himself and frequently loses sleep because of nightmares he has about U.S. marines capturing and torturing his family members. He begins having sexual troubles with his wife, a problem likewise afflicting other Egyptian males since the invasion. The film treats the problem as an indictment of the older generation and the nation's widespread impotence in the face of political aggression and the stagnant Mubarak regime.

Shaker eventually devises another clever solution, this time aimed at preventing a future U.S. invasion. Recalling a particularly talented former student whose accomplishments in the sciences set him apart from his peers at the school, the headmaster asks him to help create a weapon to deter the American superpower. One of Shaker's friends learns about these efforts and tries to assure him that Egypt has already developed such a weapon; the nation's "unconcern and passivity," he argues, are a sure sign that they already have such technology. Yet another friend tells Shaker that Cairo's black cloud, which has darkened the skies above the city for several years in the late fall and often poses a dangerous health risk for Egyptians, is not smog caused by farmers burning stubble in the fields after the harvest, as is popularly believed, but must be caused by radiation from the government's "secret underground testing."[44] Finally, another friend reminds him of a recent power outage, one that he insists was not just another blackout of the type the country frequently experiences but must have been the result of military efforts to develop the weapon. The men's proof for the weapon plan draws on instances of inefficiencies or failures in the nation's infrastructure—signs that the older generation is still too easy on the Mubarak administration and prefers to remain passive in the misguided belief that the government is actually working on solutions to deter a U.S. invasion.

While the older generation of Egyptians comes under fire from the filmmaker, the younger generation is also criticized for wasting its political potential. Shaker locates his gifted former student, Tarek Abdel Samad, only to discover that the young man prefers to put his efforts into smoking hashish with friends and lying to his family about work rather than into conducting research at the university. The headmaster eventually persuades Tarek to help him work on developing the weapon, taking matters into his own hands when he finally realizes that the government has no plans to protect them. Tarek soon falls in love with Shaker's daughter, Mohie, who, like other women in the film, is more engaged in political

Fig. 17. Young Egyptians gathering to prepare materials for the antiwar movement in *The Night Baghdad Fell* (directed by Mohamed Amin, 2005), from the DVD.

change than their male cohorts are. Mohie is a fearless leader who speaks her mind and doesn't let anyone deter her from her involvement in the movement. As an organizer of the protests, she sets up headquarters in the family's home, where the students busy themselves organizing the opposition on the street and on the Internet. There, hanging on the walls, are posters in Arabic and English, one of which reads "Stop Cowboy."

Later, at a demonstration in front of the American embassy, Mohie delivers a speech outlining the protesters' complaints about U.S. military aggression. "If you thought to keep us backward and oppressed," she states, "we're telling you now, we've woken up." She continues, telling the Americans, "Don't think a bunch of cowboys like you, with no history to speak of, can conquer peoples who made history. We'll always be here; you'll never wipe us out. We'll remain in spite of you." Here the term "cowboy" signifies not a hero of democracy and liberation on an international frontier but an anachronistic character who is both out of time and out of place, a figure ill fit for bringing meaningful change to current political situations in the Middle East. In the film, the freedom-bringing cowboy instead functions in the context of U.S.

East of the Spaghetti Western

imperial formations, what Ann Laura Stoler describes as continual "processes of decimation, displacement, and reclamation." As she argues, imperial formations "are relations of force. They harbor those mutant[,] rather than simply hybrid, political forms that endure beyond the formal exclusions. . . . Not least, they are states of deferral that mete out promissory notes that are not exceptions to their operation, but constitutive of them: imperial guardianship, trusteeships, delayed autonomy, temporary intervention, conditional tutelage, military takeover in the name of humanitarian words, violent intervention in the name of human rights, and security measures in the name of peace."[45] The global cowboy serves as a farcical figure in the movie, his projects of liberation and democracy revealed as just one more instance in the history of imperial formations across the region. Circulating as a local genre in Egyptian culture, the popular Western referenced in *The Night Baghdad Fell* is transformed into an instance of the war movie, its cowboy hero recast as a soldier and placed within the genre of the American combat film.

Although the cowboy hero is not a captivating figure for Egyptians in this context, it turns out that the uniformed and armed U.S. marines become so, at least for some of the female characters in the movie. In various scenes, the film subverts how imperial and sexual politics are often entangled in the context of war. Kathryn Bigelow's post-9/11 film, *The Hurt Locker*, displays combat as an erotic force for some of the soldiers after the main character, Sergeant James, experiences a sexual rush from battle. Following a particularly tense moment in which he successfully defuses an improvised explosive device, the soldier returns to his vehicle, lights a cigarette, and blows out a wave of smoke. "That was good," he tells a fellow soldier.[46] In *The Night Baghdad Fell*, Shaker encourages the young Tarek to focus all of his "urges" on creating the weapon of deterrence. Although he tries to do so, Tarek is unable to repress his fantasies about American power itself—here embodied by Secretary of State Condoleezza Rice—and dreams of watching her belly dance for him one night. Later, when he marries Mohie, he is impotent on his wedding night. Mohie finds an answer to his problem by donning the Fourteenth Airborne squadron uniform in bed, thus allowing her groom to indulge his fantasies through sexualized military role playing.

Cynthia Enloe examines the intersections of military culture and sexual politics, noting the ways war often leads to the control of male soldiers' sexualities at the same time that it places inordinate attention on certain sexual acts themselves. Enloe argues that the military both restricts soldiers' behaviors (e.g., "don't ask, don't tell") and holds the belief that men in battle need sexual access to certain women in order to be "real men."[47] As such, battle zones have seen military brothels, various forms of sexual slavery, and the rape of local women as a means of providing such sexual services for men at war.[48] In the film, newspaper reports about the gang rape of Iraqi women serve as a horrifying instance of U.S. abuses in the region and as a powerful means of motivating Egypt's anti-war movement. Yet, the film also parodies the sexual cultures of war, reversing the powers of eroticism in the process. For instance, when Mohie's mother, Maisa, finds out about her daughter's solution to Tarek's impotence, she too tries on a U.S. army uniform before she slips into bed with her husband. "Can't I go to war too?" she asks him suggestively. "Shouldn't seeing the enemy before you like this create a state of emergency?" Indeed it does, and soon Shaker declares that his impotence has been cured. "The troops are now standing at full attention," he assures his wife.

The film cuts to scenes in other bedrooms across Egypt as wives young and old don camouflage uniforms in order to aid their husbands' sexual performance and their own pleasure. Such scenes reconfigure the post-9/11 gendered rescue fantasy, with Egyptian women featured not as passive victims but as empowered and capable actors who work to save the nation from its would-be captors and to resolve the country's collective impotence. In doing so, they dismantle the military-imperial-eroticization of conquest that serves American interests. Near the end of the film, the CIA officials finally manage to capture Tarek and his father-in-law, placing both men in a psychiatric hospital, where they are finally silenced and kept out of the way, their weapon designs now unable to contribute to the nation's security efforts. The two men are later released just as the U.S. invasion of Egypt unfolds as predicted, and they are able to witness the weapon of deterrence working just as they had planned. Tarek is joined by Mohie and their young son, and the film ends in dancing, singing, and cheering as the camera focuses on the boy as a symbol of hope and the future of a free and democratic Egypt.[49]

As these instances of popular expression across the Middle East indicate, the struggle against repression in the region does not require American liberators. Pro-democracy movements such as the developments in the Arab Spring do not need U.S. cowboy saviors to provide meaning to their actions or justifications for regime change. Yet, in so far as they critically engage U.S. texts, such counternarratives often do so in ways that may elude American scholars. In "The World, the Text, and the Americanist," Brian T. Edwards notes that scholars of U.S. texts need to develop "a more supple appreciation of ways in which the multiple conditions of globalization, on both local and international levels, set a fundamentally different encounter between text and world."[50] He suggests that the issue becomes what to do "with our carefully historicized readings" of American texts "when the conditions for their circulation" are so dramatically altered, when numerous new "archives and contexts are now required to place a text in its contexts."[51] As U.S. cultural texts circulate across "contexts outside the publics they were crafted to address . . . they frequently spur on new and disruptive sets of meanings and innovations."[52] He explains that often a cultural object may circulate as a "fragment" of the original, traveling "off the expected circuits, out of legibility."[53] Such instances may lead to the "end of circulation," he argues, the place where global culture may "meet an endpoint, a dead end, from which they are difficult to translate back into global circulation."[54]

It is important to note that the ends of circulation may also occur when contemporary revisionist efforts do not become translated into English. Fewer translations of Arabic or Farsi texts make it to the American market than vice versa, while many films from the region do not play widely at the U.S. cineplex. The editors of the volume *Literature from the "Axis of Evil"* call this lack of circulation a cultural "trade deficit," whereby U.S. audiences have little exposure to other cultures, as their access to world literatures in translation steadily decreases.[55] In the case of film, for instance, *The Night Baghdad Fell* is not listed on the IMDb website but is available for online purchase at Amazon, where it is cataloged under a different title, *The Fall of Baghdad*. The critic Hosam Aboul-Ela offers a solution to the problems Americanist scholars may face in countering the ends of circulation, suggesting that Arabic may soon become just as crucial a language to study as Spanish has become for scholars working in American studies today.[56]

Edwards's observations about the "ends" of circulation play on the word to speak not just of illegibility and the endpoint of knowledge but also of productive "ends," as in the uses of these circulated texts for new purposes.[57] Studies of the meanings texts take on as they move through the Middle East, as well as of the cultures of distribution across the region, open up complicated new approaches to the history and development of the popular Western.[58] Thus, the cinematic Western's distribution through the black market in Iran as an instance of the "American anti-American film" in Mandanipour's novel transforms the genre in ways that may make Westerns more interesting and complicated to study as cultural objects. In a similar way, Italy's countercinema may travel meaningfully throughout Iran, as it does in Farhadi's film, to suggest continuities between the lack of freedom in both Iran and the United States, as well as the hypocrisy of Americans who may understand themselves as self-proclaimed providers of democracy and independence throughout the world. Such films may likewise circulate as such throughout Egypt's Arab Spring, where the "good, the bad, and the politician" may be plugged into the critical tradition of Leone's spaghetti Westerns, rather than the tradition of the Western situated in a U.S. setting. Meanwhile, in Libya, the cowboy hero may not translate quite so well but instead may be stopped in his tracks, his liberating antics proving too simplistic for the nation's unfolding pro-democracy movement. Finally, for the Western film tradition referenced in Egyptian cinema, the form's codes and conventions may face such resistance that it becomes necessary to recode and reclassify it as an entirely new local genre—in this case, as the American war film, an apt revision that dislodges the dominant post-9/11 discourse of Westerns, cowboys, and Arabs in meaningful, unexpected, and often humorous ways.

Conclusion

Once Upon a Time in the Middle East

Scholars have marshaled their expertise to argue that targeted
humiliations of subject populations, humanitarian intervention
as offensive strategy, prolonged states of emergency, and
preemptive military assault in the name of peace are neither
aberrant nor exceptional tactics of imperial regimes,
but fundamental to their governing grammar.
—ANN LAURA STOLER

Perhaps westerns will adjust to the postnational moment and
some figure from the outside (as did the Italian filmmaker
Sergio Leone in his 1968 *Once Upon a Time in the West*)
will show everyone else how to imagine it again.
—KRISTA COMER

I bring my discussion of "captivating Westerns" to a close by addressing problems surrounding captivity, freedom, and border defense
as screened in two recent global Westerns. The Mexican director
Beto Gómez's *Saving Private Perez* (2011) and "Ahlan Ezayak"—a
2007 music video by the Saudi-Kuwaiti singer Shams—disengage
from the restrictive and totalizing viewpoints often associated with
the Western during the war on terror. Both texts extend the discussion I addressed in the previous chapter by providing incisive and
humorous critiques of these uses of the genre, displacing the United

States and the cowboy hero from their position as benevolent providers of freedom and democracy in the world.[1] Such interventions operate as a way of laying bare what Vijay Prashad calls the "twin goals of supremacy and liberation" that often shape American projects of imperialism, with its "urge to liberate . . . as fundamental as the requirement to subordinate."[2] In the case of Gómez's Western, the war on terror affects a Mexican family when a gangster's younger brother goes missing in action while serving in Iraq. The gangster's aging mother, who lies sick in a hospital bed, tells her son that she will forgive him for his violent past and allow him back into the family if he brings his younger brother home alive. This remake of the Western captivity tale with its search-and-rescue mission draws attention to the problems of the militarized borderland in an age of increased security and national defense, while also addressing the larger impact of the U.S. war on terror on Mexican and Mexican American lives. Since 2001, these populations have often found themselves held captive to new forms of racial surveillance and policing as the United States reacts to increasing anxieties about possible terrorist entry through the southern border.[3] Meanwhile, in a popular music video by the Saudi-Kuwaiti singer Shams, U.S. "Lone Ranger" foreign policy also becomes subject to parody and critique. In the context of Kuwait, the emergence of this music video cannot be understood outside the discourses that framed the Gulf War of 1990–91 and the Iraq War since 2003, which featured the civilian populations of two Arab nations—first Kuwait and then Iraq—as helpless, weak, and feminized entities in need of rescue by powerful American soldier-saviors. In Shams's narrative, the logic of the 9/11 Western is reworked for a distinctly anti-imperial project in ways that recast the traditional captive victim and the typical rescuing hero. The result is a critical showdown between invading American soldiers and an avenging Arab cowgirl in the militarized desert landscapes of the Middle East.

Mexico and Iraq

In *Saving Private Perez*, when the Mexican gangster Julián Pérez (Miguel Rodarte), who is known as the "most powerful man in

Mexico," learns that his younger brother Juan (Juan Carlos Flores) has gone missing in Iraq while serving in the U.S. Army, he assembles a group of skilled outlaws to embark on a rescue mission. With his holster, hat, and cowboy boots, Julián embodies the classic Western hero, updating the role of the skilled and able gunman in what Will Wright calls the "professional plot." In these revisionist Westerns, the protagonist is a man whose life of violence places him outside society and whose primary job is to defeat the villains who are threatening the larger community. The hero, a trained and professional killer who has been marginalized by society, now finds himself defending that very social order, which in turn is portrayed as diminished and ineffective.[4] The professional plot involves the creation of a group of men, "each with a special fighting ability," who come together for battle and whose abilities and status provide a "basis for mutual respect and affection."[5] Rather than adhering to the Western's values of justice and order, these professional gunmen are disenchanted with the corruptions of society and thus commit themselves to the values of "strength, skill, enjoyment of the battle, and masculine companionship," all of which are evident in the collective "coolness, humor, and wit" they express as they face the threat of death.[6] The emergence of the professional plot may be traced to larger social disruptions in the 1960s, an era when the Western entered a new cycle that favored the breakdown of authoritative structures and a disengagement with many elements of the classic form.[7]

Taking on similar themes of political disruption and social breakdown, Beto Gómez's *Saving Private Perez* references the treatment of captivity and rescue across the U.S.-Mexico border in Richard Brooks's movie *The Professionals* (1966), a film that also provided the title Wright used to describe this tradition of Westerns. Brooks's film features a group of professional gunmen hired to find a wealthy rancher's wife who has been kidnapped by a revolutionary Mexican soldier now in hiding. The story involves numerous scenes of improbable escape that showcase instances when the hired men successfully face down groups of better-armed fighters. The plot of *The Professionals* becomes further complicated when the hired gunmen finally locate the captive ranch wife, Maria (Claudia Cardinale), and discover that she doesn't want to be rescued after all. As they eventually learn, Maria was sold into marriage by her father and prefers to stay with her alleged captor, who is actually her lover (Jack Palance). Here the larger social values that the hired professionals are meant to uphold prove to be compromised, the community bonds they are supposed to shore up not worthy of defense.

Such social and moral breakdown also marks the lives of the gunmen in *Saving Private Perez*. In Gómez's film, the group Julián hires to rescue his brother includes a prisoner in a maximum security facility who is a member of a rival drug cartel, as well as an old friend who once served in Vietnam and went on to a life of violence but now lives in comfortable retirement hiding out in Beverly Hills. After the group learns about their rescue mission, one of the hired professionals asks Julián, "Where the hell's Iraq?" His reply—"Everyone knows . . . it's right next to Kuwait, Saudi Arabia, Spain, and Holland"—is telling in its own right. While it pokes fun at the ways these men do not know the geography they are entering and cannot locate the country on a map, the conversation also provides commentary on the larger predicaments Mexico faces in the post-9/11 era. While their powerful northern neighbor fights a war against terrorism that has little or nothing to do with lives south of the border, Mexicans have been drawn into this larger conflict and forced to fight battles that are not of their own making. With a renewed panic surfacing about Latinx immigration and how it allegedly imperils the safety and future of the United States, Mexico also finds itself located in what José Fusté calls a "racial triangulation" that connects America's old and new enemies. As he points out, there is an important linkage in the post-9/11 era between how Arabs and/or Muslims are "criminalized as the foreign enemies of the United States abroad" and the ways in which contemporary "Latino/a border crossers are also criminalized as foreign enemies 'at our doorstep.'"[8]

Extending these observations, David Lloyd and Laura Pulido suggest that Latinxs in turn may have been subject to the "great-

Fig. 18. Mexicans and Iraqis in *Saving Private Perez*
(directed by Beto Gómez, 2011), from the DVD.

est collateral damage" of any group in the post-9/11 period.⁹ As
they point out,

> The inequality that characterizes U.S.-Mexico relations is fueled
> by a racism that dates back to the Spanish conquest, was solidi-
> fied during the Mexican-American War, and has continually been
> rearticulated against both Mexico and the ethnic Mexican popu-
> lation in the United States over the course of the twentieth and
> twenty-first centuries. Its latest manifestation began in the 1990s
> with the growing anti-immigration sentiment and the militariza-
> tion of the U.S.-Mexico border, both of which reached a crescendo
> in the post-9/11 era, as seen in Arizona's SB 1070, and with recent
> State Department suggestions that Mexico itself is a "failed state."¹⁰

These connections become important in Gómez's film. While
Saving Private Perez indicates that Julián's life as a violent gangster is morally indefensible, the film's critique is equally directed
toward the larger American presence that pulls Mexican lives into
its global orbit. While the promise of greater economic opportunities initially draws the younger brother Juan into service in the
U.S. Army and he is later kidnapped by a radical faction of armed
rebels, so the older brother Julián decides to enter the lucrative

but dangerous international drug trade, which becomes a powerful force in the borderlands during the era of the North American Free Trade Agreement and globalization.

These geopolitical remappings of the post–Cold War period
militarize the borderlands in ways that profoundly affect Mexican and Mexican American lives. In *Saving Private Perez*, the professional gunmen find an unexpected ally in the Russian bandit
Sasha Boginski, who locates weapons for them in Istanbul and
secures their safe passage from Turkey to Iraq. "We'll travel the traditional way," Sasha tells the hired professionals. What follows is a
deliberately staged over-the-the top sequence featuring the group
slowly making their way across the desert on camels in a sand-
storm, a scene that is reminiscent of David Lean's neo-imperial
Western, *Lawrence of Arabia* (1962). The movie offers other cinematic references as well, from war films to spaghetti Westerns and
from martial arts films to African American neo-noir. The title of
Gómez's movie, for instance, recalls the triumphant and improbable rescue plot of Stephen Spielberg's World War II film *Saving
Private Ryan* (1998). At another point, Gómez's film features a bus
that pulls out to reveal a row of hired killers in a scene replaying
an iconic moment in Sergio Leone's *Once Upon a Time in the West*
(1968), when a train moves away to reveal the figure of Harmon-
ica, played by Charles Bronson. Finally, another visual sequence
involves a battle scene in Iraq that slows down the action as a way
of mingling fight scenes from Ang Lee's *Crouching Tiger, Hidden
Dragon* (2000), with the sideways exchange of gunfire capturing a
moment from the Hughes brothers' *Menace II Society* (1993).

In the "making-of-the-movie" featurette included in the DVD
version, the director describes *Saving Private Perez* as a modern-
day Western and a film about family as it searches for forgiveness
and redemption. The movie concludes on this note, with news
reporters covering the successful rescue of the captive Mexican soldier by the hired professionals. While the film implicitly critiques
government failures to curb poverty and corruption and likewise
ends with an intertitle explaining that Julián died three months
later in a bloody ambush along with other drug dealers, Mexico

is also redeemed at the end of the story. Television reporters at the close of the film celebrate the rescue mission, noting that Mexican forces were able to get in and out of Iraq quickly, completing their mission of finding the soldier without entering a war that isn't in their own interests. At the same time, the television reporters imply that the United States has not been quite as effective, having become involved in a prolonged military engagement and having yet to determine its own exit strategy. By the end of *Saving Private Perez*, the Western's frequent divisions between savagery and civilization are dismantled, as a new cast of heroes appears on-screen in a transformation that counters the vilification of Mexicans and Mexican Americans and that also avoids demonizing Arabs and Muslims as new enemies in the war on terror.

Arab Cowgirls and the Global Frontier

In the music video "Ahlan Ezayak" featuring the Saudi-Kuwaiti singer Shams, a similar disruption of the savagery/civilization binary provides a critical take on the United States' post-9/11 global mission. Early in Shams's music video, words at the top of the screen credit the singer along with the "featured artist" George W. Bush, who had, at the time the video was first posted in 2007, entered the second half of his second term in office. The president's simulated appearance in the video is a clever reversal of the manner in which U.S. foreign policy has played out in the Middle East. Just as the administration often inserted itself into political matters across the region without prior support or approval, so the music video features the unwitting participation of members of the Bush administration in a counternarrative that centers on an avenging cowgirl who seeks justice in the war on terror and whose actions ultimately lead to the defeat of the American hyperpower.

"Ahlan Ezayak" is Egyptian-Arabic slang for "Hi, how are you?"[11] The music video soon cuts to the figure who will eventually emerge as the Arab "cowgirl" in this desert showdown. First, however, she is positioned in front of the White House delivering speeches at press conferences or against various backdrops across Iraq and the Middle East. Meanwhile, the president's face appears as a digitized

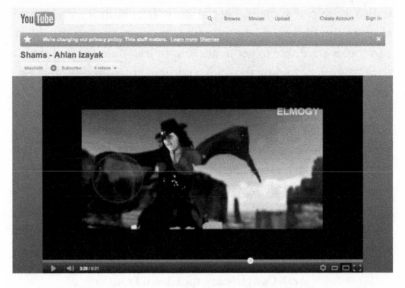

Fig. 19. The avenging Arab "cowgirl" in Shams's "Ahlan Ezayak" music video (2007), from YouTube.

cardboard cut-out, a political figure who is not fully in control of his actions and policies. The point is emphasized later in the video as the woman unmasks the figure, revealing underneath the faces of Donald Rumsfeld and Condoleezza Rice as the real powers in charge of the administration's actions in the region. Functioning as a satire about the cowboy hero on the new global frontier, the music video turns 9/11 discourses against themselves, staging a desert battle in which the Arab cowgirl is forced to secure the conditions for freedom and democracy across the Middle East. The video has gained popularity on the Internet, where it has been described as a protest song and where it has garnered several thousand hits on the many different versions posted online, including one featuring English translations of the lyrics. The music video has also sparked a lively discussion about its portrayal of the United States and the Iraq War in online comments posted in both Arabic and English on YouTube.[12]

As the "featured artist" in the music video, the former president is seen bobbing to the music along with the pop singer, who eventually takes over the podium and the command of the microphone, thus usurping the administration's power and, by extension, the power of American media in determining and directing news coverage of the Middle East. Struggles over representation appear center stage in the video, which offers a critical montage of key moments in U.S.–Middle East relations. The video begins with the camera zooming in on various stories featured in Arabic-language newspapers, each of which offers a counterperspective on the debates and struggles shaping politics and life in the region. At one point, a figure representing Secretary of State Condoleezza Rice appears as Lady Liberty in gown and torch, dancing to the music's beat in the middle of New York City's Times Square. The scene features the famous icon of American national identity, which has often been subjected to criticism in struggles and debates about citizenship, immigration, and belonging, as well as democracy, freedom, and independence. One historian has remarked that Lady Liberty herself began life as "a gift that no one wanted" after the original statue, which the French sculptor Frédéric Bartholdi initially modeled after an Egyptian *fellah*, was rejected for the opening of the Suez Canal.[13]

Here American liberty is depicted as a gift that Arab populations also do not particularly wish to receive. As such, the image provides an instance of the diverse and conflicted understandings that often reshape U.S. national icons, narratives, and values as they move across international spaces. Brian T. Edwards and Dilip Parameshwar Gaonkar examine this discrepancy, addressing what they call the "vernacular" approach to interpreting American foundational texts. For the critics, local or nation-based readings frequently provide provincial and limited ways of understanding the circulation of U.S. cultural texts in global contexts. In turn, they suggest that scholars adopt a more "cosmopolitan" reading of the field's foundational stories as these narratives travel and gain new meanings across the world.[14] As shown in the music video, such narrow, vernacular understandings of Lady Liberty as a symbol of freedom do not travel particularly well in the post-9/11 Middle

East but are often subjected to scrutiny and critique by populations vilified in the war on terror.

Later in the video, Secretary of State Rice reappears in an arena as a professional boxer dressed in a flowing robe, calling to mind an Apollo Creed/Rocky Balboa rematch as the singer and the secretary of state fight it out once again on a global stage. In the scene, the Arab protagonist, as Apollo Creed, proves to be a formidable foe to defeat, as are the lingering humiliations of the "Vietnam syndrome," which are recalled here through references to the 1976 movie. In another scene, the music video's heroine appears on the White House lawn, her body stretched across large block letters that spell out "GUANTANAMO." The character is featured in the odalisque position often favored in orientalist art traditions in Europe and the United States, her body draped across the word "Guantanamo" as a reminder of the Arab and Muslim captives in the war on terror. Later the video takes on racial profiling as well, setting one scene in a jail as two females in Bedouin clothing are photographed in a mug shot after their arrest.

In the music video, the American presence in Iraq appears not as a liberating force that brings freedom and democracy but as the embodiment of military aggression, political violence, and social restriction. At one point, the heroine sings and dances in the Iraqi desert while U.S. soldiers fight nearby. The soldiers seem ineffectual as they conduct their mission, stumbling aimlessly through the landscape, firing shots that miss their mark, and falling over each other as they engage in a futile battle against their desert enemy. Again, large block letters appear in the background of the music video, this time spelling out "DEMOCRACY." Eventually, the female protagonist fights off an approaching American marine, who falls into the desert sand, defeated by the blow of her arm. It is significant that the music video figures the conflict in gendered terms; in the colonial fantasies that shape U.S. justifications for invading Iraq, the Middle East is often imagined as a place of subservient, oppressed women needing to be saved from despotic male leaders.[15] In the video, however, the U.S. hero offers no political salvation. Instead, American militarized masculinity undergoes scrutiny

Fig. 20. The female figure counters cowboy diplomacy in Shams's "Ahlan Ezayak" music video (2007), from YouTube.

in a scene that cuts to images of Sylvester Stallone's iconic character, John Rambo. The scene depicts Rambo as the poster boy for failed U.S. interventions across the world, a figure who has not weathered the years too well. Indeed, Rambo appears in the video as a scrawny, over-the-hill mercenary of a bygone era, a shirtless gunman with atrophied muscles who is still determined to enact vengeance against his enemies, blasting his machine gun across the jungle, letting out a crazed laugh as he takes aim against his global enemies.

Toward the end of the video, the Arab cowgirl experiences political victory. In her western-style hat and dark clothing, she stands on a platform in the desert, looking face to face at the U.S. president, her cowboy opponent. He advances toward her, only to have her knock him off the platform. He plunges downward, ending up on his back in the desert sand. Block letters spelling out "LIB-ERTY" fall, landing on top of him as jail bars come down. The music video closes with a final image that announces the end of cowboy diplomacy in the Middle East, exposing the project as an ineffective and counterproductive foreign policy.

Ultimately, these two global Westerns disengage from the narrowly defined and limiting scripts that cast rigid divisions between heroes and outlaws in the war on terror. By foregrounding the per-

Fig. 21. Liberty behind bars in Shams's "Ahlan Ezayak"
music video (2007), from YouTube.

spective of those populations who were targeted after 9/11, these
texts question how the Western has been recently deployed in
international contexts, refuse their restrictive forms of morality,
and reimagine a vastly different purpose for the genre. In doing
so, these revisionist narratives reactivate the ideological diversity
and fluidity of meanings that—as I have argued throughout this
study—have been central to the genre from its very beginnings.
Recently, certain uses of the Western ignored the complexities of
meaning inscribed in its plots, overlooking how writers and filmmakers throughout history have often employed the form to ask
difficult questions about the limits of the American civilizing mission, the problems of using violence to resolve political disputes, the
underside of hypermasculine imperatives, and the consequences
of dehumanizing and dispossessing racial, national, or ethnic Others. In that sense, these global Westerns struggle against another
form of captivity, rescuing the genre from its state of confinement
in order to imagine new ways of understanding how populations
might interact and treat each other in ever-changing and unequal
global contexts.

Conclusion

NOTES

Introduction

1. For more on the Western as a genre able to address a number of competing positions and issues, see Robinson, *Having It Both Ways*; Tatum, "Problem of the Popular in the New Western History," 164; and Campbell, *Rhizomatic West*, 130.

2. For an overview of captivity as a central element in popular Westerns, see Countryman, "Captivity Narratives," 78–81.

3. Baepler, *White Slaves, African Masters*, xii.

4. Sayre, "Renegades from Barbary," 348.

5. Sayre, "Renegades from Barbary," 349.

6. Amy Kaplan examines transnational and imperial elements of the Western in "Romancing the Empire." For a reading of *Ben Hur* (1959) as a Western set in the Middle East, see Allmendinger, *Ten Most Wanted*, 105–22.

7. Gregory, *Colonial Present*, 11.

8. Gregory, *Colonial Present*, 10.

9. El Hamamsy and Soliman, "Introduction," 6.

10. See Rowe, "American Orientalism after Said."

11. I borrow the notion of "having it both ways" from Forrest G. Robinson, who describes a similar strategy of evasion in popular Westerns in *Having It Both Ways*.

12. E. Wright, *Generation Kill*, 360; Buzzell, *My War*, 258.

13. Pritchard, *Ambush Alley*, 305. For critical studies of the Jessica Lynch story, see Woods, "Cowboys, Indians, and Iraq"; Tucker and Walton, "From General's Daughter to Coal Miner's Daughter"; and Faludi, *Terror Dream*, 165–95.

14. Byrd, *Transit of Empire*, xiii.

15. Byrd, *Transit of Empire*, xii–xiii.

16. Crawford, *Last True Story I'll Ever Tell*, 33, 54.

17. Filkins, *Forever War*, 310.

18. Abrams, *Fobbit*, 20, 47 (italics in original).

19. I thank Van Zimmerman for offering the term "entrepreneurial Western" to me. For a reading of capitalist development in the genre, see also French, *Westerns*, 143.

20. Abrams, *Fobbit*, 52, 170–71.

21. Naylor, *Not a Good Day to Die*, 285.

22. Fick, *One Bullet Away*, 122.

23. Goodman, *Translating Southwestern Landscapes*, 42.

24. Francaviglia, *Go East, Young Man*, viii.

25. For an astute reading of a similar comparative logic in the exploration of the American Southwest, see Lubin, "'We Are All Israelis.'"

26. Fountain, *Billy Lynn's Long Halftime Walk*, 222.

27. Fountain, *Billy Lynn's Long Halftime Walk*, 2 ("nina leven," "terrRist," "currj"), 148 ("*acks* of *sack-rih-fice*"), 38 ("*soooh-preeeeeme* sacrifice," "dih-mock-cruh-see"), 219 ("dubya em dees").

28. Fountain, *Billy Lynn's Long Halftime Walk*, 174.

29. Fountain, *Billy Lynn's Long Halftime Walk*, 172–73.

30. Fountain, *Billy Lynn's Long Halftime Walk*, 193.

31. Gibson, *Pattern Recognition*, 37, 55, 60.

32. Proulx, "Tits-Up in a Ditch," 184, 189, 194, 195.

33. Proulx, "Tits-Up in a Ditch," 203, 214.

34. Proulx, "Tits-Up in a Ditch," 218.

35. Proulx, "Tits-Up in a Ditch," 214.

36. LeMenager, "Imagining the Frontier," 515, 516.

37. Ghosh, "Petrofiction," 75.

38. Vitalis, "Wallace Stegner's Arabian Discovery," 410.

39. Vitalis, "Wallace Stegner's Arabian Discovery," 408. Recently, scholars in environmental humanities have revisited Stegner's account. See, for instance, Ziser, "Oil Desert," 81; and LeMenager, *Living Oil*, 94. The novelist Philipp Meyer also examines the oil encounter in his novel about Texas, frontier violence, and capitalist development. See Meyer, *Son*, 85, 503.

40. Barnes, *In the Kingdom of Men*, 55.

41. Barnes, *In the Kingdom of Men*, 71.

42. Barnes, *In the Kingdom of Men*, 75.

43. Barnes, *In the Kingdom of Men*, 142.

44. Barnes, *In the Kingdom of Men*, 259.

45. Barnes, *In the Kingdom of Men*, 260.

46. Barnes, *In the Kingdom of Men*, 234.

47. Shohat and Alsultany, "Cultural Politics of 'the Middle East,'" 27.

48. Behdad, *Forgetful Nation*, ix.

49. R. Wilson, "Afterword," 212.

50. Riverbend, *Baghdad Burning*, 261. Sara Spurgeon has recently offered important insights into twenty-first-century global studies of the frontier in "Incidentally Western."

51. Riverbend, *Baghdad Burning II*, 44.

52. Rice's visit is recounted in a *Ynetnews* article entitled "Playing Wild West in West Bank."

53. Lynch, "'Nothing But Land,'" 377.

54. Darwish, "Speech of the Red Indian." For a useful related discussion of U.S. frontier discourses in the Middle East, see W. J. T. Mitchell, "Holy Landscapes."

55. Deloria, *Playing Indian*, 37.

56. For a discussion of how a nineteenth-century European fascination with Native Americans led to other instances of "playing Indian," see Rydell and Kroes, *Buffalo Bill in Bologna*, 107–17. For more on practices of survivance, see Vizenor, *Manifest Manners*.

57. Lubin, "'We Are All Israelis,'" 673.

58. For useful overviews of the genre in literary history, see Slotkin, *Gun-fighter Nation*. For the emergence of the genre in film, see Simmon, *Invention of the Western Film*.

59. For a representative list, see Drinnon, *Facing West*; Bold, "Rough Riders at Home and Abroad"; Shohat, *Taboo Memories, Diasporic Voices*; Fusté, "Containing Bordered 'Others' in La Frontera and Gaza," 814; and Sabine, "Home and Abroad."

60. Dyer, *White*, 33.

61. Hassan, *Immigrant Narratives*, 9.

62. Shohat and Stam, *Unthinking Eurocentrism*, 2.

63. Shohat and Stam, *Unthinking Eurocentrism*, 2; Comer, "West," 239.

64. Laachir and Talajooy, *Resistance in Middle Eastern Culture*, 2.

1. "I Longed to Be an Arab"

1. G. White, *Eastern Establishment*, 6.

2. G. White, *Eastern Establishment*, 21.

3. G. White, *Eastern Establishment*, 7.

4. Bold, *Frontier Club*, xvii.

5. Bold, *Frontier Club*, xviii.

6. Bold, *Frontier Club*, xvii.

7. Wills, "Nervous Origins of the American Western," 293. See also Tuttle, "Rewriting the West Cure."

8. Wills, "Nervous Origins of the American Western," 293.

9. Wills, "Nervous Origins of the American Western," 294.

10. Wills, "Nervous Origins of the American Western," 295.

11. Said, *Out of Place*, 232.

12. Simmon, *Invention of the Western Film*, 22.

13. Arthur Schlesinger Jr., quoted in French, "Western," 14; Newman, *Wild West Movies*, 2.

14. Denning, *Mechanic Accents*, 20. John G. Cawelti notes connections between the colonial adventure novels by authors such as H. Rider Haggard and the codes and conventions of the Western in his *Six-Gun Mystique Sequel*, 25. Marta Kvande and Sara Spurgeon have argued a case for recognizing the birth of the Western in Charlotte Lennox's novel *The Life of Harriot Stuart* (1750), which provides the first fictionalized account of captivity while addressing the experience of creolization in the colonies. See Kvande and Spurgeon, "Removes of Harriot Stuart."

15. Altman, *Film/Genre*, 36.

16. Altman, *Film/Genre*, 37–38. Of course, as Christopher Frayling points out, by the 1960s spaghetti Westerns complicated this link between the genre's film production and American landscapes. See Frayling, *Spaghetti Westerns*.

17. Pratt, "Arts of the Contact Zone." Shelley Streeby traces the emergence of what she calls the "Mexican Western" in reading an inter-American popular culture that "invites the rethinking of models of the 'West' that isolate the U.S. nation-state from other imperial, national, and cultural histories." Streeby, *American Sensations*, 247.

18. Slotkin, *Gunfighter Nation*, 149.

19. Ella Shohat makes a similar case in *Taboo Memories, Diasporic Voices*, 17–69.

20. Cawelti, *Six-Gun Mystique Sequel*, 45. There are some distinctions to be made between different imperial practices and productions of orientalist discourse. While the Western helped circulate ideas about the moral certainty of U.S. expansion, due in part to the elevated qualities of its hero, scholars have noted that, in some cases, American nation-building during the late nineteenth century faced racial conflicts and concerns about whiteness that helped distinguish it from European imperialism and orientalist representation in the same time period. Scholars have argued that some U.S. expansionists in the late nineteenth century wanted to avoid arguments about "racial uplift," "manifest destiny," or the "white man's burden" in order to sidestep a larger racial panic that was developing over empire. As Eric T. L. Love argues, for instance, some expansionists recognized the potential the language might have in hindering imperialist projects, especially as fears circulated that expansionism would increase the nation's nonwhite population. Love indicates that even as these expansionists were not themselves antiracist, some of them tried to avoid using race-based arguments in advancing their cause. In this way, it may be difficult to argue for a simple, direct correspondence between European and U.S. imperialism and orientalism, although moments of overlap and similarity exist that are certainly worth noting. See Love, *Race over Empire*, xi–xx, 120. For a related discussion of racial discourses and American national identity in this context, see Gerstle, *American Crucible*.

21. Cawelti, *Six-Gun Mystique Sequel*, 25.

22. Cracroft, "American West of Karl May," 252.

23. May, *Jack Hildreth on the Nile*, 2.

24. For a useful discussion of May's writing in the context of the European scramble for Africa, see Ferens, "Confidence Man in Africa."

25. Roosevelt, *Diaries of Boyhood and Youth*, 276.

26. Nance, *How the Arabian Nights Inspired the American Dream*, 19.

27. Roosevelt, *Diaries of Boyhood and Youth*, 283.

28. Obenzinger, *American Palestine*, xvii–xviii.

29. Obenzinger, *American Palestine*, 5.

30. Obenzinger, *American Palestine*, xii.

31. Twain, *Innocents Abroad*, 411.

32. Twain, *Innocents Abroad*, 486.

33. Twain's lampooning of William C. Prime is addressed in Regan, "Heroism."

34. Prime, *Boat Life in Egypt and Nubia*, 416.

35. Prime, *Boat Life in Egypt and Nubia*, 103–4.

36. Prime, *Tent Life in the Holy Land*, 197.

37. Twain, *Innocents Abroad*, 532.

38. Twain, *Innocents Abroad*, 520.

39. Twain, *Innocents Abroad*, 591.

40. Twain, *Innocents Abroad*, 540.

41. The term "Arab-as-Indian" comes from Lubin, "'We Are All Israelis,'" 688. For an astute analysis of Twain's "comparative racialization" for another literary context, see Hsu, "Vagrancy and Comparative Racialization."

42. Twain, *Innocents Abroad*, 486.

43. Twain, *Innocents Abroad*, 514, 546.

44. Twain, *Innocents Abroad*, 472, 473.

45. Twain, *Innocents Abroad*, 473.

46. Obenzinger, *American Palestine*, 164.

47. Twain, *Innocents Abroad*, 547.

48. Twain, *Innocents Abroad*, 477.

49. Twain, *Innocents Abroad*, 477.

50. Obenzinger, *American Palestine*, 157–58, 179.

51. Grey, *Wildfire*, 16. The Arab reference likewise appears briefly in Grey, *Young Lion Hunter*, 141. See a discussion of Grey's treatment of Mormonism in Handley, *Marriage, Violence, and the Nation*, 97–124.

52. Twain, *Roughing It*, 158. See also the discussion in Bold, "Rough Riders at Home and Abroad."

53. Taylor and Maar, *American Cowboy*, 64.

54. Taylor and Maar, *American Cowboy*, 64.

55. Roosevelt, *Ranch Life and the Hunting-Trail*, 6.

56. Bold, *Frontier Club*, 91.

57. Bold, *Frontier Club*, 91–92.

58. For more on the invention of the term "Middle East," see Marr, "Strangers in the Spider's House," 191.

59. Nicholas, *Becoming Western*, 2–3.

60. Wister quoted in Bold, *Selling the Wild West*, 38.

61. Nicholas, *Becoming Western*, 3–4.

62. Wister, "Evolution of the Cow-Puncher," 614.

63. Wister, "Evolution of the Cow-Puncher," 603–4.

64. Wister, "Evolution of the Cow-Puncher," 604.

65. Wister, "Evolution of the Cow-Puncher," 612.

66. Colley, "La Jineta," 32.

67. Colley, "La Jineta," 34–35.

68. At one point in "Evolution of the Cow-Puncher," Wister mentions in passing that the superiority of the American horses of the western plains, whose intelligence, after having run "wild for a century or two" and after having "gathered the sundry experiences of war and peace, of being stolen, and of being abandoned in the show at inconvenient distances from home," brings them "a wit sharper than the street Arab's" (608). Here the author references an Arab presence through a fleeting allusion to a particular group of urban immigrants who were called "street Arabs," a term that, beginning in the nineteenth century, was used to describe first-generation Syrian immigrants who often worked as pack peddlers in U.S. cities. "Street Arabs" became the phrase used to describe itinerant merchants who were often associated with the chaos of urban spaces and who carried the threatening prospect of racial otherness and nonassimilation into American culture. For more on the figure of the "street Arab" in nineteenth-century American literature, see Berman, *American Arabesque*, 179–84.

69. Ackerman, *American Orientalists*, 162.

70. For a discussion of U.S. orientalist painters and the American West, see Dippie, "Visual West," 680–86.

71. Simmon, *Invention of the Western Film*, 52.

72. Simmon, *Invention of the Western Film*, 39.

73. Nemerov, *Frederic Remington and Turn-of-the-Century America*, 97.

74. For a discussion of melancholy and mourning in Remington's work, see Nemerov, *Frederic Remington and Turn-of-the-Century America*, 146–47; and Tatum, *In the Remington Moment*, 88–95.

75. Wister quoted in Samuels and Samuels, *Frederic Remington*, 168.

76. Bigelow, *Seventy Summers*, 312.

77. Bigelow, *Seventy Summers*, 312.

78. Bigelow, "French Fighters in Africa," 368.

79. Bigelow, "French Fighters in Africa," 369.

80. Bigelow, "French Fighters in Africa," 372.

81. Bigelow, *Seventy Summers*, 315.

82. Berger, *About Looking*, 6–10.

83. Lears, *No Place of Grace*, xv.

84. Remington, "Gallop through the Midway," 111.

85. Tatum, *In the Remington Moment*, 104.

86. Remington, "Gallop through the Midway," 112.

87. Remington, "Gallop through the Midway," 112.

88. Papanikolas, "Cowboy and the Gaucho," 179.

89. Papanikolas, "Cowboy and the Gaucho," 179.

90. Remington, "Gallop through the Midway," 111.

91. Remington, "Gallop through the Midway," 112.

2. From the Moors

1. Campbell, *Rhizomatic West*, 2. For an overview of transnational critiques of the West as a bounded region, see Anzaldúa, *Borderlands/La Frontera*; Saldívar, *Border Matters*; Lowe, *Immigrant Acts*; King, *Truth about Stories*; and Wrobel and Steiner, *Many Wests*.

2. The "frontier thesis" is outlined in Frederick Jackson Turner's essay, "The Significance of the Frontier in American History" (1893), included in Turner, *Frontier in American History*, 1–38. For representative critiques of the Turnerian model from the perspective of transnational studies, see Tatum, "Postfrontier Horizons"; Campbell, *Rhizomatic West*; Comer, "Exceptionalism, Other Wests, Critical Regionalism"; and Kollin, "Global West."

3. See Willis, *Portents of the Real*, 125; and Kollin, "Introduction," ix–x. Pres. Barack Obama's administration deployed the rhetoric as well, adopting the code name "Geronimo" in spring 2011 to refer to the capture and killing of Osama bin Laden.

4. I borrow the term "un-American" from Kim Newman's study of international Westerns in *Wild West Movies*. Wai Chee Dimock also uses the term "un-American" in her discussion of Washington Irving in "Hemispheric Islam."

5. Dimock, "Hemispheric Islam," 32.

6. Dimock, "Hemispheric Islam," 33.

7. Many of these popular terms are themselves imprecise. For instance, the "Middle East" as a signifier for a particular transnational region, insofar as it often also includes North Africa, is geographically imprecise. Ella Shohat and Evelyn Alsultany note what they call the "inaccuracy and even Orientalist history of the term 'Middle East'" yet are compelled to use the concept, as it speaks to a diversity that is otherwise difficult to address. As they explain, the term "evokes the variegated identities, including Amazigh/Berbers, Arab-Christians, Arab-Jews, Armenians, Chaldeans, Copts, Druze, Kurds, Iranians, Nubians, Turks, which do not easily fall under the 'Arab-Muslim' rubric." The term also speaks to "the complexity of Middle Eastern diasporic formations within and in relation to diverse spaces—at their point of departure and at their point of

arrival, as well as in their continuous multiple cross-border movements." Shohat and Alsultany, "Cultural Politics of the Middle East,'" 20–21. The concept of Old and New Worlds is also problematic, encoding a colonizer's view of the so-called "discovery" of the Americas.

8. The list may be found online at "Mrs. Laura Bush's Family Favorites."

9. The term "Arab world" has been widely critiqued. Joseph A. Massad describes the concept as a "colonial appellation" in *Desiring Arabs*, 2. The term likewise carries hints of the "clash of civilizations" discourse and empties out the national, religious, and other forms of diversity found among Arab populations across the world. See Said, "Window on the World."

10. Shohat, "Sephardic-Moorish Atlantic," 51.

11. Shohat, "Sephardic-Moorish Atlantic," 55.

12. Shohat, "Sephardic-Moorish Atlantic," 50. Elsewhere, Robert Stam and Ella Shohat argue that Columbus may be seen as the "ur-orientalist" through his active role in "globalizing Iberian Orientalist discourses by linking the *indias occidentales* and the *indias orientales*." Stam and Shohat, "Whence and Whither Postcolonial Theory?," 373.

13. Shohat, "Sephardic-Moorish Atlantic," 59.

14. Shohat, "Sephardic-Moorish Atlantic," 47.

15. Stoler, "Introduction," 3.

16. Critics have discussed the scene in different manners. For a study of imperialism and orientalism in Cather's novel, see Goodman, *Translating Southwestern Landscapes*, 140, 153–64; and Godfrey, "Willa Cather's *Death Comes for the Archbishop*." For an analysis of large-scale history, time, and space in Cather's work, see Daiches, *Willa Cather*; and Tsunoda, "Study on Willa Cather's *Death Comes for the Archbishop*." For a reading of Spanish North America more generally, see Broncano, "Willa Cather's Hispanic Epiphanies." For a cosmopolitan reading of the bell and analysis of how Cather "conflates Christianity and Islam," see Reynolds, *Willa Cather in Context*, 160–61. For a discussion of the "blended sounds" of the bell interconnecting different histories and cultural experiences, see Dean, *Travel Narratives from New Mexico*, 60–62. For an analysis of estrangement and interconnection, master narratives, and religious difference, see S. Wilson, "Material Objects as Sites of Cultural Mediation." For a reading of everyday practices and the uses of objects as signs and agents of historical change, see Lima, "Willa Cather's Rewriting of the Historical Novel."

17. Cather, *Death Comes for the Archbishop*, 44.

18. Cather, *Death Comes for the Archbishop*, 44.

19. Cather, *Death Comes for the Archbishop*, 45.

20. Cather, *Death Comes for the Archbishop*, 44.

21. Stoler, "Introduction," 21.

22. Stoler, "Introduction," 9.

23. Stoler, "Introduction," 7.

24. Klaus P. Stich argues a similar point, writing that for Father Vaillant "the bell's original purpose and dedication complements its present service in his proselytizing mission in New Mexico." Stich, "Cather's 'Midi Romanesque,'" 60.

25. For more on the microranking of whiteness in the twentieth-century United States, see Mills, *Racial Contract*, 78–81; and Flory, "Ethnicity and Race in American Film Noir," 391–96.

26. Cather, *Death Comes for the Archbishop*, 5.

27. For further discussion, see Stam and Shohat, "Whence and Whither Post-colonial Theory?," 373.

28. For more on the complexities of racial classification across the Mediterranean, see Hassan, *Immigrant Narratives*, 15.

29. Cather, *Death Comes for the Archbishop*, 4.

30. B. Brown, *Material Unconscious*, 4.

31. B. Brown, *Material Unconscious*, 14.

32. B. Brown, *Material Unconscious*, 5.

33. Cather, "Novel Démeublé," 43.

34. Cather, "Novel Démeublé," 45.

35. Cather, "Novel Démeublé," 50.

36. Cather, "Novel Démeublé," 48.

37. Cather, "Novel Démeublé," 51.

38. Cather describes the essay as the "best paper" among the pieces published in *Not under Forty* in her letter to Alfred Knopf dated May 1, 1936, in Jewell and Stout, *Selected Letters of Willa Cather*, 515.

39. This body of work is vast; for a representative list of queer scholarship about Cather, see O'Brien, "'Thing Not Named'"; Sedgwick, "Across Gender, Across Sexuality"; Lindemann, *Willa Cather*; Goldberg, *Willa Cather and Others*; Hackett, "Jezebel and Sapphira"; and Nealon, *Foundlings*, 61–97.

40. Nealon, *Foundlings*, 62.

41. Cather, "Novel Démeublé," 47.

42. See Stout, "Introduction."

43. Cather, "Novel Démeublé," 45.

44. For textual references to *The Arabian Nights*, Holy Land tours, Egyptian mummies and obelisks, orientalist painting, and Arabian spices in Cather's work, see March and Arnold, *Reader's Companion to the Fiction of Willa Cather*.

45. Nealon, *Foundlings*, 63.

46. Nealon, *Foundlings*, 71.

47. Nealon, *Foundlings*, 68.

48. Nealon acknowledges that marriage is a plotline in Thea's life story but that it is largely downplayed by Cather and is relegated to a minor role in the novel. See Nealon, *Foundlings*, 73–74.

49. Cather quoted in Nealon, *Foundlings*, 72.

50. Nealon, *Foundlings*, 72.

51. Nealon, *Foundlings*, 73, 74.

52. For more on Egyptomania in the United States, see Schueller, *American Orientalisms*; and Brier, *Egyptomania*.

53. For further discussion of the Anglo construction of the desert Southwest, see Goodman, *Translating Southwestern Landscapes*, xvi–xvii.

54. Cather, *Death Comes for the Archbishop*, 27, 28.

55. See, for instance, Auerbach, *Explorers in Eden*; and Francaviglia, *Go East, Young Man*, 126–54.

56. Obenzinger, *American Palestine*, 5. For more on how cultural production about the Holy Land played into post–World War II negotiations of U.S. national identity, see McAlister, *Epic Encounters*, 43–83.

57. Cather, *Death Comes for the Archbishop*, 30.

58. Cather, *Death Comes for the Archbishop*, 95.

59. Quayson, "Sighs of History," 360.

60. Cather to Elizabeth Shepley Sergeant, April 20, 1912, in Jewell and Stout, *Selected Letters of Willa Cather*, 150.

61. Cather to Elizabeth Shepley Sergeant, April 20, 1912, in Jewell and Stout, *Selected Letters of Willa Cather*, 151.

62. Cather, *Death Comes for the Archbishop*, 183.

63. Lubin, "'We Are All Israelis,'" 688.

64. Flint and Flint, *Documents of the Coronado Expedition*, 381.

65. Shohat and Stam, *Unthinking Eurocentrism*, 60. Nadine Naber likewise points out that various "scholars have argued that images of 'the Arab' are rooted in images of the 'Muslim' as a dark and evil Other that were transposed from the Byzantines to western Europeans and European colonists during the period of the rise of Islam and later, to the Americas." Naber, "Introduction," 23.

66. Rana, "Story of Islamophobia," 150.

67. Rana, "Story of Islamophobia," 151.

68. Rana, "Story of Islamophobia," 152.

69. Cather, *Death Comes for the Archbishop*, 100.

70. Mignolo, *Idea of Latin America*, 8. He notes that Fanon describes the colonial experience as a "suffocation," while Anzaldúa depicts it as an "open wound," 74.

71. Mignolo, *Idea of Latin America*, 8.

72. Mignolo, *Idea of Latin America*, 11.

73. Cather, *Death Comes for the Archbishop*, 274.

74. Cather, *Death Comes for the Archbishop*, 275.

75. Cather, *Death Comes for the Archbishop*, 276.

76. B. Brown, *Sense of Things*, 86.

77. B. Brown, *Sense of Things*, 127.

78. Fischer, "Pastoralism and Its Discontents," 36–37.

79. Cather to Sarah Orne Jewett, October 24, 1908, in Jewell and Stout, *Selected Letters of Willa Cather*, 116–17.

80. Cather to Alfred A. Knopf, April 19, 1938, in Jewell and Stout, *Selected Letters of Willa Cather*, 546.

81. Cather to Alfred A. Knopf, April 19, 1938, in Jewell and Stout, *Selected Letters of Willa Cather*, 547.

82. Comer, "Taking Feminism and Regionalism to the Third Wave," 113–14.

83. Comer, "Taking Feminism and Regionalism to the Third Wave," 113–14.

84. Nabhan, "Arabic in the Saddle." See also Colley, "Desert Shall Bloom."

85. For a useful discussion of national identity and the discursive function of authenticity in western American cultural production, see Handley and Lewis, *True West*, 1–20.

86. R. W. B. Lewis, *American Adam*, 5.

87. Wills, "Nervous Origins of the American Western."

88. Majid, *We Are All Moors*, x.

89. Majid, *We Are All Moors*, 62.

3. On Savagery and Civilization

1. Gualtieri, *Between Arab and White*, 33.

2. Gualtieri, *Between Arab and White*, 13.

3. Gualtieri, *Between Arab and White*, 7.

4. Gualtieri, *Between Arab and White*, 6.

5. Gualtieri, *Between Arab and White*, 33.

6. See Kasson, *Buffalo Bill's Wild West*, 4, 190.

7. Reddin, *Wild West Shows*, 128.

8. Semmerling, *"Evil" Arabs in American Popular Film*, 30–36.

9. French, "Western," 14.

10. Corkin, *Cowboys as Cold Warriors*, 3.

11. Corkin, *Cowboys as Cold Warriors*, 69.

12. McAlister, *Epic Encounters*, 11. In a similar way, Timothy Marr offers the terms "domestic orientalism" and "comparative orientalism" to speak of particular variations on the discourse. See Marr, *Cultural Roots of American Islamicism*, 11.

13. D. Brown, *American West*, 385; Reddin, *Wild West Shows*, 98.

14. Cox, *Dime Novel Companion*, 43.

15. Cox, *Dime Novel Companion*, 134.

16. Cox, *Dime Novel Companion*, 209.

17. Moses, *Wild West Shows and the Images of the American Indians*, 190–91.

18. G. Hamid, *Circus*, 34. For a useful discussion of Hamid, see also Nance, *How the Arabian Nights Inspired the American Dream*, 117–18, 131–33.

19. G. Hamid, *Circus*, 38.

20. Moses, *Wild West Shows*, 190.

21. "Buffalo Bill's Wild West Combined with Pawnee Bill's Great Far East 1909 Courier," 1.

22. "Buffalo Bill's Wild West Combined with Pawnee Bill's Great Far East 1909 Courier," 16.

23. Magee, *Irving Berlin's American Musical Theater*, 33.

24. Rydell, "Buffalo Bill's Wild West," 109.

25. Rydell, "Buffalo Bill's Wild West," 109–10.

26. Rydell, "Buffalo Bill's Wild West," 110.

27. Fields and Fields, *Annie Get Your Gun*, 13.

28. Prats, *Invisible Natives*, 2.

29. See, for instance, El-Din Aysha, review of *Hidalgo*. I thank Emad El-Din Aysha for providing me with a copy of that film review. For a discussion of the uses of the Western in the war on terrorism, see Metz, "'Mother Needs You.'" For a discussion of Hollywood's representations of Islam in the post-9/11 era, see Steinberg, "French Fries, Fezzes, and Minstrels."

30. Hopkins's autobiography was reissued by the Long Riders' Guild Press with supporting materials that document many of its apparent fabrications. See Hopkins, *Hidalgo and Other Stories*.

31. Said, *Out of Place*, 200–201.

32. Shirley R. Steinberg explains that Hollywood films about the Middle East often introduce an Arab sidekick for the Anglo hero: "Loyal and faithful to death, the Tonto-ized friend is simpler, devoutly Muslim, full of Islamic platitudes and premonitions." Steinberg, "French Fries, Fezzes, and Minstrels," 127.

33. Sharif quoted in Ghonaim, "From the Golden Crescent of Paris . . . and Back," 15.

34. Rosen, "Making of Omar Sharif," 20.

35. Rosen, "Making of Omar Sharif," 18.

36. Rosen, "Making of Omar Sharif," 19.

37. Sharif and Guinchard, *Eternal Male*, 15–16, quoted in Caton, *"Lawrence of Arabia,"* 56.

38. For an incisive reading of the film, see Banerjee and Sommerschuh, "From Sheikh to Terrorist?," 117–20.

39. For a useful discussion of the "Indian sympathy film," see Jojola, "Absurd Reality II"; and Buscombe, *"Injuns!,"* 101–50.

40. Mills, *Racial Contract*. For a discussion of the racial classification of people of the Middle East in the United States, see also McAlister, *Epic Encounters*, 37–39.

41. Cornell and Hartman, *Ethnicity and Race*, 177–78.

42. See Morgenstern, "Viggo of Arabia." Ward Churchill refers to *Dances with Wolves* as "Lawrence of South Dakota" in his book *Fantasies of the Master Race*, 239–42.

43. Sandler, *Galloping across the U.S.A.*, 8.

44. The name may also call to mind the Treaty of Guadalupe Hidalgo, which ended the U.S.-Mexico War in 1848 and ceded half a million square miles of Mexican land to the United States, including parts of the current states of Col-

orado, Arizona, and New Mexico, as well as all of the present-day states of California, Nevada, and Utah.

45. R. White, *"It's Your Misfortune and None of My Own,"* 226.

46. Wittliff, *Vaquero.*

47. See Shora, *Arab-American Handbook*, 95.

48. The literature on the contested meanings of the Statue of Liberty is vast. For a representative overview, see Trachtenberg, *Statue of Liberty*; Bodnar, "Symbols and Servants"; Wallace, "Hijacking History"; Babcock, "Taking Liberties"; and Dillon and Kotler, *Statue of Liberty Revisited.*

49. Vecoli, "Lady and the Huddled Masses," 39.

50. Bartholdi quoted in Moreno, *Statue of Liberty Encyclopedia*, 32.

51. Grigsby, "Out of Earth," 44.

52. Pasha quoted in Robinson-Dunn, *Harem, Slavery, and British Imperial Culture*, 9.

53. For a discussion of Egypt as contested geography, see Lewis and Wigen, *Myth of Continents*, 115–19; and McAlister, *Epic Encounters*, 27–29. For a discussion of Suez Canal history, see Powell, *Different Shade of Colonialism*; and Vatikiotis, *History of Modern Egypt.*

54. Emad El-Din Aysha makes this point in his review of *Hidalgo.*

55. Cawelti, *Six-Gun Mystique Sequel*, 24.

56. Tompkins, *West of Everything*, 14, 47–67.

57. See the IMDb filmography at "Zuleikha Robinson."

58. See "Repeat Offender (Women of Cover)." For a discussion of the Bush administration's appropriation of feminism in the post-9/11 era, see Ferguson and Marso, "Introduction."

59. Shohat, *Taboo Memories, Diasporic Voices*, 11, 39. Mohja Kahf points out that the rescue fantasy can be traced back to the Middle Ages in European representations of Islam in *Western Representations of the Muslim Woman.*

60. Goldstein quoted in Ferguson and Marso, "Introduction," 3.

61. El-Din Aysha, review of *Hidalgo*, 8.

62. El-Din Aysha, review of *Hidalgo*, 8.

63. For a discussion of antimodern modernism, see Lears, *No Place of Grace*, 57. For more on modernists as melancholic writers, see Chow, *Writing Diaspora*, 3–4.

64. See supporting material published in Hopkins, *Hidalgo and Other Stories*. For analyses of the historical function of Westerns, as well as the interplay between history, ideology, and narrative in the genre, see the essays in Walker, *Westerns*. Although I point out problems in treating the source material for *Hidalgo* as an authoritative historical document, I also agree with William R. Handley and Nathaniel Lewis that efforts focusing solely on exposing myths of the West replay the larger (and futile) search for authenticity that structures regional discourse. For more on this topic, see Handley and Lewis, "Introduction."

4. Persian Peddler, Egyptian Elixir

1. Rodgers and Hammerstein, *Oklahoma!*, xvi.

2. Carter, *Oklahoma!*, xi.

3. Carter, *Oklahoma!*, xi.

4. Kantor and Maslon, *Broadway*, 188.

5. Buscombe, "*Oklahoma!*"

6. Rodgers and Hammerstein, *Oklahoma!*, 25.

7. Joseph Roach discusses the romance plot in Riggs's original play as part of a "pastoral idyll" that treats Oklahoma as "synecdoche for the United States as a whole." Roach, "World Bank Drama," 180. Vickie Olsen likewise argues that the drama provides a "golden version of a courageous frontier territory which is transformed into civilized statehood through patriarchal power." Olsen, "'Persian Good-Bye' and the '*Oklahoma!* Hello,'" 273–74. Andrea Most also contends that the romantic conflicts in the musical are not merely about "the importance of choice and freedom" but carry a larger collective importance about "melding. . . . differences into a unified loving American community." Most, "'We Know We Belong to the Land,'" 79. Examining conflicts about U.S. participation in World War II and its new global role, Bruce Kirle argues that the musical stages encounters between fragmentation and resolution as a way of solving wartime tensions between isolationists and interventionists, and between conservatives and New Dealers. See Kirle, "Reconciliation, Resolution, and the Political Role of *Oklahoma!*," 251.

8. Knapp, *American Musical and the Formation of National Identity*, 124.

9. Womack, *Red on Red*, 281.

10. Womack, *Red on Red*, 279.

11. Womack, *Red on Red*, 285 (first quote), 286 (second and third quotes).

12. Als, "America, America." The article "Updated *Oklahoma!* Has a Lone Star Accent" points out that a Latinx actor had been cast in the lead.

13. Dyer, *White*, 33–34.

14. Dyer, *White*, 34

15. Dyer, *White*, 35.

16. Sandra Baringer offers brief observations about the neglect of the Syrian peddler in the play's source materials. See Baringer, "*Oklahoma!* and Assimiliation," 452.

17. Campbell, *Rhizomatic West*, 3.

18. Campbell, *Rhizomatic West*, 7.

19. For useful discussions of the diverse geographies and cultures of the region, see Wrobel and Steiner, *Many Wests*.

20. Weaver, foreword to *Cherokee Night and Other Plays*, ix–x.

21. Braunlich, *Haunted by Home*, 31.

22. Braunlich, *Haunted by Home*, 3.

23. Weaver, foreword to *Cherokee Night and Other Plays*, xix.

24. Deloria, *Indians in Unexpected Places*, 79–80.

25. Weaver, foreword to *Cherokee Night and Other Plays*, xi.

26. For more on the figure of the Syrian peddler in American culture, see Hassan, *Immigrant Narratives*, 14, 79–84; Neff, *Becoming American*, 180–81; and Sherman, Whitney, and Guerrero, *Prairie Peddlers*. Other immigrant groups, including Greeks, Italians, Armenians, and eastern European Jews, also worked as peddlers in the United States. See Neff, *Becoming American*, 129. For a discussion of Syrian peddlers in Oklahoma, see Caldwell, "From the Hills of Lebanon."

27. For more on the life and work of Syrian peddlers, see Neff, *Becoming American*, 128–266.

28. Neff, *Becoming American*, 137.

29. Riggs, *Knives from Syria*, 5.

30. Riggs, *Knives from Syria*, 6.

31. Riggs, *Knives from Syria*, 7–8.

32. Riggs, *Knives from Syria*, 18.

33. For a discussion of the influence of the *Arabian Nights* tales in American culture, see Nance, *How the Arabian Nights Inspired the American Dream*.

34. Riggs, *Knives from Syria*, 17.

35. Riggs, *Knives from Syria*, 20.

36. Riggs, *Knives from Syria*, 23.

37. Riggs, *Knives from Syria*, 25.

38. Riggs, *Knives from Syria*, 26.

39. Braunlich, *Haunted by Home*, 82.

40. This theme is also noted in Braunlich, *Haunted by Home*, 16.

41. Justice, *Our Fire Survives the Storm*, 94.

42. Womack, *Red on Red*, 274–75.

43. Womack, *Red on Red*, 275.

44. Borowitz, "'Pore Jud Is Daid,'" 157.

45. Borowitz, "'Pore Jud Is Daid,'" 158.

46. Borowitz, "'Pore Jud Is Daid,'" 170.

47. Borowitz, "'Pore Jud Is Daid,'" 179.

48. Weaver, *That the People May Live*, 99–100.

49. Riggs, *Cherokee Night and Other Plays*, 103. See also Womack, *Art as Performance, Story as Criticism*, 116.

50. Roger Cushing Aikin points out too that the change in name from "Jeeter" in *Green Grow the Lilacs* to "Jud" in *Oklahoma!* may have come about in order to avoid confusion with another Broadway character at the time, namely Jeeter Lester from Erskine Caldwell's *Tobacco Road* (1932). See Aikin, "Was Jud Jewish?," 281.

51. Aikin, "Was Jud Jewish?," 282. See also Hoffman, *Great White Way*, 59.

52. Aikin, "Was Jud Jewish?," 283.

53. Most, "'We Know We Belong to the Land,'" 83.

54. Most, "'We Know We Belong to the Land,'" 83. Kirle argues that Ali Hakim is "written in the tradition of the Jewish star comics of the 1920s and 1930s . . . a comic, vaudevillian character . . . [who] undercuts American anti-Semitic rhetoric during World War II" and who "negates the notion that the Jew is a menace to American communal values." He also suggests that Jud may be regarded as a "stereotypical celluloid Indian," the "primitive, violent" character in classic Westerns. He notes that Trevor Nunn's Broadway revival of the show, staged just six months after 9/11, cast Ali Hakim not as Persian but as Arab, thus countering the racial profiling of Arabs in general after September 11. Kirle, "Reconciliation, Resolution, and the Political Role of *Oklahoma!*," 261, 263, 271–72.

55. Most, "'We Know We Belong to the Land,'" 77.

56. Most, "'We Know We Belong to the Land,'" 84.

57. Most argues that the peddler's Jewish identity is further confirmed by the invitations sent out on the occasion of the musical's first anniversary. In them, Oscar Hammerstein listed himself as "Mister Ali Hakimstein." Most, "'We Know We Belong to the Land,'" 84. For this anecdote, Most cites Wilk, *OK!*, 256.

58. Behdad, *Forgetful Nation*, 8.

59. Behdad, *Forgetful Nation*, xii, 4.

60. Behdad, *Forgetful Nation*, 9.

61. Behdad, *Forgetful Nation*, 11.

62. For a useful overview of this history, see Hassan, *Immigrant Narratives*, 14–18.

63. Sherman, Whitney, and Guerrero, *Prairie Peddlers*, 104.

64. Neff, *Becoming American*, 135. See also Caldwell, "From the Hills of Lebanon," 16.

65. Neff, *Becoming American*, 175.

66. Sherman, Whitney, and Guerrero, *Prairie Peddlers*, 101–8.

67. Aryain, *From Syria to Seminole*. For a discussion of another Syrian peddler, George Haddad, who also wrote an autobiography, see Hassan, *Immigrant Narratives*, 82–84.

68. Pate, introduction to *From Syria to Seminole*, xxiv.

69. Aryain, *From Syria to Seminole*, 68.

70. Aryain, *From Syria to Seminole*, 50.

71. Aryain, *From Syria to Seminole*, 57.

72. Aryain, *From Syria to Seminole*, 54.

73. Aryain, *From Syria to Seminole*, 54–55.

74. Aryain, *From Syria to Seminole*, 54.

75. Sherman, Whitney, and Guerrero, *Prairie Peddlers*, 115.

76. Sherman, Whitney, and Guerrero, *Prairie Peddlers*, 110.

77. Lowe, "Intimacies of Four Continents," 193, 207.

78. Lowe, "Intimacies of Four Continents," 193, 195.

79. Lowe, "Intimacies of Four Continents," 202–3.

80. Lowe, "Intimacies of Four Continents," 203.

81. Hassan, *Immigrant Narratives*, 16. See also Haney López, *White by Law*.

82. Majaj, "Arab-Americans and the Meaning of Race," 321, quoted in Hassan, *Immigrant Narratives*, 16.

83. Hassan, *Immigrant Narratives*, 15.

84. Hassan, *Immigrant Narratives*, 15.

85. Haney López, *White by Law*, 6.

86. Haney López, *White by Law*, 68.

87. Haney López, *White by Law*, 6.

88. Haney López, *White by Law*, 6.

89. Haney López, *White by Law*, 67.

90. Haney López, *White by Law*, 74.

91. Haney López, *White by Law*, 75. The Dow case has been widely discussed by scholars; see also Naber, "Introduction," 21, 39; and Gualtieri, *Between Arab and White*, 66–84.

92. For demographic information about Iranian immigration in the United States, see Bozorgmehr and Sabagh, "High Status Immigrants."

93. For an overview of this history, see Bozorgmehr and Sabagh, "High Status Immigrants."

94. I borrow the term "microranking of whiteness" from Flory, "Ethnicity and Race in Film Noir." John Tehranian points out that many Iranian Americans have often self-identified as white; he notes that the 2000 census allowed them to identify as "other" than white, but few Iranian Americans choose to do so. As he also points out, many older Iranian Americans often refer to themselves as the "first Aryans," with the word *Iran* deriving from the Sanskrit word meaning "Land of the Aryans." Among the younger generation, however, this racial identification with whiteness may be changing as the population becomes more politicized on the topic of race. See Tehranian, *Whitewashed*, 85–87.

95. Tehranian points to the overlooked religious diversity among Iranians and Iranian Americans, noting that Los Angeles County, for instance, is home to more than thirty-five thousand Iranian American Jews. See Tehranian, *Whitewashed*, 176.

96. For a discussion of the Persian label and negative treatment of Iranians in the United States, see Karim and Rahimieh, "Introduction," 8.

97. Riggs, *Green Grow the Lilacs*, 31.

98. Riggs, *Green Grow the Lilacs*, 33.

99. Riggs, *Green Grow the Lilacs*, 35.

100. Riggs, *Green Grow the Lilacs*, 37.

101. Dyer, *White*, 48.

102. Peiss, *Hope in a Jar*, 9.

103. Peiss, *Hope in a Jar*, 41.

104. Riggs, *Green Grow the Lilacs*, 37.

105. Riggs, *Green Grow the Lilacs*, 38.

106. See Shohat, *Taboo Memories, Diasporic Voices*, 166–200.

107. Shohat, *Taboo Memories, Diasporic Voices*, 5–6.

108. Shohat, *Taboo Memories, Diasporic Voices*, 15, 21.

109. For overviews of Egyptomania and American orientalism, see McAlister, *Epic Encounters*; Little, *American Orientalism*; and Lant, "Curse of the Pharaoh."

110. Neff, *Becoming American*, 170.

111. Neff, *Becoming American*, 171.

112. Neff, *Becoming American*, 172.

113. Twain, *Innocents Abroad*, 248, 294.

114. Twain, *Innocents Abroad*, 201–2.

115. Halberstam, "Not So Lonesome Cowboys," 190.

116. Boone, "Vacation Cruises," 90.

117. Massad, *Desiring Arabs*, 47.

118. Roediger, *Working toward Whiteness*.

119. Most also notes these lyrics but argues they foreground Ali as the "good Jew" who can be assimilated more easily than can Jud, the "bad Jew." See Most, "'We Know We Belong to the Land,'" 80.

120. See Mills, *Racial Contract*, 78–81.

121. For a discussion of how the Orient is positioned as a space of hypersexuality, see Said, *Orientalism*, 188–90.

5. Specters of Loss

1. Campbell, "The Western," 36. For more on early post-9/11 Westerns, see Metz, "'Mother Needs You.'" For more on how Westerns on television differ somewhat from film in employing post-9/11 critiques, see Zinder, "Osama bin Laden Ain't Here."

2. The Western in this sense shares much with film noir, which, as Dan Flory argues, also has the ability to operate across the political spectrum in telling both progressive and regressive stories about nation, race, and belonging. See Flory, *Philosophy, Black Film, Film Noir*, 24–25, 309; and M. Davis, *City of Quartz*, 41.

3. Tatum, "Problem of the Popular in the New Western History," 164.

4. Tatum, "Problem of the Popular in the New Western History," 167.

5. Tatum, "Problem of the Popular in the New Western History," 168.

6. Tatum, "Problem of the Popular in the New Western History," 169.

7. F. G. Robinson, *Having It Both Ways*, 3, 112–16.

8. F. G. Robinson, *Having It Both Ways*, 1.

9. McGill, "Keeping It under Their Hat," 12.

10. See Faludi, *Terror Dream*; Peebles, *Welcome to the Suck*; Takacs, "Contemporary Politics of the Western Form"; Woods, "Cowboys, Indians, and Iraq"; and Tucker and Walton, "From General's Daughter to Coal Miner's Daughter."

11. For more on Boal's experiences in Iraq, see Zenilman, "Inside *The Hurt Locker*." Many critics have noted connections between *The Hurt Locker* and *The*

Searchers. Bob Mondello, for instance, argues that Bigelow's film "could have starred John Wayne." Mondello, *"The Hurt Locker."*

12. Bold, "Westerns," 318.

13. Castronovo, "Imperialism, Orientalism, and Empire," 545.

14. Taubin, *Taxi Driver,* 20.

15. The death of Richard Davis later became the subject of a book-length study; see McCain, *Murder in Baker Company.*

16. Tatum, "'Mercantile Ethics,'" 78.

17. The term "geography of hope" comes from Wallace Stegner, *Where the Bluebird Sings to the Lemonade Springs,* xxi. For a useful outline of various revisionist strategies employed by post–World War II counter-Westerns, see Campbell, *Post-Westerns.*

18. John Markert addresses the film's use of the David and Goliath story in a different way, as a narrative about Hank going up against America itself and the "unbending bureaucratic system" he faces in trying to find out about his son Mike. See the discussion in Markert, *Post-9/11 Cinema,* 244.

19. Kimmel, *Guyland,* 55.

20. Worden, *Masculine Style,* 1.

21. Lutz, "Living Room Terrorists," 223.

22. Polan, "Movies, a Nation, and New Identities," 232.

23. Lowe, "Intimacy of Four Continents," 206.

24. Crockatt, *After 9/11,* 30.

25. Kellner, *Cinema Wars,* 1.

26. Prince, *Firestorm,* 80.

27. Prince, *Firestorm,* 2, 293.

28. Johnson, "Amanpour."

29. For overviews of the Bush administration's attempts at censoring discussion of 9/11, see Dawson and Schueller, "Introduction," 20–21; and Giroux, "U.S. University under Siege."

30. Atkinson, "Duty Calls," 32. For an analysis of how the technologies of war operate as the driving force of modern culture with no real distinction emerging between war and peacetime after World War II, see Virilio and Lotringer, *Pure War.*

31. For more on the commercial and critical reception of these films, see Markert, *Post-9/11 Cinema,* 209–13.

32. Martin Barker discusses problems with the popular reception of Iraq War films in *"Toxic Genre,"* 1–16.

33. Byron, *"The Searchers."* Byron's essay is addressed in Henderson, *"The Searchers,"* 48.

34. As documentaries about 9/11 were made in greater numbers and tended to do better critically and commercially than narrative films, it is notable that

these opening elements provide an important, documentary feel to the movie. See Markert, *Post-9/11 Cinema*, 244.

35. In his review of various books on the Iraq invasion, Eric Walberg also recognizes how Manifest Destiny and the Indian Wars serve as a backdrop to the events of *The Hurt Locker*; he reads the film differently, however, arguing that it removes the real victims of war from the story, while serving as an instance of "occupiers' angst." For an astute analysis of various Orwellian aspects of the Iraq invasion and his reading of the film, see Walberg, "American Art of War."

36. For information on film grosses, see the *IMDb.com* piece, "*True Grit*."

37. For a discussion of the Coen brothers' various revisions of the Western over the years, see the roundtable discussion in Campbell et al., "From *Blood Simple* to *True Grit*."

38. Tompkins, *West of Everything*, 15.

39. Tompkins, *West of Everything*, 51.

40. L. C. Mitchell, *Westerns*, 99. Sue Matheson also finds problems with Tompkins's observations about language in the Western but offers a different argument by reading *True Grit* through Mikhail Bahktin's theories of dialogism; for more on this argument, see Matheson, "Professional Western Revived."

41. L. C. Mitchell, *Westerns*, 95.

42. L. C. Mitchell, *Westerns*, 98.

43. L. C. Mitchell, *Westerns*, 127.

44. Harper, "Trends in Recent American Fiction," 220.

45. Howard Harper argues that, while Mattie claims to be providing a simple, straightforward account of the events, the fact that the story is "not an account of the existential *Angst* which Mattie felt, nor a lament over the epistemological limits of her subjectivity and the consequent ambiguities of her narrative, nor even much concern with the philosophical or cultural implications of it all," indicates problems with her point of view. Mattie is thus an unreliable narrator because her story does in fact "have profound cultural and philosophical implications." See Harper, "Trends in Recent American Fiction," 219.

46. Melnick, *9/11 Culture*, 131.

47. Melnick, *9/11 Culture*, 136.

48. Weber, *Imagining America at War*, 6.

49. Connaughton, "Charles Portis," 6:266.

50. Tartt, afterword to *True Grit*, 232.

51. See, for instance, Tanner, *Reign of Wonder*.

52. Melnick, *9/11 Culture*, 17, 22.

53. For more discussion of gender in the film, see Campbell et al., "From *Blood Simple* to *True Grit*," 321–22.

54. Mann, "Manhood, Sexuality, and Nation in Post-9/11 United States," 179.

55. For an overview of cross-dressing in the Western, see Modleski, *Old Wives' Tales and Other Women's Stories*, 149–78. For a related overview of gender trouble in the Western, see Halberstam, "Not So Lonesome Cowboys." Scenes of cross-dressing females have been central to the Western since the days of the dime novel; for early histories of cross-dressed heroines, see Bold, "Westerns," 318–19.

56. A. Davis, "Vocabulary for Feminist Praxis," 21.

57. A. Davis, "Vocabulary for Feminist Praxis," 23–24.

58. Faludi, *Terror Dream*, 16.

59. Armond White notes how the Coens' remake of *True Grit* borrows visual iconography from *The Searchers*, particularly in the scene in which Rooster looks into an abandoned mineshaft, his silhouette a reminder of the final image of Ford's film. Just as Ethan Edwards, now an outsider to the American family on the range, is framed by the door of the frontier home, so Cogburn is unable to reenter domestic life himself. See A. White, "Gritty and Good."

60. Melnick notes that Ethan's fate is often overlooked in some critical studies of the film's renewed life in post-9/11 arts; see the discussion in Melnick, *9/11 Culture*, 129.

61. Handley, "Popular Western," 438.

62. Simmon, *Invention of the Western Film*, xiv.

6. East of the Spaghetti Western

1. Mandanipour, *Censoring an Iranian Love Story*, 182.

2. Mandanipour, *Censoring an Iranian Love Story*, 93.

3. For an astute discussion of Nafisi's memoir in the context of neoliberal strategies of soft power, see Rowe, "Reading *Reading Lolita in Tehran* in Idaho," 261.

4. Behdad and Williams, "Neo-Orientalism," 284, 285.

5. Behdad and Williams, "Neo-Orientalism," 286. For a related critique, see Bahramitash, "Saving Iranian Women."

6. Behdad and Williams, "Neo-Orientalism," 287.

7. Mandanipour, *Censoring an Iranian Love Story*, 200.

8. Khatib, *Filming the Modern Middle East*, 121.

9. Mandanipour, *Censoring an Iranian Love Story*, 93.

10. Mandanipour, *Censoring an Iranian Love Story*, 94.

11. Mandanipour, *Censoring an Iranian Love Story*, 95.

12. Chude-Sokei, "'But I Did Not Shoot the Deputy,'" 167.

13. Chude-Sokei, "'But I Did Not Shoot the Deputy,'" 137.

14. Chude-Sokei, "'But I Did Not Shoot the Deputy,'" 139.

15. Fisher, *Radical Frontiers in the Spaghetti Western*, 3.

16. Chude-Sokei, "'But I Did Not Shoot the Deputy,'" 147.

17. Chude-Sokei, "'But I Did Not Shoot the Deputy,'" 162.

18. Farhadi quoted in Bell, "Scenes from a Marriage," 39.

19. Hayoun, "Is There a Lesson for the U.S. in Iran's Oscar-Nominated *A Separation*?"

20. Hayoun, "Is There a Lesson for the U.S. in Iran's Oscar-Nominated *A Separation*?"

21. Simmon, *Invention of the Western Film*, 18.

22. R. Hamid, "Freedom and Its Discontents," 40.

23. For a discussion of the title's significance, see Mourad, "Between *Asmaa* and *Tahrir 2011*"; and Vivarilli, "Tahrir Square Doc Takes Spaghetti Western Route."

24. This information comes from "*Tahrir 2011*," at the YouTube website.

25. Tawil-Sour, "Egypt's Uprising and the Shifting Spatialities of Politics."

26. Tawil-Sour, "Egypt's Uprising and the Shifting Spatialities of Politics," 164.

27. Edwards, "Tahrir," 495.

28. Salvatore, "Elusive Subject of Revolution," cited in Tawil-Sour, "Egypt's Uprising and the Shifting Spatialities of Politics," 161.

29. El Hamamsy and Soliman, "Introduction," 12.

30. For the different ways the pro-democracy movement unfolded across nations, see El Hamamsy and Soliman, "Introduction," 11–12.

31. Matar, *In the Country of Men*, 163.

32. Matar, *In the Country of Men*, 197.

33. Matar, *In the Country of Men*, 198.

34. Khadra, *Sirens of Baghdad*, 175.

35. Khadra, *Sirens of Baghdad*, 127.

36. Blasim, *Corpse Exhibition and Other Stories of Iraq*, 107.

37. The film is sold in the United States through Rotana distribution under the title *The Fall of Baghdad*.

38. Klinger, "Local Genres." Klinger's essay is cited in Barker, "*Toxic Genre*," 130.

39. Klinger, "Local Genres," 134.

40. Klinger, "Local Genres," 134.

41. Klinger, "Local Genres," 134–35.

42. Klinger, "Local Genres," 135.

43. Klinger, "Local Genres," 145.

44. Cairo's black cloud has appeared for some years and serves as a further sign of the government's ongoing stagnation and apathy. See Bakr, "Stopping the Clouds."

45. Stoler, "Introduction," 8.

46. Markert, *Post-9/11 Cinema*, 245.

47. Enloe, *Maneuvers*, 55.

48. Enloe, *Maneuvers*, 7, 81, 108–52. See also Enloe, *Nimo's War*, 59, 165–66.

49. Some U.S. reviewers regarded *The Night Baghdad Fell* as a "wildly" anti-American film; see, for instance, Williams, "In Egyptian Movies, Curses!"; and Fisher, "Place of Dreams, a Source of Villainy." The film was not without its crit-

ics in Egypt as well; at least one reviewer faulted the film for what he called its "extremely superficial and simple-minded" vision of politics; Hani Mustafa suggested that the film remains "closer to fantasy than realism," with the end result proving to be "extremely mediocre." See Mustafa, "Black Comedy, Black Drama."

50. Edwards, "World, the Text, and the Americanist," 232.

51. Edwards, "World, the Text, and the Americanist," 232–33.

52. Edwards, "World, the Text, and the Americanist," 234.

53. Edwards, "World, the Text, and the Americanist," 235, 241.

54. Edwards, "Tahrir," 500.

55. Mason, Felman, and Schnee, "Editors' Note," xiii.

56. Hosam Aboul-Ela made this comment at a talk sponsored by the Department of English and Comparative Literature, American University in Cairo, spring 2008.

57. Edwards, "Tahrir," 501.

58. Dudley Andrew argues that the politics of distribution is currently a defining element in world cinema studies and that the "real film wars have been waged less over production than over competition for audiences." Andrew, "Atlas of World Cinema," 11.

Conclusion

1. Many thanks to José Aranda for bringing Beto Gómez's film to my attention. I first viewed Shams's music video on Egyptian television in February 2007 in a café in Cairo.

2. Prashad, "Orientalism," 177.

3. For more on the militarization of the border and racial panics after 9/11 involving fears that al-Qaeda will enter the United States through Mexico, see Urrea, *Devil's Highway*, 34, 204–5.

4. W. Wright, *Six Guns and Society*, 85.

5. W. Wright, *Six Guns and Society*, 86.

6. W. Wright, *Six Guns and Society*, 86–87.

7. W. Wright, *Six Guns and Society*, 88.

8. Fusté, "Containing Bordered 'Others' in La Frontera and Gaza," 812.

9. Lloyd and Pulido, "In the Long Shadow of the Settler," 804.

10. Lloyd and Pulido, "In the Long Shadow of the Settler," 795.

11. See Shams, "Ahlan Ezayak." For an English translation of the song, see "Ahlan Ezayak translated to English" on YouTube. (Note: various spellings of the song title may exist due to different transliterations of Arabic.)

12. For a description of "Ahlan Ezayak" as a "song of opposition, protest, and resistance," see the blog entries at "Shams—Ahlan Ezayak," *Woody Guthrie's Guitar*. See also "Kuwaiti Singer's Video Satirizes the Bush War."

13. Zerilli, "Democracy and National Fantasy," 171, quoted in Lemke, "Liberty," 193.

14. Edwards and Gaonkar, "Introduction."

15. Orientalism figures the East as weak, dependent, and feminized, in need of help from the more powerful, hypermasculine Occident. See Said, *Orientalism*, 206.

BIBLIOGRAPHY

Visual Media

"Ahlan Ezayak translated to English." YouTube music video. Posted June 4, 2007. http://www.youtube.com/watch?v=XNDxdWxeQRU.

Annie Get Your Gun. Directed by George Sidney. Warner Brothers, 1950.

Argo. Directed by Ben Affleck. Warner Brothers, 2012.

Hidalgo. Directed by Joe Johnston. Touchstone Pictures, 2004.

Homeland. Fox 21 Television Studios, 2011.

The Hurt Locker. Directed by Kathryn Bigelow. Summit Entertainment, 2008.

In the Valley of Elah. Directed by Paul Haggis. Warner Brothers, 2007.

Lawrence of Arabia. Directed by David Lean. Columbia Pictures, 1962.

The Night Baghdad Fell. Directed by Mohammed Amin. El Arabia, 2005.

Oklahoma! Directed by Fred Zinnemann. Magna Theatre Corporation and Rodgers and Hammerstein Productions, 1955.

Saving Private Perez. Directed by Beto Gómez. Lions Gate, 2011.

The Searchers. Directed by John Ford. Warner Brothers, 1955.

A Separation. Directed by Asghar Farhadi. Sony Pictures Classic, 2011.

Shams. "Ahlan Ezayak (feat. George Bush)." YouTube music video. Posted February 16, 2007. http://www.youtube.com/watch?v=Q4qJOYKHEF0.

Tahrir 2011: The Good, the Bad, and the Politician. Directed by Ayten Amin, Tamer Ezzat, and Amr Samala. 2011.

"*Tahrir 2011*." YouTube. Posted January 26, 2012. http://www.youtube.com/watch?v=FGz2bYKyeHw.

Taken. Directed by Pierre Morel. Twentieth Century Fox, 2008.

True Grit. Directed by Ethan Coen and Joel Coen. Paramount, 2010.

The Wind and the Lion. Directed by John Milius. Warner Brothers, 1975.

Published Sources

Abrams, David. *Fobbit*. New York: Black Cat, 2012.

Ackerman, Gerald M. *American Orientalists*. Paris: Art Creation Realisation, 1994.

Aikin, Roger Cushing. "Was Jud Jewish? Property, Ethnicity, and Gender in *Oklahoma!*" *Quarterly Review of Film and Video* 22, no. 3 (2005): 277–83.

Allmendinger, Blake. *Ten Most Wanted: The New Western Literature*. New York: Routledge, 1998.

Als, Hilton. "America, America: Two Plays about the Country's Complexities." *New Yorker*, December 13, 2010. http://www.newyorker.com/magazine/2010/12/13/america-america.

Altman, Rick. *Film/Genre*. London: BFI, 1999.

Andrew, Dudley. "An Atlas of World Cinema." *Framework* 45, no. 2 (2004): 9–23.

Anzaldúa, Gloria. *Borderlands/La Frontera: The New Mestiza*. San Francisco: Aunt Lute Press, 1987.

Aryain, Ed. *From Syria to Seminole: Memoir of a High Plains Merchant*. Edited by J'Nell Pate. Lubbock: Texas Tech University Press, 2006.

Atkinson, Michael. "Duty Calls: *Zero Dark Thirty*." *Sight and Sound* 23, no. 2 (2013): 30–33.

Auerbach, Jerold S. *Explorers in Eden: Pueblo Indians and the Promised Land*. Albuquerque: University of New Mexico Press, 2011.

Babcock, Barbara A. "Taking Liberties, Writing from the Margins, and Doing It with a Difference." *Journal of American Folklore* 100, no. 398 (1987): 390–411.

Baepler, Paul, ed. *White Slaves, African Masters: An Anthology of American Barbary Coast Narratives*. Chicago: University of Chicago Press, 1999.

Bahramitash, Roksana. "Saving Iranian Women: Orientalist Feminism and the Axis of Evil." In *Security Disarmed: Critical Perspectives on Gender, Race, and Militarism*, edited by Julie Novkov, Sandra Morgen, and Barbara Sutton, 101–10. New Brunswick: Rutgers University Press, 2008.

Bakr, Mahmoud. "Stopping the Clouds." *Al-Ahram Weekly*, October 29–November 4, 2009. http://weekly.ahram.org.eg/2009/970/en81.htm.

Banerjee, Mita, and Günther Sommerschuh. "From Sheikh to Terrorist? Arab Characters in American Film." In *Arab American Literature and Culture*, edited by Alfred Hornung and Martina Kohl. Heidelberg: Universitätsverlag, 2012.

Barker, Martin. *A "Toxic Genre": The Iraq War Films*. London: Pluto, 2011.

Baringer, Sandra. "*Oklahoma!* and Assimilation." *PMLA* 113, no. 3 (1998): 452–55.

Barnes, Kim. *In the Kingdom of Men*. New York: Knopf, 2013.

Behdad, Ali. *A Forgetful Nation: On Immigration and Cultural Identity in the United States*. Durham: Duke University Press, 2005.

Behdad, Ali, and Juliet Williams. "Neo-Orientalism." In *Globalizing American Studies*, edited by Brian T. Edwards and Dilip Parameshwar Gaonkar, 283–99. Chicago: University of Chicago Press, 2010.

Bell, James. "Scenes from a Marriage." *Sight and Sound* 21, no. 7 (July 2011): 38–39.

Berger, John. *About Looking*. New York: Pantheon, 1980.

Berman, Jacob Rama. *American Arabesque: Arabs, Islam, and the Nineteenth-Century Imaginary*. New York: New York University Press, 2012.

Bigelow, Poultney. "French Fighters in Algeria." *Harper's New Monthly Magazine* 90 (February 1895): 366–77.

———. *Seventy Summers*. New York: Longmans, Green, 1925.

Blasim, Hassan. *The Corpse Exhibition and Other Stories of Iraq*. Translated by Jonathan Wright. New York: Penguin, 2013.

Bodnar, John. "Symbols and Servants: Immigrant America and the Limits of Public History." *Journal of American History* 73, no. 1 (1986): 137–51.

Boehmer, Elleke. *Colonial and Postcolonial Literature: Migrant Metaphors*. Oxford: Oxford University Press, 2005.

Bold, Christine. *The Frontier Club: Popular Westerns and Cultural Power, 1880–1920*. Oxford: Oxford University Press, 2013.

———. "The Rough Riders at Home and Abroad: Cody, Roosevelt, Remington, and the Imperialist Hero." *Canadian Review of American Studies* 18, no. 3 (1987): 321–50.

———. *Selling the Wild West: Popular Western Fiction, 1860–1960*. Bloomington: Indiana University Press, 1987.

———. "Westerns." In *The Oxford History of Popular Print Culture*. Volume 6, *U.S. Popular Print Culture 1860–1920*, edited by Christine Bold, 317–36. Oxford: Oxford University Press, 2012.

Boone, Joseph A. "Vacation Cruises; or, the Homoerotics of Orientalism." PMLA 110, no. 1 (1995): 89–107.

Borowitz, Albert. "'Pore Jud Is Daid': Violence and Lawlessness in the Plays of Lynn Riggs." *Legal Studies Forum* 27, no. 1 (2003): 157–84.

Bozorgmehr, Medhi, and Georges Sabagh. "High Status Immigrants: A Statistical Profile of Iranians in the United States." *Iranian Studies* 21, no. 3–4 (1988): 5–36.

Braunlich, Phyllis Cole. *Haunted by Home: The Life and Letters of Lynn Riggs*. Norman: University of Oklahoma Press, 2002.

Brier, Bob. *Egyptomania: Our Three Thousand Year Obsession with the Land of the Pharaohs*. New York: Palgrave Macmillan, 2013.

Broncano, Manuel. "Willa Cather's Hispanic Epiphanies and *The Professor's House*." In *Willa Cather: A Writer's World*, edited by John J. Murphy, Françoise Palleau-Pain, and Robert Thacker, 379–95. Lincoln: University of Nebraska Press, 2010.

Brown, Bill. *The Material Unconscious: American Amusement, Stephen Crane, and the Economics of Play*. Cambridge MA: Harvard University Press, 1997.

———. *A Sense of Things: The Object Matter of American Literature*. Chicago: University of Chicago Press, 2003.

Brown, Dee. *The American West*. New York: Simon and Schuster, 1994.

"Buffalo Bill's Wild West Combined with Pawnee Bill's Great Far East 1909 Courier." Buffalo: Courier Co. of Buffalo, 1910. Repository Collection: MS 6 William F. Cody Collection, Buffalo Bill Historical Center, Cody WY. Online Collection.

Buscombe, Edward. *"Injuns!" Native Americans in the Movies*. London: Reaktion Books, 2006.

———. *"Oklahoma!" The BFI Companion to the Western*, edited by Edward Buscombe, 287. New York: Da Capo, 1988.

Buzzell, Colby. *My War: Killing Time in Iraq*. New York: Berkley Trade, 2006.

Byrd, Jodi. *The Transit of Empire: Indigenous Critiques of Colonialism*. Minneapolis: University of Minnesota Press, 2011.

Byron, Stuart. *"The Searchers*: Cult Movie of the New Hollywood." *New York Magazine*, March 5, 1979, 45–48.

Caldwell, Tom. "From the Hills of Lebanon: The Syrian-Lebanese in Oklahoma." *Chronicles of Oklahoma* 64, no. 2 (1986): 14–33.

Campbell, Neil. *Post-Westerns: Cinema, Region, West*. Lincoln: University of Nebraska Press, 2013.

———. *The Rhizomatic West: Representing the American West in a Transnational, Global, Media Age*. Lincoln: University of Nebraska Press, 2008.

———. "The Western." In *A Companion to 20th-Century United States Fiction*, edited by David Seed, 36–47. Malden MA: Wiley Blackwell, 2010.

Campbell, Neil, Susan Kollin, Lee Clark Mitchell, and Stephen Tatum. "From *Blood Simple* to *True Grit*: A Conversation about the Coen Brothers' Cinematic West." *Western American Literature* 48, no. 3 (2013): 312–40.

Carter, Tim. *Oklahoma! The Making of an American Musical*. New Haven: Yale University Press, 2007.

Castronovo, Russ. "Imperialism, Orientalism, and Empire." In *The Cambridge History of the American Novel*, edited by Leonard Cassuto, Clare Virginia Eby, and Benjamin Reiss, 537–52. Cambridge: Cambridge University Press, 2011.

Cather, Willa. *Death Comes for the Archbishop*. 1927. Reprint, New York: Vintage, 1990.

———. "The Novel Démeublé." In *Not under Forty*. 1936. Reprint, New York: Knopf, 1988.

Caton, Steven. *"Lawrence of Arabia": A Film's Anthropology*. Berkeley: University of California Press, 1999.

Cawelti, John G. *The Six-Gun Mystique Sequel*. Bowling Green OH: Popular Press, 1999.

Chow, Rey. *Writing Diaspora: Tactics of Intervention in Contemporary Cultural Studies*. Bloomington: Indiana University Press, 1993.

Chude-Sokei, Louis. "'But I Did Not Shoot the Deputy': Dubbing the Yankee Frontier." In *The Worlding Project: Doing Cultural Studies in the Era of Globalization*, edited by Rob Wilson and Christopher Leigh Connery, 133–70. Berkeley CA: North Atlantic Books, 2007.

Churchill, Ward. *Fantasies of the Master Race: Literature, Cinema, and the Colonization of American Indians*. San Francisco: City Lights, 2001.

Colley, Charles C. "The Desert Shall Bloom: North African Influence on the American Southwest." *Western Historical Quarterly* 14, no. 3 (1983): 277–90.

———. "La Jineta: The Art of Moorish Horsemanship in the New World." *El Palacio Magazine: Art, History, and Culture of the Southwest* 76 (Summer 1969): 31–35.

Comer, Krista. "Exceptionalism, Other Wests, Critical Regionalism." *American Literary History* 23, no. 1 (2011): 159–73.

———. "Taking Feminism and Regionalism to the Third Wave." In *A Companion to the Regional Literatures of America*, edited by Charles L. Crow, 111–28. Malden MA: Blackwell, 2003.

———. "West." In *Keywords for American Cultural Studies*, edited by Bruce Burgett and Glenn Hendler, 238–42. New York: New York University Press, 2007.

Connaughton, Michael. "Charles Portis." In *Dictionary of Literary Biography: American Novelists since World War II*, edited by James E. Kibler Jr., 6:264–68. Detroit: Gale, 1980.

Corkin, Stanley. *Cowboys as Cold Warriors: The Western and U.S. History*. Philadelphia: Temple University Press, 2004.

Cornell, Stephen, and Douglas Hartman. *Ethnicity and Race: Making Identity in a Changing World*. 2nd ed. London: Pine Forge, 2007.

Countryman, Edward. "Captivity Narratives." In *The BFI Companion to the Western*, edited by Edward Buscombe, 78–81. New York: Da Capo, 1998.

Cox, J. Randolph. *The Dime Novel Companion: A Sourcebook*. Westport CT: Greenwood, 2000.

Cracroft, Richard. "The American West of Karl May." *American Quarterly* 19, no. 2 (1967): 249–58.

Crawford, John. *The Last True Story I'll Ever Tell: An Accidental Soldier's Account of the War in Iraq*. New York: Riverhead, 2006.

Crockatt, Richard. *After 9/11: Cultural Dimensions of American Global Power*. New York: Routledge, 2007.

Daiches, David. *Willa Cather: A Critical Introduction*. Westport CT: Greenwood Press, 1971.

Darwish, Mahmoud. "Speech of the Red Indian." In *The Adam of Two Edens*, edited by Munir Akash and Daniel Moore, 129–45. Syracuse: Syracuse University Press, 2001.

Davis, Angela. "A Vocabulary for Feminist Praxis: On War and Radical Critique." In *Feminism and War: Confronting U.S. Imperialism*, edited by Robin L. Riley, Chandra Talpade Mohanty, and Minnie Bruce Pratt, 19–26. London: Zed Books, 2008.

Davis, Mike. *City of Quartz: Excavating the Future in Los Angeles*. New York: Verso, 1990.

Dawson, Ashley, and Malini Johar Schueller. "Introduction: Rethinking Imperialism Today." In *Exceptional State: Contemporary U.S. Culture and the New Imperialism*, edited by Ashley Dawson and Malini Johar Schueller, 1–36. Durham: Duke University Press, 2007.

Dean, John Emory. *Travel Narratives from New Mexico: Reconstructing Identity and Truth*. Amherst NY: Cambria, 2009.

Deloria, Philip. *Indians in Unexpected Places*. Lawrence: University Press of Kansas, 2006.

———. *Playing Indian*. New Haven: Yale University Press, 1998.

Denning, Michael. *Mechanic Accents: Dime Novels and Working Class Culture in America*. 2nd ed. London: Verso, 1998.

Dillon, Wilton S., and Neil G. Kotler, eds. *The Statue of Liberty Revisited*. Washington DC: Smithsonian Institution Press, 1994.

Dimock, Wai Chee. "Hemispheric Islam: Continents and Centuries for American Literature." *American Literary History* 21, no. 1 (2009): 28–52.

Dippie, Brian W. "The Visual West." In *The Oxford History of the American West*, edited by Clyde Milner, Carol A. O'Connor, and Martha A. Sandweiss, 675–707. New York: Oxford University Press, 1996.

Drinnon, Richard. *Facing West: The Metaphysics of Indian-Hating and Empire Building*. New York: Plume, 1980.

Dyer, Richard. *White*. New York: Routledge, 1997.

Edwards, Brian T. "Logics and Contexts of Circulation." In *A Companion to Comparative Literature*, edited by Ali Behdad and Dominic Thomas, 454–72. Malden MA: Blackwell, 2011.

———. "Tahrir: Ends of Circulation." *Public Culture* 23, no. 3 (2011): 493–504.

———. "The World, the Text, and the Americanist." *American Literary History* 25, no. 1 (2013): 231–46.

Edwards, Brian T., and Dilip Parameshwar Gaonkar. "Introduction: Globalizing American Studies." In *Globalizing American Studies*, edited by Brian T. Edwards and Dilip Parameshwar Gaonkar, 13–30. Chicago: University of Chicago Press, 2010.

El-Din Aysha, Emad. Review of *Hidalgo*. *Egyptian Gazette*, June 17, 2004, 8.

El Hamamsy, Walid, and Mounira Soliman. "Introduction: Popular Culture—A Site of Resistance." In *Popular Culture in the Middle East and North Africa*, edited by Walid El Hamamsy and Mounira Soliman, 1–16. New York: Routledge, 2013.

Enloe, Cynthia. *Maneuvers: The International Politics of Militarizing Women's Lives*. Berkeley: University of California Press, 2000.

———. *Nimo's War: Making Feminist Sense of the Iraq War*. Berkeley: University of California Press, 2010.

Faludi, Susan. *The Terror Dream: Fear and Fantasy in Post-9/11 America*. New York: Metropolitan Books, 2007.

Ferens, Dominika. "A Confidence Man in Africa: Karl May and the German Colonial Enterprise." *Werkwinkel: Journal of Low Countries and South African Studies* 3, no. 1 (2008): 89–110.

Ferguson, Michaele L., and Lori Jo Marso. "Introduction: Feminism, Gender, and Security in the Bush Administration." In *W Stands for Women: How the George W. Bush Presidency Shaped a New Politics of Gender*, edited Michaele L. Ferguson and Lori Jo Marso, 1–16. Durham: Duke University Press, 2007.

Fick, Nathaniel. *One Bullet Away: The Making of a Marine Officer*. New York: Mariner Books, 2006.

Fields, Dorothy, and Herbert Fields. *Annie Get Your Gun: As a Straight Play without Music*. Chicago: Dramatic Publishing, 1952.

Filkins, Dexter. *The Forever War*. New York: Vintage, 2008.

Fischer, Mike. "Pastoralism and Its Discontents: Willa Cather and the Burden of Imperialism." *Mosaic* 23, no. 1 (1990): 31–44.

Fisher, Austin. *Radical Frontiers in the Spaghetti Western: Politics, Violence, and Popular Italian Cinema*. 2011. Reprint, London: I. B. Tauris, 2014.

Fisher, Max. "A Place of Dreams, a Source of Villainy: How Foreign Movies Portray America." *The Atlantic*, September 4, 2012. http://www.theatlantic.com /international/archive/2012/09/a-place-of-dreams-a-source-of-villainy-how -foreign-movies-portray-america/261876/.

Flint, Richard, and Shirley Cushing Flint, eds. *Documents of the Coronado Expedition, 1539–1542: "They Were Not Familiar with His Majesty, nor Did They Wish to Be His Subjects."* Albuquerque: University of New Mexico Press, 2012.

Flory, Dan. "Ethnicity and Race in American Film Noir." In *A Companion to Film Noir*, edited by Andrew Spicer and Helen Hanson, 387–404. Malden MA: Blackwell, 2013.

———. *Philosophy, Black Film, Film Noir*. University Park: Pennsylvania State University Press, 2008.

Fountain, Ben. *Billy Lynn's Long Halftime Walk*. New York: HarperCollins, 2012.

Francaviglia, Richard V. *Go East, Young Man: Imagining the American West as the Orient*. Logan: Utah State University Press, 2011.

Frayling, Christopher. *Spaghetti Westerns: Cowboys and Westerns from Karl May to Sergio Leone*. 1981. Reprint, London: I. B. Taurus, 2006.

French, Philip. "The Western." In *The Observer Book of Film*, edited by Carl Wilkinson, 14. Reading: Cox and Wyman / Observer Books, 2007.

———. *Westerns*. New York: Viking, 1973.

Fusté, José I. "Containing Bordered 'Others' in La Frontera and Gaza: Comparative Lessons on Racializing Discourses and State Violence." *American Quarterly* 62, no. 4 (2010): 811–19.

Gerstle, Gary. *American Crucible: Race and Nation in the Twentieth Century*. Princeton: Princeton University Press, 2001.

Ghonaim, Yazmin. "From the Golden Crescent of Paris . . . and Back." *Cineaste* 29, no. 2 (2004): 14–17.

Ghosh, Amitav. "Petrofiction: The Oil Encounter and the Novel." In *The Imam and the Indian*. Hyderabad: Sangam Books, 2002.

Gibson, William. *Pattern Recognition*. New York: Berkley, 2003.

Giroux, Henry A. "The U.S. University under Siege: Confronting Academic Freedom." In *A Concise Companion to American Studies*, edited by John Carlos Rowe, 407–31. Malden MA: Wiley-Blackwell, 2010.

Godfrey, Kathleen. "Willa Cather's *Death Comes for the Archbishop*: The Weight of Orientalism." *Southwestern American Literature* 25, no. 2 (2000): 7–14.

Goldberg, Jonathan. *Willa Cather and Others*. Durham: Duke University Press, 2001.

Goodman, Audrey. *Translating Southwestern Landscapes: The Making of an Anglo Literary Region*. Tucson: University of Arizona Press, 2002.

Gregory, Derek. *The Colonial Present: Afghanistan, Palestine, Iraq*. Malden MA: Wiley Blackwell, 2004.

Grey, Zane. *Wildfire*. 1910. Reprint, Rockville MD: Arc Manor, 2008.

———. *The Young Lion Hunter*. New York: Harper and Brothers, 1911.

Grigsby, Darcy Grimaldi. "Out of Earth: Egypt's Statue of Liberty." In *Edges of Empire: Orientalism and Visual Culture*, edited by Jocelyn Hackforth-Jones and Mary Roberts, 38–69. London: Blackwell, 2005.

Gualtieri, Sarah M. A. *Between Arab and White: Race and Ethnicity in the Early Syrian American Diaspora*. Berkeley: University of California Press, 2009.

Hackett, Robin. "Jezebel and Sapphira: Willa Cather's Monstrous Sapphists." In *Sapphic Primitivism: Productions of Race, Class, and Sexuality in Key Works of Modern Fiction*, 121–46. New Brunswick: Rutgers University Press, 2004.

Halberstam, Judith [Jack]. "Not So Lonesome Cowboys: The Queer Western." In *The Brokeback Book: From Story to Cultural Phenomenon*, edited by William R. Handley, 190–204. Lincoln: University of Nebraska Press, 2011.

Hamid, George A. *Circus, as Told to His Son, George A. Hamid Jr*. New York: Sterling, 1950.

Hamid, Rahul. "Freedom and Its Discontents: An Interview with Asghar Farhadi." *Cineaste* 37, no. 1 (2011): 40–42.

Handley, William R. *Marriage, Violence, and the Nation in the American Literary West*. Cambridge: Cambridge University Press, 2002.

———. "The Popular Western." In *A Companion to the Modern American Novel, 1900–1950*, edited by John T. Matthews, 437–53. Malden MA: Wiley-Blackwell, 2009.

Handley, William R., and Nathaniel Lewis, eds. *True West: Authenticity and the American West*. Lincoln: University of Nebraska Press, 2004.

Haney López, Ian F. *White by Law: The Legal Construction of Race*. New York: New York University Press, 1996.

Harper, Howard H., Jr. "Trends in Recent American Fiction." *Contemporary Literature* 12, no. 2 (1971): 204–29.

Hassan, Waïl. *Immigrant Narratives: Orientalism and Cultural Translation in Arab American and Arab British Literature*. Oxford: Oxford University Press, 2011.

Hayoun, Massoud. "Is There a Lesson for the U.S. in Iran's Oscar-Nominated *A Separation?*" *The Atlantic*, February 12, 2012. http://www.theatlantic.com/entertainment/archive/2012/02/is-there-a-lesson-for-the-us-in-irans-oscar-nominated-a-separation/253018/.

Henderson, Brian. "*The Searchers*: An American Dilemma." In *"The Searchers": Essays and Reflections on John Ford's Classic Western*, edited by Arthur M. Eckstein and Peter Lehman, 47–73. Detroit: Wayne State University Press, 2004.

Hoffman, Warren. *The Great White Way: Race and the American Musical*. New Brunswick: Rutgers University Press, 2014.

Hopkins, Frank T. *Hidalgo and Other Stories*. N.p.: Long Riders' Guild Press, 2004.

Hsu, Hsuan. "Vagrancy and Comparative Racialization in *Huckleberry Finn* and 'Three Vagabonds of Trinidad.'" *American Literature* 81, no. 4 (2009): 687–717.

Jewell, Andrew, and Janis Stout, eds. *The Selected Letters of Willa Cather*. New York: Knopf, 2013.

Johnson, Peter. "Amanpour: CNN Practiced Self-Censorship." *USA Today*, September 14, 2003. www.usatoday.com/life/columnist/mediamix/2003–09-media-mix_x.htm.

Jojola, Ted. "Absurd Reality II: Hollywood Goes to the Indians." In *Hollywood's Indian: The Portrait of the Native American in Film*, edited by Peter C. Rollins and John E. O'Connor, 12–26. Lexington: University Press of Kentucky, 2003.

Justice, Daniel Heath. *Our Fire Survives the Storm: A Cherokee Literary History*. Minneapolis: University of Minnesota Press, 2006.

Kahf, Mohja. *Western Representations of the Muslim Woman: From Termagant to Odalisque*. Austin: University of Texas Press, 1999.

Kantor, Michael, and Laurence Maslon. *Broadway: The American Musical*. New York: Bulfinch, 2004.

Kaplan, Amy. "Romancing the Empire: The Embodiment of American Masculinity in the Popular Historical Novel of the 1890's." *American Literary History* 2, no. 4 (1990): 659–90.

Karim, Persis M., and Nasrin Rahimieh. "Introduction: Writing Iranian Americans into the American Literature Canon." *MELUS* 33, no. 2 (2008): 7–16.

Kasson, Joy. *Buffalo Bill's Wild West: Celebrity, Memory, and Popular History*. New York: Hill and Wang, 2000.

Kellner, Douglas. *Cinema Wars: Hollywood Film and Politics in the Bush-Cheney Era*. Malden MA: Wiley-Blackwell, 2010.

Khadra, Yasmina. *The Sirens of Baghdad*. Translated by John Cullen. New York: Anchor, 2007.

Khatib, Lina. *Filming the Modern Middle East: Politics in the Cinemas of Hollywood and the Arab World*. London: I. B. Taurus, 2006.

Kimmel, Michael. *Guyland: The Perilous World Where Boys Become Men*. New York: Harper Perennial, 2009.

King, Thomas. *The Inconvenient Indian: A Curious Account of Native People in North America*. Toronto: Doubleday Canada, 2012.

———. *The Truth about Stories: A Native Narrative*. Minneapolis: University of Minnesota Press, 2008.

Kirle, Bruce. "Reconciliation, Resolution, and the Political Role of *Oklahoma!* in American Consciousness." *Theatre Journal* 55, no. 2 (2003): 251–74.

Klinger, Barbara. "Local Genres: The Hollywood Adult Film in the 1950s." In *Melodrama: Stage, Picture, Screen*, edited by Jacky Bratton, Jim Cook, and Christine Gledhill, 134–46. London: British Film Institute, 1994.

Knapp, Raymond. *The American Musical and the Formation of National Identity*. Princeton: Princeton University Press, 2005.

Kollin, Susan. "The Global West: Temporality, Spatial Politics, and Literary Production." In *A Companion to the Literature and Culture of the American West*, edited by Nicolas S. Witschi, 514–27. Malden MA: Wiley-Blackwell, 2011.

———. "Introduction: Postwestern Studies; Dead or Alive." In *Postwestern Cultures: Literature, Theory, Space*, edited by Susan Kollin, xi–xix. Lincoln: University of Nebraska Press, 2007.

"Kuwaiti Singer's Video Satirizes the Bush War." *The Nation*, February 5, 2008. www.thenation.com/blog/kuwaiti-singers-video-satirizes-bush-war.

Kvande, Marta, and Sara Spurgeon. "The Removes of Harriot Stuart: Charlotte Lennox and the Birth of the Western." In *Before the West Was West: Critical Essays on Pre-1800 Literature of the American Frontiers*, edited by Amy T. Hamilton and Tom J. Hillard, 213–38. Lincoln: University of Nebraska Press, 2014.

Laachir, Karima, and Saeed Talajooy, eds. *Resistance in Middle Eastern Culture: Literature, Cinema, and Music*. New York: Routledge, 2013.

Lant, Antonia. "The Curse of the Pharaoh: Or, How Cinema Contracted Egyptomania." *October* 59 (Winter 1992): 87–112.

Lears, T. J. Jackson. *No Place of Grace: Anti-Modernism and the Transformation of American Culture, 1880–1920*. 1981. Reprint, Chicago: University of Chicago Press, 1994.

LeMenager, Stephanie. "Imagining the Frontier." In *The Cambridge History of the American Novel*, edited by Leonard Cassuto, Clare Virginia Eby, and Benjamin Reiss, 515–36. Cambridge: Cambridge University Press, 2011.

———. *Living Oil: Petroleum Culture in the American Century*. Oxford: Oxford University Press, 2014.

Lemke, Sieglinde. "Liberty: A Transnational Icon." In *Reframing the Transnational Turn in American Studies*, edited by Winfried Fluck, Donald E. Pease, and John Carlos Rowe, 193–208. Hanover NH: Dartmouth College Press, 2011.

Lewis, Martin W., and Karen E. Wigen. *The Myth of Continents: A Critique of Metageography*. Berkeley: University of California Press, 1997.

Lewis, R. W. B. *The American Adam: Innocence, Tragedy, and Tradition in the Nineteenth Century*. Chicago: University of Chicago Press, 1956.

Lima, Enrique. "Willa Cather's Rewriting of the Historical Novel in *Death Comes for the Archbishop*." *Novel: A Forum on Fiction* 46, no. 2 (2013): 179–92.

Lindemann, Marilee. *Willa Cather: Queering America*. New York: Columbia University Press, 1999.

Little, Douglas. *American Orientalism: The United States and the Middle East since 1945*. Chapel Hill: University of North Carolina Press, 2008.

Lloyd, David, and Laura Pulido. "In the Long Shadow of the Settler: On Israeli and U.S. Colonialisms." *American Quarterly* 62, no. 4 (2010): 795–809.

Love, Eric T. L. *Race over Empire: Racism and U.S. Imperialism, 1865–1900*. Chapel Hill: University of North Carolina Press, 2004.

Lowe, Lisa. *Immigrant Acts: On Asian American Cultural Politics*. Durham: Duke University Press, 1996.

———. "The Intimacies of Four Continents." In *Haunted by Empire: Geographies of Intimacy in North American History*, edited by Ann Laura Stoler, 191–212. Durham: Duke University Press, 2006.

Lubin, Alex. "'We Are All Israelis': The Politics of Colonial Comparisons." *South Atlantic Quarterly* 107, no. 4 (2008): 671–90.

Lutz, Catherine. "Living Room Terrorists." In *Security Disarmed: Critical Perspectives on Gender, Race, and Militarism*, edited by Julie Novkov, Barbara Sutton, and Sandra Morgen, 223–30. New Brunswick: Rutgers University Press, 2008.

Lynch, Tom. "'Nothing But Land': Women's Narratives, Gardens, and the Settler-Colonial Imaginary in the US West and the Australian Outback." *Western American Literature* 48, no. 4 (2014): 374–99.

Magee, Jeffery. *Irving Berlin's American Musical Theater*. Oxford: Oxford University Press, 2012.

Majaj, Lisa Suhair. "Arab-Americans and the Meaning of Race." In *Postcolonial Theory and the United States: Race, Ethnicity, and Literature*, edited by Amritjit Singh and Peter Schmidt, 320–37. Jackson: University of Mississippi Press, 2000.

Majid, Anouar. *We Are All Moors: Ending Centuries of Crusades against Muslims and Other Minorities*. Minneapolis: University of Minnesota Press, 2009.

Mandanipour, Shahriar. *Censoring an Iranian Love Story*. Translated by Sara Khalil. New York: Vintage, 2009.

Mann, Bonnie. "Manhood, Sexuality, and Nation in Post-9/11 United States." In *Security Disarmed: Critical Perspectives on Gender, Race, and Militarization*, edited by Julie Novkov, Barbara Sutton, and Sandra Morgen, 179–97. New Brunswick: Rutgers University Press, 2008.

March, John, and Marilyn Arnold. *A Reader's Companion to the Fiction of Willa Cather*. Westport CT: Greenwood, 1993.

Markert, John. *Post-9/11 Cinema: Through a Lens Darkly*. Lanham MD: Scarecrow, 2011.

Marr, Timothy. *The Cultural Roots of American Islamicism*. Cambridge: Cambridge University Press, 2006.

———. "'Out of This World': Islamic Irruptions in the Literary Americas." *American Literary History* 18, no. 3 (2006): 542–49.

———. "Strangers in the Spider's House: Transcultural Intelligence in American-(Middle)-Eastern Encounters." *American Literary History* 23, no. 1 (2011): 189–204.

Mason, Alane, Dedi Felman, and Samantha Schnee. "Editors' Note." In *Literature from the Axis of Evil: Writing from Iran, Iraq, North Korea, and Other Enemy Nations*, edited by Words without Borders, xiii–xxi. New York: New Press, 2006.

Massad, Joseph A. *Desiring Arabs*. Chicago: University of Chicago Press, 2007.

Matar, Hisham. *In the Country of Men*. 2006. Reprint, New York: Dial, 2007.

Matheson, Sue. "The Professional Western Revived: Southern Diaspora, Frontier Heteroglossia, and Audience Nostalgia in *True Grit* (2010)." In *Contemporary Westerns: Film and Television since 1990*, edited by Andrew Patrick Nelson, 77–92. London: Scarecrow, 2013.

May, Karl. *Jack Hildreth on the Nile*. 1899. Reprint, Whitefish MT: Kessinger Publishing, 2004.

McAlister, Melani. *Epic Encounters: Culture, Media, and U.S. Interests in the Middle East since 1945*. 2001. Reprint, Berkeley: University of California Press, 2005.

McCain, Cilla. *Murder in Baker Company: How Four American Soldiers Killed One of Their Own*. Chicago: Chicago Review Press, 2010.

McGill, Hannah. "Keeping It under Their Hat." *Sight and Sound* 23, no. 2 (2013): 12–13.

Melnick, Jeffrey. *9/11 Culture*. Malden MA: Wiley-Blackwell, 2009.

Metz, Walter. "'Mother Needs You': The Melodramatics of the Post-9/11 Western." In *A Family Affair: Cinema Calls Home*, edited by Murray Pomerance, 63–76. London: Wallflower, 2008.

Meyer, Philipp. *The Son*. New York: Ecco, 2013.

Mignolo, Walter. *The Idea of Latin America*. Malden MA: Blackwell, 2005.

Mills, Charles. *The Racial Contract*. Ithaca: Cornell University Press, 1997.

Mitchell, Lee Clark. *Westerns: Making the Man in Fiction and Film*. Chicago: University of Chicago Press, 1996.

Mitchell, W. J. T. "Holy Landscapes: Israel, Palestine, and the American Wilderness." *Critical Inquiry* 26, no. 2 (2000): 193–223.

Moaveni, Azadeh. *Lipstick Jihad: A Memoir of Growing Up Iranian in America and American in Iran*. New York: Public Affairs, 2005.

Modleski, Tania. *Old Wives' Tales and Other Women's Stories*. New York: New York University Press, 1998.

Mondello, Bob. "*The Hurt Locker*: An Explosive Look at the Iraq War." *National Public Radio*, June 26, 2009. http://www.npr.org/templates/story/story.php?story Id=105755842.

Moreno, Barry. *The Statue of Liberty Encyclopedia*. New York: Simon and Schuster, 2000.

Morgenstern, Joe. "Viggo of Arabia: In *Hidalgo* Tale of Mideast Horse Race, Mortenson Hits Quicksand." *Wall Street Journal*, March 5, 2004. http://online.wsj.com/article/sb107844111452346991.html.

Moses, L. G. *Wild West Shows and the Images of American Indians, 1883–1933*. Albuquerque: University of New Mexico Press, 1996.

Most, Andrea. "'We Know We Belong to the Land': The Theatricality of Assimilation in Rodgers and Hammerstein's *Oklahoma!*" *PMLA* 113, no. 1 (1998): 77–89.

Mourad, Sarah. "Between *Asmaa* and *Tahrir 2011*." *Al-Ahram Weekly*, January 5–11, 2012. http://weekly.ahram.org.eg/2012/1079/ee2.html.

"Mrs. Laura Bush's Family Favorites." George W. Bush Presidential Library and Museum, July 29, 2013. www.georgewbushlibrary.smu.edu/Teachers/The-First-Lady-and-Education/Laura-W-Bush-Favorites.aspx.

Mustafa, Hani. "Black Comedy, Black Drama: Screen of Discontent: Hani Mustafa on Films of the Revolution." *Al-Ahram Weekly*, April 17, 2013. http://weekly.ahram.org.eg/News/2270/23/Black-comedy,-black-drama.aspx.

Naber, Nadine. "Introduction: Arab Americans and U.S. Racial Formations." In *Race and Arab Americans before and after 9/11: From Invisible Citizens to Visible Subjects*, edited by Amaney Jamal and Nadine Naber, 1–45. Syracuse: Syracuse University Press, 2008.

Nabhan, Gary Paul. "Arabic in the Saddle." *Saudi Aramco World*, March–April 2007. www.saudiaramcoworld.com/issue/200702/.

Nafisi, Azar. *Reading Lolita in Tehran: A Memoir in Books*. New York: Random House, 2003.

Nance, Susan. *How the Arabian Nights Inspired the American Dream, 1790–1935*. Chapel Hill: University of North Carolina Press, 2009.

Naylor, Sean. *Not a Good Day to Die: The Untold Story of Operation Anaconda*. New York: Berkley Trade, 2006.

Nealon, Christopher. *Foundlings: Lesbian and Gay Historical Emotion before Stonewall*. Durham: Duke University Press, 2001.

Neff, Alexa. *Becoming American: The Early Arab Immigrant Experience*. Carbondale and Edwardsville: Southern Illinois University Press, 1985.

Nemerov, Alexander. *Frederic Remington and Turn-of-the-Century America*. New Haven: Yale University Press, 1995.

Newman, Kim. *Wild West Movies: Or How the West Was Found, Won, Lost, Lied About, Filmed, and Forgotten*. London: Bloomsbury, 1991.

Nicholas, Liza. *Becoming Western: Stories of Culture and Identity in the Cowboy State*. Lincoln: University of Nebraska Press, 2006.

Obenzinger, Hilton. *American Palestine: Melville, Twain, and the Holy Land Mania*. Princeton: Princeton University Press, 1999.

O'Brien, Sharon. "'The Thing Not Named': Willa Cather as a Lesbian Writer." *Signs: Journal of Women in Culture and Society* 9, no. 4 (1984): 576–99.

Olsen, Vickie. "The 'Persian Good-Bye' and the '*Oklahoma!* Hello': The Monogamous Ideal in the Postwar American Film Musical." In *Estudios de la mujer en el ámbito de los países de habla inglesa II*, edited by Josephine Bregazzi, Isabel Durán, Dámaso López, Félix Martín, Joanne Neff, Esther Sánchez-Pardo, Beatriz Villacañas, and Estefanía Villalba, 270–77. Madrid: Universidad Complutense de Madrid, 1996.

Papanikolas, Zeese. "The Cowboy and the Gaucho." In *Reading "The Virginian" in the New West*, edited by Melody Graulich and Stephen Tatum, 175–97. Lincoln: University of Nebraska Press, 2003.

Pate, J'Nell, ed. Introduction to *From Syria to Seminole: Memoir of a High Plains Merchant*, by Ed Aryain. Lubbock: Texas Tech University Press, 2006.

Peebles, Stacey. *Welcome to the Suck: Narrating the Soldier's Experience in Iraq*. Ithaca: Cornell University Press, 2011.

Peiss, Kathy. *Hope in a Jar: The Making of America's Beauty Culture*. New York: Metropolitan, 1998.

"Playing Wild West in the West Bank." *Ynetnews*, January 14, 2007. www.ynetnews .com/articles/0,7340,l-3352236,00.html.

Polan, Dana. "Movies, a Nation, and New Identities." In *American Cinema of the 2000s: Themes and Variations*, edited by Timothy Corrigan, 216–38. New Brunswick: Rutgers University Press, 2012.

Powell, Eve Troutt. *A Different Shade of Colonialism: Egypt, Great Britain, and the Mastery of the Sudan*. Berkeley: University of California Press, 2003.

Prashad, Vijay. "Orientalism." In *Keywords for American Cultural Studies*, edited by Bruce Burgett and Glenn Hendler, 174–77. New York: New York University Press, 2007.

Prats, Armando José. *Invisible Natives: Myth and Identity in the American Western*. Ithaca: Cornell University Press, 2002.

Pratt, Mary Louise. "Arts of the Contact Zone." *Profession* 91 (1991): 33–40.

Prime, William Cowper. *Boat Life in Egypt and Nubia*. New York: Harper and Brothers, 1857.

———. *Tent Life in the Holy Land*. New York: Harper and Brothers, 1857.

Prince, Stephen. *Firestorm: American Film in the Age of Terrorism*. New York: Columbia University Press, 2009.

Pritchard, Tim. *Ambush Alley: The Most Extraordinary Battle of the Iraq War*. New York: Presidio, 2005.

Proulx, Annie. "Tits-Up in a Ditch." In *Fine Just the Way It Is: Wyoming Stories 3*, 177–221. New York: Scribner, 2008.

Quayson, Ato. "The Sighs of History: Postcolonial Debris and the Question of (Literary) History." *New Literary History* 43, no. 2 (2012): 359–70.

Rana, Junaid. "The Story of Islamophobia." *Souls: A Critical Journal of Black Politics, Culture, and Society* 9, no. 2 (2007): 148–61.

Reddin, Paul. *Wild West Shows*. Urbana: University of Illinois Press, 1999.

Regan, Robert. "Heroism." In *The Routledge Encyclopedia of Mark Twain*, edited by J. R. LeMaster and James D. Wilson, 355–59. New York: Routledge, 1993.

Remington, Frederic. "A Gallop through the Midway." In *The Collected Writings of Frederic Remington*, edited by Peggy Samuels and Harold Samuels, 111–13. Garden City NY: Doubleday, 1979.

"Repeat Offender (Women of Cover)." *Dubyaspeak*, accessed May 16, 2008. www.dubyaspeak.com/repeatoffender.phtml?offense=cover.

Reynolds, Guy. *Willa Cather in Context: Progress, Race, Empire*. New York: St. Martin's, 1996.

Riggs, Lynn. *The Cherokee Night and Other Plays*. Norman: University of Oklahoma Press, 2003.

———. *Green Grow the Lilacs: A Play*. New York: S. French, 1931.

———. *Knives from Syria*. New York: Samuel French, 1928.

Riverbend. *Baghdad Burning: Girl Blog from Iraq*. New York: Feminist Press, 2005.

———. *Baghdad Burning II: More Girl Blog from Iraq*. New York: Feminist Press, 2006.

Roach, Joseph. "World Bank Drama." In *Shades of the Planet: American Literature as World Literature*, edited by Wai Chee Dimock and Lawrence Buell, 171–83. Princeton: Princeton University Press, 2007.

Robinson, Forrest G. *Having It Both Ways: Self-Subversion in Western Popular Classics*. Albuquerque: University of New Mexico Press, 1996.

Robinson-Dunn, Diane. *The Harem, Slavery, and British Imperial Culture: Anglo-Muslim Relations in the Late Nineteenth Century*. Manchester: Manchester University Press, 2006.

Rodgers, Richard, and Oscar Hammerstein. *Oklahoma! The Complete Book and Lyrics of the Broadway Musical*. 1943. Reprint, New York: Applause Theatre and Cinema Books, 2010.

Roediger, David. *Working toward Whiteness: How America's Immigrants Became White; The Strange Journey from Ellis Island to the Suburbs*. New York: Basic Books, 2006.

Roosevelt, Theodore. *Diaries of Boyhood and Youth*. New York: Charles Scribner's Sons, 1928.

———. *Ranch Life and the Hunting-Trail*. New York: Century, 1888.

Rosen, Miriam. "The Making of Omar Sharif: An Interview." *Cineaste* 17, no. 1 (1989): 18–20.

Rowe, John Carlos. "American Orientalism after Said." In *Popular Culture in the Middle East and North Africa: A Postcolonial Outlook*, edited by Walid El Hamamsy and Mounira Soliman, 183–96. New York: Routledge, 2013.

———. "Reading *Reading Lolita in Tehran* in Idaho." *American Quarterly* 59, no. 2 (2007): 253–75.

Rydell, Robert W. "Buffalo Bill's Wild West: The Racialisation of the Cosmopolitan Imagination." In *Colonial Advertising and Commodity Racism*, edited by Wulf D. Hund, Michael Pickering, and Anandi Ramamurthy, 97–118. Zurich: Lit Verlag, 2013.

Rydell, Robert W., and Rob Kroes. *Buffalo Bill in Bologna: The Americanization of the World, 1869–1922*. Chicago: University of Chicago Press, 2005.

Sabine, Paul. "Home and Abroad: The Two 'Wests' of Twentieth-Century United States History." *Pacific Historical Review* 66, no. 3 (1997): 305–41.

Said, Edward. *Orientalism*. New York: Vintage, 1978.

———. *Out of Place: A Memoir*. New York: Vintage, 1999.

———. "A Window on the World." *Guardian*, August 1, 2003. http://www.theguardian.com/books/2003/aug/02/alqaida.highereducation.

Saldívar, José David. *Border Matters: Remapping American Cultural Studies*. Berkeley: University of California Press, 1997.

Salvatore, Armando. "The Elusive Subject of Revolution." *The Eminent Frame* (blog), Social Science Research Council, February 16, 2011. http://blogs.ssrc.org/tif/2011/02/16/the-elusive-subject-of-revolution/.

Samuels, Peggy, and Harold Samuels. *Frederic Remington: A Biography*. New York: Doubleday, 1982.

Sandler, Martin W. *Galloping across the U.S.A.: Horses in American Life*. Oxford: Oxford University Press, 2003.

Sayre, Gordon. "Renegades from Barbary: The Transnational Turn in Captivity Studies." *American Literary History* 22, no. 2 (2010): 347–59.

Schueller, Malini Johar. *American Orientalisms: Race, Nation, and Gender in Literature, 1790–1890*. Ann Arbor: University of Michigan Press, 2001.

Sedgwick, Eve Kosofsky. "Across Gender, Across Sexuality: Willa Cather and Others." *South Atlantic Quarterly* 88, no. 1 (1989): 53–72.

Semmerling, Tim. *"Evil" Arabs in American Popular Film*. Austin: University of Texas Press, 2007.

"Shams—'Ahlan Ezayak.'" *Woody Guthrie's Guitar* (blog). February 28, 2012. http://woodyguthriesguitar.blogspot.com/2007/07/ahlan-izayak-shams.html.

Sharif, Omar, and Marie-Thérèse Guinchard. *The Eternal Male: Omar Sharif; My Own Story*. London: W. H. Allen, 1977.

Sherman, William C., Paul L. Whitney, and John Guerrero. *Prairie Peddlers: The Syrian-Lebanese in North Dakota*. Bismarck ND: University of Mary Press, 2002.

Shohat, Ella. "The Sephardic-Moorish Atlantic: Between Orientalism and Occidentalism." In *Between the Middle East and the Americas: The Cultural Poli-*

tics of Diaspora, edited by Evelyn Azeeza Alsultany and Ella Shohat, 42–64. Ann Arbor: University of Michigan Press, 2013.

———. *Taboo Memories, Diasporic Voices*. Durham: Duke University Press, 2006.

Shohat, Ella, and Evelyn Alsultany. "The Cultural Politics of 'the Middle East' in the Americas: An Introduction." In *Between the Middle East and the Americas: The Cultural Politics of Diaspora*, edited by Evelyn Azeeza Alsultany and Ella Shohat, 3–41. Ann Arbor: University of Michigan Press, 2013.

Shohat, Ella, and Robert Stam. *Unthinking Eurocentrism: Multiculturalism and the Media*. New York: Routledge, 1994.

Shora, Nawar. *The Arab-American Handbook: A Guide to Arab, Arab-American, and Muslim Worlds*. Seattle: Cune, 2008.

Simmon, Scott. *The Invention of the Western Film: A History of the Genre's First Half-Century*. Cambridge: Cambridge University Press, 2003.

Slotkin, Richard. *Gunfighter Nation: The Myth of the Frontier in Twentieth-Century America*. 1992. Reprint, Norman: University of Oklahoma Press, 1998.

Spurgeon, Sara. "Incidentally Western." Unpublished paper delivered at a meeting of the Western Literature Association, Berkeley CA, October 10, 2013.

Stam, Robert, and Ella Shohat. "Whence and Whither Postcolonial Theory?" *New Literary History* 43, no. 2 (2012): 371–90.

Stegner, Wallace. *Where the Bluebird Sings to the Lemonade Springs: Living and Writing in the West*. 1992. Reprint, New York: Modern Library, 2002.

Steinberg, Shirley R. "French Fries, Fezzes, and Minstrels: The Hollywoodization of Islam." In *9/11 in American Culture*, edited by Norman K. Denzin and Yvonna S. Lincoln, 123–28. Lanham MD: Altamira/Rowman and Littlefield, 2003.

Stich, Klaus P. "Cather's 'Midi Romanesque': Missionaries, Myth, and the Grail in *Death Comes for the Archbishop*." *Studies in the Novel* 38, no. 1 (2006): 56–73.

Stoler, Ann Laura. "Introduction: The Rot Remains; From Ruins to Ruination." In *Imperial Debris: On Ruins and Ruination*, edited by Ann Laura Stoler, 1–38. Durham: Duke University Press, 2013.

Stout, Janis P. "Introduction: For Use, for Pleasure, for Status; The Object World of Willa Cather." In *Willa Cather and Material Culture: Real-World Writing, Writing the Real World*, edited by Janis P. Stout, 1–14. Tuscaloosa: University of Alabama Press, 2005.

Streeby, Shelley. *American Sensations: Class, Empire, and the Production of Popular Culture*. Berkeley: University of California Press, 2002.

Takacs, Stacy. "The Contemporary Politics of the Western Form: Bush, *Saving Jessica Lynch*, and *Deadwood*." In *Reframing 9/11: Film, Popular Culture, and the "War on Terror,"* edited by Jeff Birkenstein, Anna Froula, and Karen Randell, 153–63. New York: Continuum, 2010.

Tanner, Tony. *The Reign of Wonder: Naivety and Reality in American Literature*. Cambridge: Cambridge University Press, 1977.

Tartt, Donna. Afterword to *True Grit*, by Charles Portis, 225–35. 1968. Reprint, New York: Overlook, 2010.

Tatum, Stephen. *In the Remington Moment*. Lincoln: University of Nebraska Press, 2010.

———. "'Mercantile Ethics': *No Country for Old Men* and the Narcocorrido." In *Cormac McCarthy: "All the Pretty Horses," "No Country for Old Men," "The Road,"* edited by Sara L. Spurgeon, 77–93. New York: Continuum, 2011.

———. "Postfrontier Horizons." *Modern Fiction Studies* 50, no. 2 (2004): 460–68.

———. "The Problem of the Popular in the New Western History." In *The New Western History: The Territory Ahead*, edited by Forrest G. Robinson, 153–90. Tucson: University of Arizona Press, 1998.

Taubin, Amy. *Taxi Driver*. London: BFI, 2000.

Tawil-Sour, Helga. "Egypt's Uprising and the Shifting Spatialities of Politics." *Cinema Journal* 52, no. 1 (2012): 160–66.

Taylor, Lonn, and Ingrid Maar. *The American Cowboy*. New York: HarperCollins, 1983.

Tehranian, John. *Whitewashed: America's Invisible Middle Eastern Minority*. New York: New York University Press, 2008.

Tompkins, Jane. *West of Everything: The Inner Life of Westerns*. New York: Oxford University Press, 1993.

Trachtenberg, Marvin. *The Statue of Liberty*. New York: Penguin, 1976.

"True Grit." *IMDb.com*, accessed September 12, 2013. http://www.imdb.com/title /tt1403865/?ref_=fn_al_tt_1.

Tsunoda, Shunji. "A Study on Willa Cather's *Death Comes for the Archbishop*." *Studies in English Language and Literature* 37 (1994): 194–201.

Tucker, Bruce, and Priscilla L. Walton. "From General's Daughter to Coal Miner's Daughter: Spinning and Counterspinning Jessica Lynch." *Canadian Review of American Studies* 36, no. 3 (2006): 311–30.

Turner, Frederick Jackson. *The Frontier in American History*. 1920. Reprint, Tucson: University of Arizona Press, 1986.

Tuttle, Jennifer. "Rewriting the West Cure: Charlotte Perkins Gilman, Owen Wister, and the Sexual Politics of Neurasthenia." In *The Mixed Legacy of Charlotte Perkins Gilman*, edited by Catherine J. Golden and Joanna Schneider Zangrando, 103–21. Newark: University of Delaware Press, 2000.

Twain, Mark. *The Innocents Abroad, or The New Pilgrims' Progress*. 1869. Reprint, New York: Dover, 2003.

———. *Roughing It*. 1872. Reprint, New York: Signet, 1962.

"Updated *Oklahoma!* Has a Lone Star Accent," *Houston Chronicle*, July 11, 2011. www.chron.com/life/article/Updated-Oklahoma-has-a-Lone-Star-accent -2081331.php.

Urrea, Luis Alberto. *The Devil's Highway: A True Story*. New York: Back Bay Books, 2004.

Vatikiotis, P. J. *A History of Modern Egypt*. Baltimore: Johns Hopkins University Press, 1991.

Vecoli, Rudolph J. "The Lady and the Huddled Masses: The Statue of Liberty as a Symbol of Immigration." In *The Statue of Liberty Revisited*, edited by Wilton S. Dillon and Neil G. Kolter, 39–70. Washington DC: Smithsonian Institution Press, 1993.

Virilio, Paul, and Sylvère Lotringer. *Pure War: Twenty-Five Years Later*. Translated by Mark Polizzotti. Los Angeles: Semiotext(e), 2008.

Vitalis, Robert. "Wallace Stegner's Arabian Discovery: The Imperial Blind Spots in a Continental Vision." *Pacific Historical Quarterly* 76, no. 3 (August 2007): 405–38.

Vivarilli, Nick. "Tahrir Square Doc Takes Spaghetti Western Route." *Variety*, September 8, 2011. http://variety.com/2011/film/news/tahrir-square-doc-takes-spaghetti-western-route-1118042431/.

Vizenor, Gerald. *Manifest Manners: Narratives on Postindian Survivance*. Lincoln: University of Nebraska Press, 1999.

Walberg, Eric. "The American Art of War." *Al-Ahram Weekly*, May 13–19, 2010. http://weekly.ahram.org.eg/2010/998/cu3.htm.

Walker, Janet, ed. *Westerns: Films through History*. New York: Routledge, 2001.

Wallace, Mike. "Hijacking History: Ronald Reagan and the Statue of Liberty." *Radical History Review* 37 (January 1987): 119–30.

Weaver, Jace. Foreword to *The Cherokee Night and Other Plays*, by Lynn Riggs. Norman: University of Oklahoma Press, 2003.

———. *That the People May Live: Native American Literatures and Native American Community*. Oxford: Oxford University Press, 1997.

Weber, Cynthia. *Imagining America at War: Morality, Politics, and Film*. New York: Routledge, 2005.

White, Armond. "Gritty and Good." *New York Press*, December 21, 2010. www.nypress.com/article-21986-gritty-and-good.html.

White, G. Edward. *The Eastern Establishment and the Western Experience: The West of Frederic Remington, Theodore Roosevelt, and Owen Wister*. New Haven: Yale University Press, 1968.

White, Richard. *"It's Your Misfortune and None of My Own": A New History of the American West*. Norman: University of Oklahoma Press, 1991.

Wilk, Max. *OK! The Story of Oklahoma!; A Celebration of America's Beloved Musical*. New York: Applause Books 2002.

Will, Barbara. "The Nervous Origins of the American Western." *American Literature* 70, no. 2 (1998): 293–316.

Williams, Daniel. "In Egyptian Movies, Curses! We're the Heavies." *Washington Post*, March 26, 2006. http://www.washingtonpost.com/wpdyn/content/article/2006/03/19/ar2006031901037.html.

Willis, Susan. *Portents of the Real: A Primer for Post-9/11 America*. London: Verso, 2005.

Wilson, Rob. "Afterword: Worlding as Future Tactic." In *The Worlding Project: Doing Cultural Studies in the Era of Globalization*, edited by Rob Wilson and Christopher Leigh Connery, 209–23. Berkeley CA: North Atlantic Books, 2007.

Wilson, Sarah. "Material Objects as Sites of Cultural Mediation in *Death Comes for the Archbishop*." In *Willa Cather and Material Culture: Real-World Writing, Writing the Real World*, edited by Janis P. Stout, 171–87. Tuscaloosa: University of Alabama Press, 2005.

Wister, Owen. "The Evolution of the Cow-Puncher." *Harper's Magazine*, September 1895, 602–17.

Wittliff, Bill. *Vaquero: Genesis of the Texas Cowboy*. Austin: University of Texas Press, 2004.

Womack, Craig. *Art as Performance, Story as Criticism: Reflections on Native Literary Aesthetics*. Norman: University of Oklahoma Press, 2009.

———. *Red on Red: Native American Literary Separatism*. Minneapolis: University of Minnesota Press, 1999.

Woods, Gioia. "Cowboys, Indians, and Iraq: Jessica Lynch, Lori Piestewa, and the Great American Makeover." *Studies in Popular Culture* 29, no. 1 (2006): 17–39.

Worden, Daniel. *Masculine Style: The American West and Literary Modernism*. New York: Palgrave Macmillan, 2011.

Wright, Evan. *Generation Kill: Devil Dogs, Iceman, Captain America, and the New Face of American War*. 2004. Reprint, New York: Berkley Trade, 2008.

Wright, Will. *Six Guns and Society: A Structural Study of the Western*. Berkeley: University of California Press, 1977.

Wrobel, David, and Michael Steiner, eds. *Many Wests: Place, Culture, and Regional Identity*. Lawrence: University Press of Kansas, 1997.

Zenilman, Avi. "Inside *The Hurt Locker*." *New Yorker*, July 10, 2009. http://www .newyorker.com/news/news-desk/inside-the-hurt-locker.

Zerilli, Linda. "Democracy and National Fantasy: Reflections on the Statue of Liberty." In *Cultural Studies and Political Theory*, edited by Jodi Dean, 167–88. Ithaca: Cornell University Press, 2000.

Zinder, Paul. "Osama bin Laden Ain't Here: *Justified* as a 9/11 Western." In *Contemporary Westerns: Film and Television since 1990*, edited by Andrew Patrick Nelson, 119–34. Lanham MD: Scarecrow, 2013.

Ziser, Michael. "The Oil Desert." In *American Studies, Ecocriticism, and Citizenship: Thinking and Acting in the Local and Global Commons*, edited by Joni Adamson and Kimberly N. Ruffin, 76–86. New York: Routledge, 2013.

"Zuleikha Robinson." *IMDb.com*, May 25, 2008. http://www.imdb.com/name /nm0733196/filmoyear.

INDEX

Page numbers in italic indicate illustrations.

In the Postwestern Horizons series

*María Amparo Ruiz de Burton: Critical
and Pedagogical Perspectives*
Edited by Amelia María de la Luz Montes and
Anne Elizabeth Goldman

To order or obtain more information on these or other University of Nebraska Press
titles, visit nebraskapress.unl.edu.

CPSIA information can be obtained
at www.ICGtesting.com
Printed in the USA
LVHW091312030419
612827LV00001B/211/P

9 781496 214232